Wildfire: Church Growth in Korea

Church Growth Series

Wildfire: Church Growth in Korea

by

Roy E. Shearer

William B. Eerdmans Publishing Company
Grand Rapids, Michigan

Foreword

Here is a significant book on a basic subject, the fashion in which the Christian Church grows. If the world be viewed as a whole, as, from the perspective of the Divine purpose, it must be, the Church clearly continues the amazing growth that it has displayed during the past four centuries. Because of the explosion of population, especially in Asia, where Christians have never been more than small minorities, percentage-wise they constitute a smaller proportion of mankind than they did fifty years ago. But they are more widely distributed than ever. In some areas, notably in sub-Saharan Africa, their numbers are rapidly mounting, and, in spite of surging anti-imperialism and anti-colonialism, and in part because of them, the Church is becoming more deeply rooted among more peoples, especially in Asia and Africa, than ever before. The Institute of Church Growth, at whose instance and under whose auspices Mr. Shearer has written, is committed to discovering the reasons why the Church grows rapidly in some places and more slowly or not at all in other regions. By church growth is meant not only mounting numbers but also intelligent Christian commitment and indigenous leadership.

Mr. Shearer comes to his study with excellent qualifications. He has been and is a Presbyterian missionary in Korea, the land to which he addresses himself. In conformity with high scholarly standards, he has gone to first-hand sources of information. He has acquainted himself with the pertinent material in print, including books, periodicals, and reports. He has also gone extensively into the files of correspondence in the archives of what was formerly the Board of Foreign Missions of the Presbyterian Church in the United States of America, now the Commission on Ecumenical Mission and Relations of the United Presbyterian Church. In a wise effort to avoid ill-grounded generalizations he has confined his account to the record of the mission with which he has been connected, that of the Northern Presbyterians. But he has

5

sought to give perspective and inclusive coverage by brief summaries of the missions of other Presbyterian churches and of the American Methodists. He notes that the Presbyterians have laid more emphasis on evangelism than have Methodists, and that, in comparison with the Presbyterians, the Methodists have stressed education. In general, the study is confined to the years before the defeat of Japan and the division of the country by the Russians and Americans at the thirty-eighth parallel.

As all familiar with the history of missions in the past ten decades know, the growth of the Church in Korea has been striking. Mr. Shearer rightly believes that significant growth has been through the Holy Spirit, as all true church growth has always been and is. However, with similar insight, he points out that it has been conditioned by the environment. He shows that in Korea the "higher religions," Buddhism and Confucianism, have long been decadent and that the vacuum has been filled by Shamanism, closely akin to animism. It is among peoples of animistic cults that in the past two centuries the Church has registered its chief gains — as among the Bataks, the Karens, the hill peoples and depressed classes of India, the islands of the Pacific, and sub-Saharan Africa. That partly accounts for the advance in Korea. Mr. Shearer notes that in Korea progress has not been uniform. It has varied with political events and from area to area. It has been more marked in the Northwest than in the South. This he suggests may have been because the former region has been more prosperous than the latter and has had better education. He is of the opinion that a cause usually ascribed for growth, the Nevius method, devised by a missionary to China who visited Korea at a formative period, was not as potent as is sometimes thought. He is quite aware, however, that "self-propagation" by Korean Christians, laity as well as clergy, which is in accord with the principles of Nevius, has been a major factor. Although not primarily due to Nevius, it was probably reinforced by the impulse given by him. The author notes that the growth of the Church was not infallibly associated with "revivals." Rather, these deepened the life of the

Church and were not immediately productive of augmented growth. Growth has usually been by families and by villages. Here, then, is one of the most thoughtful and dependable studies of church growth in recent years.

Kenneth Scott Latourette
Sterling Professor of Missions and Oriental History,
Emeritus, in Yale University

Preface

This study of church growth in Korea comes out of a personal need to answer a persistent question: How, if possible, can a Western missionary actually be involved in helping a younger Church to grow? My first furlough afforded the time to study this question, and the Institute of Church Growth, in Eugene, Oregon, was the setting for the research. Although the complete answer will not be found in this book, the question has been partially answered by study of how the Church grew in the past and of what roles were played in this growth by missionaries and national Christians.

At the outset it must be affirmed that God gave the growth to the Church in Korea. I say this not only because it is part of our Biblical faith, but also because during the study I became increasingly aware that this Church in Korea grew as no mere human institution could grow. While using human instruments in the environment of human society, the Holy Spirit alone caused men's hearts to turn to Christ the Savior. In order, then, to learn how we can be better instruments for His use in church extension today, I have tried to obtain through this study a clear understanding of how and why these human agents affected church growth in past years.

While attempting a brief survey of the major Protestant Churches in Korea, I have concentrated on the Presbyterian Church for two reasons. First, it has had the greatest numerical growth of all denominations in Korea. Second, as a United Presbyterian missionary, I naturally started searching for material in the New York mission headquarters of my own Church. After I had spent a few days photographing and collecting material from the rich resources of its files and library, it became evident to me that I would have to spend the remainder of the time I had allotted for study putting together a picture of how this one denomination worked for the growth of the Korean Presbyterian Church. There was no time left for intensive research on the three

9

other mission areas of the Presbyterian Church in Korea, nor of other missions in the country. I hope that the areas of the Korean Church not thoroughly studied here will soon receive the attention they deserve.

The basic statistics for this study were taken from photocopies of the diligently kept statistics of the General Assembly of the Presbyterian Church in Korea. Reports and letters of the early missionaries from the beginning of the mission until 1911 were studied from microfilm copies at the United Presbyterian Library in New York City. Personal reports of the missionaries from 1911 until the present were searched for information concerning the growth of the Presbyterian Church in Korea. Background information came from the annual reports of the Board of Foreign Missions of the Presbyterian Church in the U. S. A. and from the many books published on the missionary movement in Korea.

The term "church growth," used throughout this writing, means primarily numerical church growth. Numerical church growth and spiritual church growth are not mutually exclusive. A statement from a World Council of Churches-sponsored study on church growth says,

> Numerical expansion and quality of Christian life are not alternatives, but correlatives, inasmuch as each is vitally related with the other. Again and again, it has been shown that the spontaneous expansion of a church quickens its own spiritual life; on the other hand a church which is truly growing in grace thereby grows in concern for its missionary outreach.*

To be concerned for the numerical growth of the Church is simply to heed the instruction which Paul gave Timothy: to pray for the salvation of all men because God desires not a few but "desires all men to be saved" (I Timothy 2:4).

Throughout this writing, growth will be given as percentage increase per decade. Although the period being considered is other than a decade, the percentage growth will be given

*"The Growth of the Church," a statement drawn up by a special consultation convened by the W. C. C. Department of Missionary Studies (Iberville, Quebec: July 31 — August 2, 1963).

as if that growth continued for ten years, thus making all percentages comparable.

For the help they rendered in collecting materials for this study, I wish to acknowledge the assistance of Mr. Yang Sun Kim, Director of the Christian Museum in Seoul, Korea, Miss Catherine Brown of the United Presbyterian Library staff in New York City, and Mrs. Roy K. Smith, retired missionary to Korea, now of Duarte, California.

I appreciate the valuable comments given me by the following men, who read the manuscript: Dr. Kenneth S. Latourette, Dr. Richard H. Baird, Dr. L. George Paik, Dr. W. Stanley Rycroft, Dr. Horace G. Underwood, Dr. Francis Kinsler, Dr. Allen D. Clark, and Dr. Samuel H. Moffett.

Thanks go to Dr. Donald McGavran, Director of the Institute of Church Growth, and to Dr. Alan Tippett, also of the Institute, who were constant companions in the search for the true meaning of the data with which I came in contact day by day.

I appreciate the editing ability of Mrs. Thomas R. Loree, who put hard work on the manuscript, and I also acknowledge to the reader the important task done by my wife at the typewriter.

Contents

List of Tables

15

List of Figures

Chapter I. The Setting for Rapid Growth

STUDENTS OF THE MISSIONARY MOVEMENT KNOW THE STORY OF the rapid growth of the Church in Korea. Few however, realize that this growth was not country-wide, but geographically limited. Many Christians pray for an increase of the Church by a repetition of the famous 1907 Korean revival, but that revival actually did not cause the great, historic church growth. It has been said that the reason for the Church's fast growth was the "Nevius Method," but that is not the entire truth either. We are deeply concerned that new Christians be won and new churches be planted, but the oral tradition and promotional literature of church leaders and missionaries of the Presbyterian Church in Korea are an inadequate base on which to build future policy for planting churches. A truer picture of the growth of the Church in Korea can be seen in the candid observations in letters and reports of the participants in that growth. These observations must be sought and compared with the accurate statistical records of church membership. In this way I have attempted to find an accurate picture of how, why, and where the Church in Korea grew like WILDFIRE.[1]

But first let me briefly introduce this unique Korea to those of you who are not familiar with her. Most visitors to Korea see only her several large cities, where economic conditions are not the best, but where large department stores, hurrying people, taxis, traffic policemen, slums and an expanding population, all of which are common to many urban areas of the world, can be seen. True, some cities of the world lack Korea's roasted-squid vendors, its fragrant, medicinal herb shops, and the lovely brocade costumes of the Korean women, which make the cities of proud little Korea distinctive. All over the country, a visitor finds new

---

[1] D. L. Gifford, "The work in the country has spread like wildfire." Quoted from his letter to the Board of Foreign Missions of the Presbyterian Church U. S. A. (Seoul, Korea: September 1, 1896).

industrial and mining areas springing up. The infancy of these industries reminds us that industrialization is not yet complete in Korea. Dotted on the edges of the peninsula Korea, a visitor sees fishing villages where the people barely make a living from the sea.

However, the most distinctive feature of Korea is the rural area, where customs are slow to change and the way of life is still at a markedly slower pace than in the cities. A visitor to Korea's rural villages will see straw-roofed, mud-walled homes nestled closely together beside countless diked rice paddies. These homes are clustered at the base of time-worn mountains which are constantly stripped of their little pine tree covering. The pine trees are used for firewood which cooks the rice and heats the paper-covered floors of these cottages. The firewood is at a premium but is used efficiently because the cooking fire also furnishes heat by flues under the floor. These hot-floored homes are inhabited by large families whose lord is the grandfather. Actually the home is ruled by the grandmother, whose authority over her daughter-in-law and grandchildren has been unquestioned through the ages.

I. KOREAN RURAL CUSTOMS

The daughter-in-law rises with the light to begin her ritual of lighting the firewood and cooking the rice. The children awake in the same clothes they wore yesterday and will wear today and toddle outdoors to wash their faces and brush their teeth in water from the village well. These children dress in bright red and yellow silk and bow low to their grandparents on holiday mornings.

The children of Korea race the dusty streets of their village in play, and their feet squish delightfully through the mud of the rice paddy dikes. They learn early to eat hot, red-peppered and heavily garlicked cabbage and oriental radishes from their richly fertilized family gardens. Korean children learn early to maintain the natural squatting position practiced by their elders (U. S. college students call it "hunkering") which is at once convenient for work on the ground level and comfortably relaxing. The girls learn to stand and walk with straight backs as they carry pottery jars or other containers on their heads to the fields or to market in the next town. The little boys are throughly spoiled (Westerners would say) by their devoted mothers, who keep them to breast for a number of years before weaning them to rice, garlic, and red pepper.

The fathers toil in their precious, high-yielding rice paddies, maintaining the mud dikes, keeping the fields plowed and then full of water, and transplanting their carefully tended rice shoots to the paddies, working knee-deep in water full of blood-sucking leeches. They resolutely bend their backs to cut the mature rice stalks with sickles in the autumn season. They kick up their feet and beat the two-headed drum in a harvest dance of joy and go to town to drink rice wine with their friends until they make a loud and weaving journey back home.

The mothers sew the family clothes, basting the hems not with thread but with a rice paste glued with a hot iron. They pound their evenings away with two rhythmic ironing bats, sounding through the night as they beat the white, washed clothes of the family members to a shiny stiffness. In their prettiest silk, brocade satin, pastel nylon or shiny white cotton empire dresses, they parade to market with shopping baskets. They find the market place a fascinating jumble of sounds and smells and people. Both women and men have an exciting time of bargaining, gossip and conversation with neighbors from other villages — people whom they have not seen since the last market day they attended. Occurring every fifth day, market days are the country Korean means of communication which, coupled with the radio, serve in place of the United States media of magazines and television. News of families and villages is swapped in streets where cattle, vegetables, baskets and fish are sold. The market place is really like a maze of telephone lines.

Korean mothers not only walk periodically to market, but they spend most of their time in earthen-floored, sunken kitchens, producing truly enticing aromas from soybean sauce and pastes, from little green onions and garlic cloves, from red pepper paste and broiled fish right from the sea, from salty, sesame-oiled seaweed, and from tasty, hot, spicy chicken, beef, seaweed, or squid soups. Korean mothers are skillful at their unique and wonderful culinary art. Many of these mothers grieve that they cannot buy all the many varieties of foods that their country offers to feed their loved ones; they frequently must be content with only one vegetable and rice.

The boys and girls dress in faded black, cotton uniforms and trudge to the nearest school, spring, summer and fall, but not in the winter. Since the schools are unheated and cold, winter is a time for staying home where the floors are hot. The students face a scholastic competition few Americans have ever known. They memorize lectures by poor, flickering candlelight and cram for severe examinations held in countless class subjects. When failure to gain college entrance becomes known, suicides are not rare. The students consider themselves the hope of Korea. In the 1960 revolution which overthrew the Syngman Rhee regime, the tragic marching demonstrations of the college students marked the nation; their blood stained not only the streets of Korea's cities, but the memories of their grieving mothers and countrymen.

II. KOREAN RACIAL ORIGIN

The precise racial and ethnic origin of the Korean people remains a mystery enlightened only by mythology. They claim a history of over four thousand years and until very recently have used a calendar which dates from this mythical origin. Our year 1962 A.D. was the Korean year 4295. Although Koreans, Japanese and Chinese may have common ancestors, the Korean people are now a distinct people, different from either Japanese or Chinese. They are one nation with one language intelligible to all sections of their country. The language has borrowed much from Chinese and some from Japanese but still remains a distinctive Korean language with its own phonemic alphabet.

Yet within the Korean nation there seem to be different racial types. Missionaries have observed a distinct racial and temperamental difference between north and south Koreans. One anthropologist, Dixon, maintains that north-erners are a type closely related to Manchurians and that Koreans in the south are related to the Japanese.[2] The geographer Lautensach follows Erwin Balez in judging that there are two types of races in Korea. One is the "Mandschu-Korean" type with the large, slender body, flat nose, slim limbs, and narrow hips more common in the north. The second "Mongol-Malayan" type is short, the nose profile is concave, the face has a wide mouth and protruding lips, and there is a heavy-set body. This second type is found more commonly in the south. Lautensach goes on to say that the Mongol-Malayan people are related to the Japanese, whereas the Mandschu-Korean type is more closely related to Manchurians — which agrees with Dixon's theory.[3]

There is one other indication of different racial strains found in Snyder's study of blood types. Snyder calls south-erners (along with the Japanese) a "Hunan" type. The Hunan has a high frequency of Type A blood and a low frequency of Type B. But northern Koreans are the "Indo-Manchurian" type (along with the Manchus and Chinese), which contrarily has a high frequency of Type B and low frequency of Type A. Along with these extreme southern and northern types, Snyder lists four localities as areas of "middle Koreans," two of which areas are Seoul and Pyong-yang. These two and the extreme north and south with their percentages of Types A and B blood are listed as follows:[4]

[2] Roland B. Dixon, *The Racial History of Man,* pp. 286-287.

[3] Herman Lautensach, *Korea Land, Volk, Schicksal,* translated by Glenn Wass, p. 41.

[4] Laurence H. Snyder, "Human Blood Groups, their Inheritance and Racial Significance," *Source Book in Anthropology,* by A. L. Kroeber and T. T. Waterman, p. 161.

	TYPE A	TYPE B
Extreme North . . .	27.4%	34.5%
Pyongyang	29.9%	27.7%
Seoul	35.7%	25.1%
Extreme South . . .	41.5%	25.7%

SNYDER'S FREQUENCY OF BLOOD TYPE OCCURRENCE IN KOREA
TABLE I

A cultural anthropologist with whom I have discussed this theory feels that if blood types are any indication of racial characteristics, the significance of Snyder's study is that areas from Seoul and southward are similar to the Hunan and areas to the north are largely Indo-Manchurian. There is an obvious gradation from extreme south to extreme north which is borne out by these percentages. It would seem from these figures that one racial strain resided in Seoul and southward, another from Pyongyang northward, and a mixed racial strain in between. Again this theory agrees with that of Dixon and Lautensach.

Additional evidence for a difference in racial strains comes from the traditions of the people themselves. We can see an inkling of this tradition in early French Roman Catholic missionary correspondence. Father Maudant, who entered the country in 1836, writes that the Koreans belong to the Mongol race "intermixed in the north with aboriginal people and Tungus, but in the south with the Japanese."[5] Although there is no existing historical evidence for large Japanese immigration to Korea, it may be safely assumed that Father Maudant found that the Koreans themselves recognized different racial origins and ethnic differences between the north-

[5] Father Maudant, Letter written in 1836, translated from the French by Alan R. Tippett (on file at the Institute of Church Growth, Eugene, Oregon).

erners and southerners, and he expressed this recognition in his letter.

Now why go to such length to labor this point? The reason is not to prove that there is racial difference between north and south, but that where these marked physical differences occur there is a strong possibility that sharp cultural differences also occur, due to isolation and non-intermarriage between the north and south. The physical differences indicate that Korea is not made up of one homogeneous population. This is contended both by the evidence already cited and by many missionary and Korean sources like the following:

> The people in northern Korea are more aggressive and energetic than those of the south. . . . Their social customs are also different from those of the capital. There are no strict class distinctions as in Seoul and other provinces.[6]

We are mistaken if we treat all of the Korean people as coming from the same ethnic and cultural background. Even today it is possible for a Westerner to distinguish a northern Korean from his southern countryman by the slight differences in language and by a great difference in outlook on life.

One cause for these regional differences is that most Koreans have always lived outside of the large cities and so have not been under the influence of the central government.

> The Korean kingdoms were not quite so centralized as the court chronicles of the flourishing periods of unity would have us believe. . . .only in the Yi Dynasty [1392-1910] were the wide local differences in culture and dialects virtually erased.[7]

But even these differences were not completely erased. Only in recent times through migration and modern transportation

---

6 Il Seung Kay, *Christianity in Korea*, p. 214.

7 Key P. Yang and Gregory Henderson, "An Outline History of Korean Confucianism, Part I, The Early Period and Ye Factionalism," *The Journal of Asian Studies*, Vol. XVIII, No. 1 (November 1958), p. 98.

have the wide regional, cultural and ethnic differences come closer together. Still they have not entirely disappeared.

Until the tragic division brought about by the 1950 Korean War, Korea had been one state politically for hundreds of years. The political unity of Korea along with its regional cultural differences can be compared with Great Britain, whose Saxons in the south and Scots in the north have for hundreds of years been one nation with one language and one king, while maintaining their cultural differences.

III. KOREAN GEOGRAPHY

When we consider the land of Korea, both north and south, we find that she is a long, thin peninsula with an area of 85,256 square miles, which is about the size of Great Britain or the state of Utah. Northern Korea is located at the same latitude as the southern part of Oregon. This six-hundred-mile-long peninsula, seldom more than two hundred miles wide, is found in the heart of east Asia. Because of her central location, Korea has always been a buffer state. Russia borders her on the northeast, Manchuria on the north, China on the west and Japan to the southeast. Each of these powerful nations has at various times battled the others for control of Korea. Especially today her strategic position has made her a dividing line between Communist and non-Communist forces in the Far East.

Throughout the six-hundred-mile length of the peninsula there is a great variation in topography. There are broad plains in the southern part of Korea which produce the rice and other agricultural products for the Korean table. The plains are found along the coasts and between the high mountain ranges. But only one-fifth of Korea is cultivated, because of those mountains which seem to be everywhere. This terrain affects the people and their behavior, for they have always lived in the valleys where they could produce rice and grains, and they have always traveled along the valleys rather than over the mountain ranges. Because the northeast is more mountainous, it is natural to expect the population to be scarce there. The northwest section of Korea, like the south, contains more lowlands and is more densely populated. Korea has a good supply of minerals in her mountain areas; these are now being tapped. Coal, iron, tungsten, copper, graphite, magnesite, fluorspar, mica, gold and silver are found in paying quantity.[8] The bulk of mineral wealth is in north Korea, as is the large potential for hydroelectric power.

In ancient times the many Korean rivers were an important means of transportation. They are still used to some extent, but in the last fifty years some of the southern rivers have become so filled with silt that navigation is difficult and other types of transportation are now used. The ocean, which surrounds Korea on three sides, has had its influence upon the country. The Eastern Sea ("Japan Sea") with its crystal-clear waters has an abundance of fish and seaweed. The eastern tides are so small that fishing villages dot the very edge of the shoreline. The western "Yellow Sea" is yellow because of river silt, but it still provides fish. Neither seacoast has large harbors. The harbors on the eastern shore will take shallow draft ships, as will Pusan harbor in the south. The west coast is hampered by tides that can run thirty feet between high and low tide. These tides make it impossible for large freighters to dock. There are 3,479 islands dotted around Korea, mostly rimming her southern coast, and many of them are populated with fishermen.

The climate of Korea is affected by her location as a peninsula connected to a great land mass in the north and extended southward into a large body of water. The northern land mass sends down cool, dry air while the sea from the south sends up warm, moist, maritime air.

North Korean weather is affected by land monsoons that bring in this cold air from the north. Heavy winter snows and low winter temperatures to minus forty degrees Fahrenheit have been recorded, although on the northern border the average low is minus fourteen and four-tenths degrees Fahrenheit. Southern Korea is moderated by marine air in the wintertime and average southern temperature for January is just near the freezing point.

[8] Shannon McCune, *Korea's Heritage: "A Regional and Social Geography,* p. 101.

Summers are a different story because, as the warm, marine air blows from the south, most of Korea turns quite warm and — during the months of July and August — very humid. Average temperatures for July range from seventy-one and six-tenths degrees to seventy-eight and seven-tenths degrees Fahrenheit for the whole country. When the warm southern air mass strikes cool air from the Siberian continent, the pelting, heavy rains of the summer result. About half of the annual rainfall of between thirty-two and fifty-five inches will fall during July and August, causing floods and making farming extremely difficult. The rain is good for rice farming, but, because it comes all at once, the land must be irrigated.

IV. KOREAN RELIGIONS

This land of Korea also has its religious climate. A detailed study of Korea's religions can be made by reading Charles A. Clark, *Religions of Old Korea* and also Chapter Twelve of *Korea, Its Land, People, and Culture*, published in 1960 by the government of South Korea. However, out of the many sects in Korea, we shall look only at the four religions dominant prior to the coming of Protestantism. These are Buddhism, Confucianism, Shamanism and a distinctively Korean movement called *Chundokyo*.

Buddhism. Buddhism came through China to the Korean peninsula about 300 A.D. As Buddhism has done wherever it has gone, it adapted to the culture and existing religious practices of the people. From 935 A.D. to 1392 A.D., the Koryo era, it flourished to such an extent that the period is called "the Golden Age of Buddhism" in Korea. Great and lasting stone temples were built. Buddhism became the state religion; in fact, Buddhist priests were powerful manipulators of the Korean government in the Koryo era. As Buddhism exchanged its religious character for a political one, this priest-ridden government became thoroughly corrupt.[9] In 1392 the Yi Dynasty came into power, defeating the Koryo government, curbing the power of Buddhist priests and tak-

[9] L. George Paik, *The History of Protestant Missions in Korea* 1832-1910, pp. 18, 19.

ing over much of the property held by the great temples. Buddhist priests and nuns were kept out of the city of Seoul by law. The new Yi Dynasty became an advocate of the Chinese ethical system of Confucianism.

Buddhism never recovered from the blow it received at the hands of the Yi Dynasty. Some of the temples still exist today, such as the great structure in Kyungju in southeast Korea, but the temples, though maintained by resident monks, are great empty halls with the dusty smell of a glorious past. They are visited often by curious tourists but rarely by Buddhist worshipers, and the Buddhist monks are held in contempt by many Koreans today. Although I once saw a group of women wearing prayer beads on a summer pilgrimage to the beautiful temple at Mount Sorak on the east coast, most of the temples I have visited, while priests have been on duty, have been devoid of adherents.

Confucianism. Confucianism was brought into power by the Yi Dynasty in 1392. Its high, ethical system has deeply influenced the culture of Korea, but more as a philosophy than as a religion. One of the chief religious aspects of Confucianism was the governmental sacrifice (which has been discontinued) to heaven and earth at the Sajik shrine in Seoul. My wife and I lived a few blocks from this shrine in 1959. It was then part of a park in our neighborhood, with Korean children swarming over its stone foundation as they played.

The other religious aspect of Korean Confucianism is its doctrine of filial piety, symbolized by the eldest son as he worships his family's ancestors. This ancestor worship is the only actual religious element remaining. It is still common practice for most Korean families to make an annual pilgrimage to the gravemounds of their fathers and there make sacrifices of food.

Confucianism suffered under the Japanese occupation, and there was a strong attempt to bring it under the thumb of the Japanese emperor. The Confucian school in Seoul was forced into Japanese control, but after World War II this school was again opened and now has become a modern university. A professor of this university admits that Confucianism is discredited in the face of modern industrial society, but he notes that it still has students who are trying to find the essential truths through Confucian wisdom.[10]

Chundokyo. Another Korean religion is Chundokyo, literally "the heavenly way," a native movement which actually arose in the 1850s as an anti-Roman Catholic and anti-Western movement. Later it broke out as the "Tonghak Revolt" (Eastern Learning) in 1894, continuing as a religious movement with some Christian elements and with a definite patriotic message. Many of the signers of the 1919 Korean Declaration of Independence were members of the Chundokyo organization.

No Religion? The latest official government statistics of the religious bodies show that out of a South Korean population of 24,926,000 people, only 1,140,000 are Buddhist adherents, and fewer yet, 172,000 are Confucian worshipers. The Chundokyo membership is given as 22,000 and that of "Tangoonism" as 29,000. Tangoonism is a sect which thoroughly believes the well-known myth that through Tangoon, the man-god, Korea was originated. The figure for Protestant Christianity is listed as 607,000, while Roman Catholicism is 475,000. Membership definition usually differs between the Roman Catholic and Protestant Churches in that the Roman figure includes its entire believing community, while the Protestant figure generally refers to communicant membership only. The remaining sects and religions of South Korea claim only 16,000 people.[11] It can be seen on Figure 1 that the percentages of religious Koreans are low and that over ninety percent of South Koreans claim no religion at all.

Even though there are professional leaders of the religions of Korea, such as Confucianism and Buddhism, the organizations they represent have not been a strong force in Korean society since before the time when early missionaries and travelers from the West entered Korea. Because of this, the early travelers wrote that Korea was a nation without a religion. They found no temples in the capital and also found

---

[10] *Korea, Its Land, People and Culture,* p. 329.
[11] *Korea Statistical Yearbook,* p. 356.

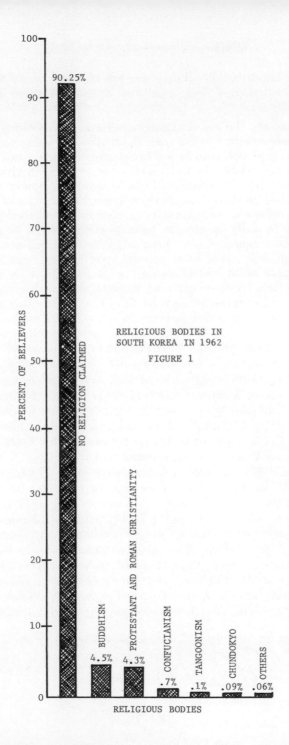

RELIGIOUS BODIES IN
SOUTH KOREA IN 1962

FIGURE 1

no priesthood there.[12]   Those writers, however, were looking
for the evidences of religion as they had known them in their
own countries.

Shamanism. To say that ninety percent of the Korean people are not religious is far from the truth. For centuries there
has been and still is a strong belief in the spirits residing in
the material world: in the rocks, trees, ground, and sky. A
priesthood for the control of these spirits is found in the
shamans or *mudang*. Animistic religion includes many types
of spirits and also includes special exercises performed by the
mudang, in order to win the favor of the spirits or heal sick-
ness. These exercises have been officially outlawed at various
times but still maintain a popular control over the Korean
people even today. Several times in the villages, I have been
lulled to sleep by the pentatonic chanting and the drum beating
of the mudang, who attempts by this behavior to drive out the
harmful spirits in a sick person. When I awoke in the morning, I again heard the rhythm of the mudang still ex-
orcising spirits. She had been continuously at work all night!

When Protestant Christianity came to Korea, it found no
strong, organized religious opposition but found instead that
Shamanism, or animism, had actually prepared the nation to
receive Christianity. I asked a Yonsei University professor
in Seoul why Christianity had made such great advances in
Korea. His answer was strange to me at the time, but I
dutifully took down his ideas and filed them away. Now that
I realize I first rejected his reasoning because of my eth-
nocentric position, I am able to understand what he meant.
He said that while Shamanism is not an organized religion,
it is one of salvation through a higher being, a religion which
holds that a person has no power in himself but needs help
from a higher being. The shamans attempt control of the
spirits around them, particularly of those spirits residing in
one who is ill. For centuries Korea had been plowed by
Shamanistic efforts to communicate with higher beings, and
when the seeds of Christianity were placed in this rich,

[12] Percival Lowell, *Choson, the Land of the Morning Calm,* pp. 181-
182.

plowed soil, they flourished and produced the fruit of Christian disciples. The populations where Shamanism flourished were prepared to believe in a higher being.

The religions of Korea did not flourish equally in all parts of the nation. Chundokyo, even though it originated in the south, had more believers in the north, as did Shamanism, while Confucianism and Buddhism seemed stronger in the south of Korea. There is, however, no strong line of demarcation, and indeed each of these religions has borrowed much from the others. Many families have maintained no strict loyalty to one religion but have combined the practices of several religions into their lives.

V. KOREAN HISTORY

All the people of Korea are justly proud of their ancient history. Tradition goes back to 2333 B.C., while recorded history begins at about the time of Christ. The modern history of Korea dates from the beginning of the Yi Dynasty in 1392, just a century before Columbus discovered the New World.[13] The Yi Dynasty came in with new reforms, drove out the corrupt Buddhists and established Confucianism. During that time the Koreans had to fight off Manchurians on one side and Japanese on the other. It is little wonder that Korea was called the "hermit nation" and was very reluctant to open up her doors to foreigners. She was afraid of outsiders. A possible oversimplification of the strife and turmoil that leads Korea to the modern era, but which nevertheless gives a fair outline of the history of her suffering, is that Korea was attacked by one nation, then Korea herself called for help from another nation, only to find that her helper gave more "help" than was asked for by taking control of the country for a while. Korea's first modern step was to sign treaties which opened her ports to Japan in 1876 and to the United States in 1882. Then other Western nations followed, and all began to walk through the opened doors into this hermit nation.

Opening of Korea to the West did not lesson the covetous-

[13] Paik, *op. cit.*, p. 14.

ness of surrounding nations for her; she was and still is a strategic piece of soil. Because of the map outlines of Korea and Japan, some Japanese have described her as a dagger pointing at the heart of Japan. In 1894 and 1895 Japan fought China, in part on Korean soil, leaving Japan in control after the fighting. But Russia also had designs on Korea and so fought them out with Japan in 1904 and 1905, again partly on Korean soil, and once again Japan was the victor. This time Japan was assured of absolute control over Korea, because of these two victories and also because of a secret agreement between the President of the United States, Theodore Roosevelt, and the Japanese government. This agreement was, in short, that the United States would respect Japan's control of Korea if Japan would respect the United States' control of the Philippines.[14] Korea was formally annexed to Japan in 1910. The dagger point at Japan's heart was turned into a stepping-stone to the Asian mainland.

Korea's long Yi Dynasty was over; she was no longer free and independent, and the rule of Japan was very harsh. Economic improvements brought in by the Japanese benefited not the Koreans but the Japanese people. Increased rice production was shipped to Japan and Korean industry was developed only to aid Japan. World War II brought even greater hardships on the Korean people as their resources of food and all kinds of metal, even to the brass spoons of the Korean table, were requisitioned for the Japanese war effort. Men were forced to go to work for Japan. The whole economy of Korea and her people suffered greatly.

At this writing Korea is still not free. Her modern history continues fresh in our minds. Once again two great foreign powers, the Communist bloc and the United Nations, fought over the little country, leaving her half-destroyed and divided into two pieces.

[14] *Ibid.*, p. 259 (From T. Dennett, "President Roosevelt's Secret Pact With Japan," *The Current History Magazine* (October, 1924), pp. 15-21.

Chapter II. Survey of Korean Political and Church History

INTO THE MIDST OF THE SUFFERING, FASCINATING, VERY OLD Korea came the message of Christianity carried by foreigners from the West, who as people of a new culture were a curiosity to the people of the old culture. As we examine the encounter of the Christian Gospel with four thousand years of Asian tradition, the historical events which intertwine with the advance of the Protestant Church in Korea become real to us. We shall first review these events briefly in their time sequence, beginning with the entrance in 1832 of Carl Gutzlaff (the first Protestant missionary, who came to Korea for just a month's visit) and continuing until the present.

The next missionary visit was made in 1865 by Robert Thomas, who the following year became the first Protestant martyr in Korea. In 1876 John McIntyre and John Ross, who like Thomas were Scots, baptized the first Korean Protestants from among those Koreans who moved to Manchuria. Korea was not yet open to foreigners, but that was changed when in 1884, two years after the first American treaty was made with Korea, an American missionary doctor, Horace Allen, went to Korea to live and work. The next year the first *ordained* Protestant missionaries of the Northern Methodist and Northern Presbyterian Churches of the United States landed in Korea together. H. G. Appenzeller was the Methodist and Horace G. Underwood the Presbyterian.

Within a few years they saw that there would be no official hindrance to preaching, and wide itineration by the missionaries began. Other missions soon began work in Korea: the Australian Presbyterian Mission in 1889, the Church of England in 1890, the American Southern Presbyterian Mission in 1892 and the Canadian Presbyterian in 1898.

Japan began her gradual absorption of Korea by defeating the mighty Chinese Army partly on Korean soil in the Sino-Japanese War of 1894. Immediately following this war in

1895, the Presbyterian Church in Korea began to expand rapidly. By 1900 missionaries with Korean assistance had completed a translation of the New Testament which was to become the foundation of the growing Church in Korea.

In 1905 Japan clinched its control of Korea by defeating Russia in the Russo-Japanese War, and the Korean people saw that they were expected to be subjects of the Japanese Empire. In these dark days the Church was growing rapidly, and in 1907 the "fire" of the Holy Spirit fell upon Korea in the form of a great revival that gave the whole Church new strength.

The year 1910 is marked by the formal annexation of Korea by Japan and the inauguration of the "Million Souls for Christ" movement, a concerted effort by the Church and missions for expansion following the great revival.

In 1912 the Japanese government tried to discredit the Christian Church indirectly by convicting 105 of its members and pastors of conspiring to murder a Japanese official. Apparently false, most of the convictions were set aside by a higher court, and those few men sentenced to prison terms were released within a few years. This incident was called the "Conspiracy Case."

With the hope of aid from the United States, the Korean people made a peaceful bid for independence in March, 1919, by street demonstrations, which were swiftly and brutally put down by the Japanese police with much bloodshed. Christians were in the forefront of this independence movement that failed politically. The following year most of the Churches found new strength and began again to grow rapidly in spite of increasing Japanese pressure.

In 1937 the Northern and Southern Presbyterian Missions began to close their schools rather than allow their faculties and student bodies to bow before the Japanese Shinto shrines, considered religious by these missions. By 1938 the Japanese government had complete control over the Protestant Churches, and membership began to decline.

Only a few missionaries were left in Korea when World War II began in 1941, and they were soon evacuated. In 1942 all the denominations in Korea were forced to amalgamate into one organization. August 15, 1945, is known as

NATION	YEAR	CHURCH
		1866 Thomas of Scotland Bible Society martyred.
		1876 McIntyre and Ross baptize Korean Protestants in Manchuria.
First Korean treaty with the United States.	1882	1884 American Protestant missionary, Dr. Allen, arrives in Korea. 1885 Ordained missionaries Appenzeller, Methodist, & Underwood, Presb., arrive. 1887 Wide missionary itineration begins. 1889 Australian Presbyterian Mission opens. 1890 Church of England Mission opens.
Tonghak rebellion occurs. Japan defeats China in war partly held in Korea.	1894	1892 Southern Presbyterian Mission opens. 1895 Explosion of growth in Churches occurs. 1898 Canadian Presbyterian Mission opens. 1900 New Testament translation completed.
Japan defeats Russia in war partly held in Korea.	1904	1907 Great Revival in Pyongyang, Korea.
Korea annexed by Japan.	1910	1910 Million Souls for Christ movement.
Conspiracy Case.	1912	1912 General Assembly of Presbyterian Church organized.
Independence Movement.	1919	1920 Most Churches begin to grow rapidly.
		1937 Northern and Southern Presbyterian Missions close schools. 1938 Church membership begins to decline.
World War II begins.	1941	1942 All denominations amalgamated into one organization.
Korea "liberated" to Russia in north and U.S.A. in south.	1945	1945 Churches in South Korea reorganized.
Republic of Korea founded.	1948	
Refugees move into south.		
Communist invasion in Korea.	1950	1951 First Presbyterian Church schism.
Armistice agreement completed.	1953	1953 Churches again grow rapidly. 1954 Reconstruction and relief funds pour into Korean Churches.

SURVEY OF KOREAN PROTESTANT CHURCH HISTORY
AND CORRESPONDING POLITICAL EVENTS.
FIGURE 2

"Liberation Day" in Korea, but only half of her was liberated. The land north of the 38th parallel was quickly put under Communist control by Russia, and refugees began to pour into South Korea. In the year of liberation the Churches of South Korea were reorganized along their original denominational patterns.

On June 25, 1950, the Communist North Koreans, who had for some time instigated border fights, attacked South Korea in full force and threw the United Nations into war against the Communist aggressors. After bloody fighting up and down the peninsula, the battle continued along a line near the thirty-eighth parallel, and by 1953 a final armistice agreement had been completed, leaving Korea divided by a demilitarized zone running across the peninsula. Each side of this zone is armed in preparation for war.

In 1951 the Korean Presbyterian Church suffered its first schism. Recurring schisms have now split the Church into four factions.

Although they do not at all correspond to these four factions, there are also four cooperating Presbyterian Churches from abroad which helped to build the Presbyterian Church in Korea. I will refer to these four missions as follows: the mission of the Presbyterian Church in the United States will be called the "Southern Presbyterian Mission." The mission of the Presbyterian Church in the United States of America (which combined in 1958 with the United Presbyterian Church of North America to form the United Presbyterian Church in the United States of America) will be called the "Northern Presbyterian Mission." The mission of the Presbyterian Church of Canada, which later became part of the United Church of Canada, will be called the "Canadian Presbyterian Mission." Finally, the Australian Presbyterian Church, which also sent a mission to Korea, is referred to as the "Australian Presbyterian Mission." All four of these missions cooperated to build the one Korean Presbyterian Church, which was united until divisions began in 1951.

In this same way the mission of the Methodist Episcopal Church in the United States will be denoted "Northern Methodist" and the Methodist Episcopal Church South, also from the United States, will be called "Southern Methodist." In 1930 the two Korean Churches established by these two missions united to form one Methodist Church in Korea, and the two parent Churches in the United States united in 1939.

Chapter III. Growth of the Presbyterian Church in Korea

THE KOREAN PRESBYTERIAN CHURCH HAS MANY TIMES BEEN noted for its remarkable growth. One wonders whether a study of its history will reveal, for our further instruction and use, the secret of the contagious spread of Christianity in Korea. From its very first days there were evidences of unusual growth in the Presbyterian Church in Korea.

I. ESTABLISHMENT OF THE PRESBYTERIAN CHURCH 1832-1895

Early Attempts at Evangelism. Only one year after arriving in Korea, Horace G. Underwood, the first ordained Presbyterian missionary, administered the sacrament of baptism in secret to Mr. Toh Sa No.[1] The date was July 11, 1886. Mr. No was the first Korean Protestant to be baptized on his native soil, but within another year a small church was organized. Because the Roman Catholic Mission had been violently persecuted by the Korean government in the previous decade and because the present laws prohibited the spread of Christianity, the quick results of the Presbyterian missionaries' efforts were surprising even to the missionaries. This rapid beginning indicates things that were to come in the growth of the Presbyterian Church in Korea, a story which has become famous around the world.

Mr. No was not the first Christian convert of Korean birth. Indeed, Roman Catholic converts suffered persecution for their faith at the hands of their countrymen in the eighteenth century. Carl Gutzlaff, a Protestant missionary from the Netherlands Missionary Society, visited Korea for a short time

---

[1] Korean names have been transposed into the Western order, with the surname, or "last name" in the final instead of the Korean primary position.

in 1832, and the Rev. Mr. R. J. Thomas visited in 1865 and again in 1866 aboard an American vessel, the *General Sherman.* Thomas had with him some Chinese Bibles for distribution in Korea. A few of these Bibles found their way into the hands of the Korean people, but not directly from Mr. Thomas, for he and the whole crew of that ship were killed when the ship was burned about September 2, 1866.[2]

Thomas was truly the first Protestant martyr for the cause of Christ in Korea. But a ship's captain, who was sent to demand redress for this action against an American ship, became convinced that "the attack on the General Sherman was made under strong provocation."[3] The immediate reason for the attack was the *General Sherman* captain's attempted kidnap of the governor of the city of Pyongyang.[4] Other suspicious circumstances surrounding the voyage, however, had already aroused Korean hostility. The *General Sherman,* loaded with guns, powder and contraband articles, was said to be dispatched for the purpose of plundering the royal tombs in Pyongyang.[5] While Thomas' mission was honorable, the mission of the crew was not, and one cannot blame the Korean people for protecting the sacred tombs of their past monarchs by attacking and burning the ship.

A year later Alexander Williamson, a missionary of the National Bible Society of Scotland residing in Chefoo and the man who had sent Thomas to Korea, came through Manchuria. At the border of Korea in 1867 he sold a number of books to Koreans, books written in the Chinese language which was intelligible only to educated Koreans.

In 1873 John Ross, a Scotch Presbyterian residing in Manchuria, made a journey to the border, where he met with Koreans and secured a man named Sang Yoon Suh to help him translate a portion of the Bible into Korean. Remaining in Manchuria, Ross and his fellow missionary, John McIntyre, translated the Gospel of Luke into Korean with the help of

[2] L. George Paik, *The History of Protestant Missions in Korea* 1832-1910, p. 45.

[3] F. A. McKenzie, *The Tragedy of Korea,* p. 11.

[4] Harry A. Rhodes, *History of the Korea Mission Presbyterian Church U. S. A. 1884-1934,* Vol. I, p. 72.

[5] McKenzie, *op. cit.,* p. 11.

Mr. Suh, who was converted and was to lead his brother and neighbors at Sorai village in northwest Korea to this new faith. Mr. Suh's brother, Kyung Jo Suh, was one of the first seven Presbyterian ministers ordained in Korea.[6]

In the winter of 1884 Ross and his colleagues visited the Korean immigrants in the northeastern valleys of Manchuria, where they baptized seventy-five men who were farmers and heads of families.[7] Thus the first Protestant Korean Christians were instructed and baptized in Manchuria, but these men served as the link for the first Protestant work in Korea proper and some of them became the foundation for the young Church in Korea.

The first Presbyterian missionary actually to arrive in Korea was Dr. Horace N. Allen, an American who came on September 20, 1884 and served as physician to the United States Legation while being under appointment by the Board of Foreign Missions of the Presbyterian Church in the U. S. A. (Northern Presbyterian). A month later Dr. Allen's family moved to Seoul from China and became the first resident missionary family in Korea. Because of government restrictions, Dr. Allen's work was limited to the American Embassy until, on December 4, 1884, there came about an event that prepared the way for open missionary work. A political revolution was attempted and the young prince, Young Ik Min, just returned from Washington, D. C., was wounded. The Secretary of the United States Legation called Dr. Allen to treat the wounded prince, who was at the point of death. Dr. Allen's successful treatment of Prince Min won the confidence of the King and Queen, who granted Dr. Allen's request to start a Royal Hospital.

The Royal Hospital was opened in the capital city of Seoul on April 10, 1885, just five days after the arrival in Korea of the young Mr. Horace G. Underwood (also Northern Presbyterian), who, although he was a minister, had studied medicine for a year and so was immediately able to help Dr. Allen in the hospital. In addition, Underwood

[6] Paik, *op. cit.*, p. 46.
[7] *Ibid.*, p. 47.

immediately began to study the language of the Koreans and he reports:

> As soon as we had secured a little knowledge of the language, we regularly went out in the lanes and byways, sitting down under some tree near a frequented road, or beside some medicinal spring to which the people were in the habit of flocking. We would take out a book and start reading and when several gathered around us to ask questions, we would attempt to explain to them the book, its truth, and what it meant.[8]

Later these street discussions developed further, and gatherings were held on larger streets or in villages. In certain sections of Seoul, street chapels were opened. The first baptism in 1886 was only the beginning, for Underwood writes from Seoul on January 22, 1887: "We are to have several baptisms on next Sunday and the men who have applied seem to be thoroughly in earnest. They are some of the offshoots, as it were, from some of Ross' work in the North."[9] There were reportedly twenty or thirty other applicants for baptism in the country who, Underwood felt sure, would come to the capital to receive baptism once they heard there was an opportunity to do so.

Early Objection to Evangelism. Even with this small precursor of the great growth of the Church to come, Dr. Allen raised objection to these early baptisms by Underwood on the grounds that baptism was beyond the work allowed by the Korean government. He thought there was not only the possibility of persecution and martyrdom but also a possibility of ruining the present hospital work. Underwood answered his objection by saying that baptism was no more "mission work" than any other witnessing done by the missionaries; it was just a seal of the Christian life. Mr. Underwood felt sure that the government, when it learned of the good of Christianity, would withdraw its restrictions as had been done in other parts of the world. "We are keeping

---

[8] Horace Grant Underwood, *The Call of Korea,* pp. 106-107.

[9] Underwood, Letter to the Board of Foreign Missions of the Presbyterian Church U. S. A. (Seoul, Korea: January 22, 1887).

good faith with the government and have not proselytized through the hospital or school and orphanage. I can see no harm in baptizing in my home."[10]

Dr. John W. Heron, who arrived in June, 1885, to assist with the medical work, also opposed the baptism of Korean Christians for fear that the wrath of the Korean government might be brought on the missionaries. In addition, the Board of Foreign Missions at home took a cautious attitude by not reporting until 1888 the statistics of baptisms that had taken place two years earlier, lest there be official re-action either from the Korean government or the United States Legation in Korea.

In fact, during the first ten years of the mission's life in Seoul, some of the missionaries continued to oppose the use of direct evangelism because of the supposed threat of the Korean government. If there were to be any kind of persecu-tion, it certainly would begin in Seoul, since the King re-sided there. Missionaries living in that city had heard of the martyrdom of Thomas and the bloody persecution of Roman Catholics twenty years before, and so were keenly aware of the new possibilities of persecution. The Rev. Mr. Samuel A. Moffett writes:

> There are at present no signs of opposition to our work, but our position here is not assured and the present King is not secure on his throne. A revolution might bring to power the man who twenty years ago had put 20,000 Christians to death.[11]

It is a simple fact, however, that the Protestant missionary movement never received any official opposition from the Korean central government. Early missionaries were not free from attacks by local bandits and from occasional, unco-operative local officials, but there were never any restrictions on missionaries living anywhere or teaching as they felt led. In 1959 the Korean government took official notice of the seventy-fifth anniversary of Protestant missions in Korea with

[10] Underwood, Letter to Dr. Horace Allen (Seoul, Korea: January 27, 1887).

[11] Samuel A. Moffett, Letter to the Board of Foreign Missions of the Presbyterian Church U. S. A. (Seoul, Korea: March 18, 1890).

a celebration expressing its appreciation for the work of the missionaries, a most unusual and perhaps unique occurrence around the world.

However, the early missionaries could not look ahead and see that national government opposition was not forthcoming. Teaching and baptizing were officially opposed by the American Legation while Mr. Underwood was traveling on passport in Korea, but he continued exploration anyway, once going across onto Chinese soil under a Chinese passport, baptizing Korean Christians there. Even though Underwood was besieged from all sides by rural people in Korea who wanted to be baptized, the mission itself opposed Underwood's travel because his teaching and baptizing enroute were, they thought, against the Korean law. Underwood says, however:

> We have found no proof whatever that the Korean officials are not prepared to admit the preaching of the Gospel. On the contrary, a deputy governor of a province and a deputy magistrate of a city, as well as a number of smaller officials are seeking baptism.[12]

These early missionaries and the Board in the United States were simply not prepared for the great response of the Korean people. Underwood says that he came to Korea "with the expectation that we would have to wait many years before we would be able to do any work, looking forward to a steady work in the line of learning the language and translating the Scriptures for several years to come."[13] This was a normal pioneer missionary attitude. What a surprise it was, therefore, to find instead such a response as that of the four men who walked 220 miles from the village of Sorai just to receive baptism from him. They reported several in their village who wanted baptism and urged Underwood to visit them.

First Protestant Churches of Seoul and Sorai. In September, 1887, the mission organized in Seoul the first Christian church on Korean soil, with a roll of fourteen members.

[12] Underwood, Letter to the Board (Seoul, Korea: October 21, 1890).
[13] *Ibid.*, June 17, 1887.

Thirteen of these men were led to Christ by a man trained
by Mr. Ross in Mukden, Manchuria.[14] Also as a result of
Ross's work, Sang Yoon Suh, the translator, was converted
in China, trained as a colporteur and later settled in Sorai
village, there winning his countrymen to Christ. Underwood
soon set off for a visit to that village, located two hundred
miles northwest of Seoul in Whanghai Province.

In Sorai Mr. Underwood found in addition to the four
baptized in Seoul, seven men ready for baptism, which he
"gladly administered." The village has been aptly called by
Dr. L. George Paik "the cradle of Protestant Christianity in
Korea."[15] Sorai produced leadership for the Presbyterian
Church all out of proportion to the size of the village. The
first church building financed entirely by the local people
was soon erected and in only a few years, the Sorai church
claimed the adults of fifty out of fifty-eight houses in the
village. The close-knit fabric of family and neighbor relations was such a useful vehicle for the Gospel that the village
became very largely Christian. In this, Sorai showed the pattern of things to come.

A few of the people of the village, having been led to
Christ, in turn led their kinsmen to a knowledge of Him and
taught them the Scriptures. They also set the pattern of
"self-support," or providing the initiative for church extension, building the church itself and providing for its ongoing.
In this village as in many other places later on, the Gospel
spread ahead of the missionaries, who, like Underwood, went
to the villages not to convert the heathen but to baptize and
instruct those who had already met Christ. This was the
beginning of another pattern, that of vast, rural missionary
itineration, made necessary by the rapid Christian conversions.

By 1890 the Northern Presbyterian Mission reported one
hundred communicant members. The missionary staff had
been augmented to three ordained American ministers working with three Korean helpers. Much of the northern terri-

[14] Annual Report of the Board of Foreign Missions of the Presbyterian Church U. S. A. (New York: 1890), p. 134.
[15] Paik, *op. cit.*, p. 131.

tory of Korea had been explored in several long trips taken
by Mr. Underwood. These exploratory trips were continued
by Mr. S. A. Moffett, Mr. J. S. Gale, and Mr. W. L. Swallen
as they came to Korea. At first this exploration was intended
to be merely a spying-out of the land. It could not remain
that for long, however, because of the demands from all
quarters for instruction and baptism. The field was beginning to open up, and 1890 saw important policy decisions
made concerning the growth of this young Church.

Early Mission Policy. One decision of policy is seen in the
words of Dr. F. F. Ellinwood, Secretary of the Board of Foreign Missions of the Presbyterian Church U.S.A., as he is
quoted by Dr. L. George Paik:

> We believe the mistake has been made in some fields of
> over-centralization. We want to inaugurate a new policy in
> Korea, that of diffusion and the widespread preaching of the
> gospel. We will locate stations throughout the entire field.[16]

Also in 1890, in response to the invitation of Korea missionaries who were impressed with the plan presented in his book
Methods of Mission Work, Dr. John L. Nevius visited Korea.
His two-week visit with the then seven young Presbyterian
missionaries had its immediate and profound effect on mission policies, an effect which lasts until the present time.
After careful consideration of the plan presented by Nevius,
the mission fully adopted his principles and put them into
practice. A review of the history of the Korea Mission until
1942 reflects how carefully they followed the main thrust of
the ideas set forth by Dr. Nevius, then in person, and later
in his book *Planting and Development of Missionary Churches.*[17] (Turn to "Nevius Method" in the glossary for its description.)

Also around 1890 it finally became apparent that the Korean
governmental rules prohibiting the progagation of the Gospel in Korea, while they were still on the books, were not
being enforced. The mission board report of 1892 states

[16] *Ibid.*
[17] Available in print today from the Presbyterian and Reformed
Publishing Co., Philadelphia, Pennsylvania.

that there had been a "general disposition to favor American influence. It would not be strange, however, if restrictive measures were rather increased. But at the same time, the mission work in Korea has taken such deep root, that there can be no other result, humanly speaking, than that of general progress."[18] So there came a new era of freedom for the missionaries to itinerate and explore Korea to the far corners, and that is what they did. Some of them record traveling one thousand miles on foot during a year. Stations were established in the major port cities of Pusan, Wonsan, and Pyongyang. The missionaries used their new-found freedom to preach and teach the Gospel. In the north there was an eager response to their message while in the south, according to the Rev. Mr. William M. Baird, the people seemed prejudiced against the Gospel and all foreign influence. He notes that few people came to see him in Pusan after they learned of his object, even though there was no outward opposition.[19] In the city of Pyongyang in the north, however, Moffett reports that he was besieged night and day by visitors in his guestroom, which served also as his temporary residence.[20]

Early Missionary Method. The use of the guestroom or *sahrang* room, as it is called in Korea, was widespread. It was a small Korean room with a heated floor and no furniture, used by the master of the house to receive guests. One of these rooms would be rented at mission expense, and a Korean evangelist who was expected to be there constantly was placed in it. Books were made available for reading and for sale. Sometimes the missionary spent two or three hours a day in the *sahrang* room talking with visitors. Later on, Christians would gather for noon-day prayer meetings and for guided study of the Bible.[21] One missionary in Seoul, along with his assistant, began the day singing hymns in their *sahrang* room and the people from the street not over

[18] Annual Report of the Board (New York: 1892).
[19] William M. Baird, Letter to the Board of Foreign Missions of the Presbyterian Church U. S. A. (Pusan, Korea: June 27, 1892).
[20] Moffett, Letter to the Board (Pyongyang, Korea: January 12, 1894).
[21] D. L. Gifford, Report of Evangelistic Work to the Board of Foreign Missions of the Presbyterian Church U. S. A. (Seoul, Korea: 1892).

ten feet away came in and looked to see what the com-
motion was. The assistant then told them that this was the
way Christians sang hymns, and with this opening he began
his preaching. Sometimes the people came inside but more
often they stood outside in the adjoining shed and listened
to the message.[22]

Some think that identification is a new concept in mission
work, but in 1892 one of the early missionaries to Korea,
Samuel A. Moffett, went far in identifying himself with the
people he was trying to lead to Christ. The 1894 Board of
Foreign Missions report says that Moffett had the true secret
of missionary success. He lived in one Korean room for two
months in the city of Pyongyang. The board cites from
Moffett's report that year:

> I am situated just at present as I have long wished to be:
> in direct contact with the people, living in the midst of
> them, meeting them every day and all day, entering into
> their lives and having them enter into mine (however in ways
> not very easy to endure). I am certainly making friends
> and having an opportunity to do a great deal of direct per-
> sonal work in preaching, instructing, enlightening and ex-
> horting.[23]

Early Converts. Dr. L. George Paik states, "The motives
that actuated the early converts were partly selfish. A large
proportion of the first Christians were household servants,
language teachers, colporteurs, and teachers in schools who
received compensation or salary."[24] This observation is reflected in the comparatively slight growth of the Church
through 1894. For instance, from 1889 until 1893 the communicant membership fluctuated between 100 and 150. The
people were being won to Christ, but on an individual basis
and not in large numbers. While there was keen interest in
the Christian faith, it can be seen on Figure 3 that there
was small growth of communicant membership of the Church.
This was evidently a time of exploration and of planting seeds

---

[22] Gifford, Letter to the Board (Seoul, Korea: January 22, 1894).
[23] Moffett, Annual Report of the Board (New York: 1894).
[24] Paik, *op. cit.*, p. 155.

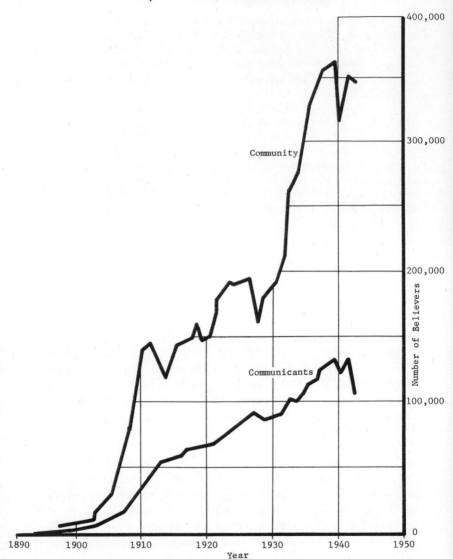

COMMUNITY AND COMMUNICANT MEMBERSHIP OF THE PRESBYTERIAN CHURCH OF KOREA
(includes the Korean Presbytery of Manchuria)

FIGURE 3

that would later bring much fruit for the kingdom of God in Korea.

II. EXPLOSION IN THE CHURCH
1895-1905

In 1895 and 1896 an explosion in the communicant membership of the Church occurred. This is illustrated in Figure 4, which is a section of Figure 3 expanded to a larger scale. The striking, upward swing in Figure 4 represents the beginning of a great movement to Christ, the sort of movement seen infrequently in modern times. Of course, the missionaries were excitedly aware of this upward swing, too. From Seoul: "The situation in Korea seems to be changing. The people, so long indifferent, seem to show signs of awakening."[25] And from Pyongyang in the annual report of 1895: "Work in Pyongyang has passed the initiatory stage and has become an established work. The Church is beginning to develop, to expand and to make itself felt as a factor in the life of the city and surrounding country." The report goes on to give the main reason for this phenomenal growth. "A cause for rejoicing is the earnest evangelistic work carried on by the members and catachumens. The men have been doing the work and we [missionaries] have been receiving calls to follow up their work." Even at this early date the Church pushed out ahead of the missionaries, who through superhuman effort took on a full load of "follow-up work," teaching and examining candidates for baptism and the catachumenate, training those won to Christ in the rudiments of the faith.

Influence of the Sino-Japanese War. This 1895 explosion in church membership may have been stimulated by the Sino-Japanese War of 1894, fought between Chinese and Japanese up and down the length of Korea. This was the first "modern war" between foreign powers fought on Korean soil. Missionaries said that had the Chinese won, mission work in Korea might have been stopped. Defeated China represented the old-line, conservative, and corrupt political

[25] S. F. Moore, Letter to the Board of Foreign Missions of the Presbyterian Church U. S. A. (Seoul, Korea: January 15, 1895).

system, but victorious Japan represented a progressive government. The conservative Koreans lined up with China, but the Koreans receptive to change and new ideas came out on top with Japan.

Did the Church Grow Too Fast? As can be seen on Figure 4, the communicant membership of the Church began to grow in 1895, and it did not slow down until 1914. At the turn of the century the Church showed better than a thirty percent increase in communicant membership for the year 1900 alone. People were flocking to the Church in tremendous numbers and the annual report of the mission board asks, "Are not these people going too fast?" The board answers itself in the words of one of its Pyongyang missionaries:

> "In the face of entire openness, of evident friendliness and a turning toward Christ, one cannot tell these people to go slowly and proceed only so fast as the few missionaries here have time to go around and instruct them. Their advances must be met on the assumption that they are made in good faith. Yet we must not shut our eyes to the fact that, if uninstructed, these people, while professing Christianity, are liable not only to fall into serious errors themselves, but to lead others into . . . lamentable mistakes."
>
> In other words, the readiness of the people is a spur to the missionary. The idea that men must be so thoroughly converted that they can go alone and grow to full stature of men in Christ Jesus without fostering care, has no place in northern Korea.[26]

Was this tremendous growth an ingathering of numbers without any spiritual foundation? Much evidence indicates that it was based firmly on spiritual foundations. No one questions the dedication of the missionaries to the Great Commission of our Lord. They were not overcome by the temptation for mere numbers, but were doing their best to make disciples of those who turned to Christ.

Returning to Figure 3, it is important to note the relationship between the Christian community and communicants. Christian *community*, synonomous in this writing with "adherents" (see glossary — "adherents") is defined by the Pres-

[26] Annual Report of the Board (New York: 1900).

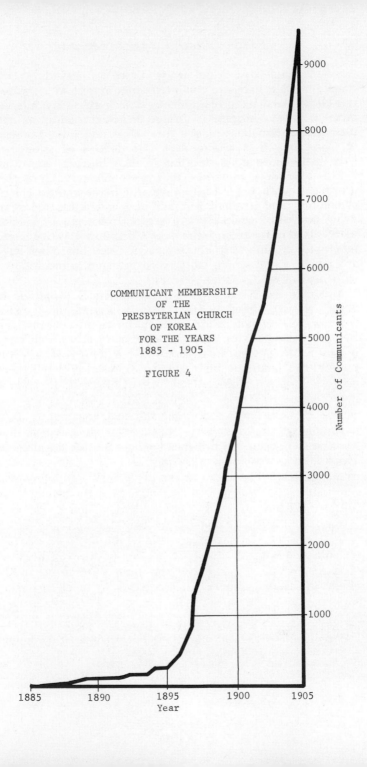

COMMUNICANT MEMBERSHIP
OF THE
PRESBYTERIAN CHURCH
OF KOREA
FOR THE YEARS
1885 - 1905

FIGURE 4

byterian Council of Missions in Korea as including communicants, all baptized children, inquirers under instruction or received on probation, regular church attenders and
others who have in some real sense detached themselves from
their old relations and placed themselves under the influence
of Christianity.[27] *Communicants* are defined as adult baptized believers in good standing in the Church.

The ratio of community to communicants in a rapidly
growing Church is very important, for if there were a large
community and a small number of communicants for any
given year, this would show a great ingathering but a poor
perfecting or training of the new Christians. A large community-to-communicant ratio can be seen in other areas
around the world where Christward movements are followed
with inadequate Christian nurture.

Although the South Sea Islands present a situation for
church growth different from that in Korea, their church
community — communicant relationship is informative. The
Rev. Mr. Alan R. Tippett, in an intensive study of a Church
in one South Pacific area, discovered a high ratio of community to communicants caused by poor perfecting and
poor leadership training of the new Christians, in spite of
many conversions from paganism. After two years of mission work there were forty-four full members out of 5,790
attending worship regularly. But after sixteen years there
were no more than 908 full members out of 19,776 adherents.
Three decades later only 4,586 out of 42,362 adherents were
communicants. The ratio of those regularly attending worship and calling themselves Christian to those brought into
full membership, after fifty years of strong intake, was eight
to one in a denomination whose figure is normally nearer
two to one. The damage was done in the first two decades,
which closed with a ratio of twenty-one to one.[28] The effects
of this community-to-communicant ratio showed up in this
South Sea Island Church in later years in block reversions

[27] Report of the Statistics Auditing Committee, Minutes of the Presbyterian Council of Missions in Korea (September, 1904).
[28] Personal interview with Alan R. Tippett, Professor at the Institute
of Church Growth in Eugene, Oregon, 1963.

from the Church into nativistic movements. Few of those who had become communicants were lost.

While no Church is able to bring into its membership one hundred percent of those coming under its influence, early Korean missionaries did a good job of training the new Christians. In 1898 the ratio between Christian community and communicants was 3.6 to 1. Between 1907 and 1942 the average ratio was 2.6 to 1, which means that for every baptized member there was an average of 1.6 other persons attending Sunday services regularly, having given up all non-Christian religious practices but not yet fully instructed to be received into full membership. Even during the period of great ingathering in 1910, for instance, the ratio of community to communicants in Korea was similar to that in 1898 (3.6 to 1). The people were not only won to Christ but they were continually being given instruction by the hard-working lay leaders and missionaries, to pass the stringent requirements leading to baptism.

III. CONFESSION AND REVIVAL
1905-1910

Even more convincing evidence for the spiritual foundation of this great growth is the fact that out of the rapidly growing Korean Church came the great "Revival of 1907." This revival has often been described as due overwhelmingly to spiritual causes. There are many non-spiritual factors also, such as the growing hopelessness of the Korean people as they began to be pressed by the Japanese.

Lack of Hope Following the Russo-Japanese War. After the Japanese had driven the Russians out of Korea in a war occurring in 1904 again on north Korean soil, they began to take over the country in a systematic way obvious to all those living in Korea. Dr. Paik, quoting the Rev. Mr. C. E. Sharp, says that the Korean people were beginning to realize the failure of the ancient civilization of their fathers in the stress of the twentieth century. They saw that nations styled Christian were the ones that possessed the highest civilization and culture and, turning from the old, they sought the new. To many of these people Christianity meant a kind of civilization only.[29] "All eyes were turned and many Christians saw in the Church the only hope of the country and . . . the country wanted a leader and the Christian Church was the strongest, most influential, single organization in Korea."[30]

Mr. Sharp gives us another example of the hopelessness that Korean people felt in the face of the Japanese, who were slowly wiping out all trace of Korean culture from the land: A magistrate attended an evening service of a Bible training class

> . . . and at the close made a few remarks to the people. In the course of his remarks he expressed a sentiment which shows the present attitude in many minds towards Christianity. "There is nothing left for us to do now but to put our trust in the Christians' God." . . . Of course this turning to Christianity does not spring from a conscious spiritual need. It is not a spiritual revival but it does mean that God is using the present political situation.[31]

Other missionaries, too, were deeply aware of other than spiritual motivations for turning to the Church. The Rev. Mr. William M. Baird was concerned that of the large numbers of people coming into the Church, some may not have been properly motivated to become Christians. This concern on the missionaries' part, as well as the concern of those of the young Church, led to action. "The missionaries have been meeting each night for the past week and praying for the Holy Spirit's blessing and the Koreans are earnestly seeking the Spirit's guidance and blessing . . . . Within the church also, the Christians are seeking earnestly for the best things."[32]

Bible Classes the Vehicle for Revival. The actual foundations of the revival, however, were not laid in a lack of spirituality but rather, in the Bible training classes. These classes, held throughout the country in both rural and urban

[29] C. E. Sharp, *Korea Mission Field* (Seoul, Korea: Evangelical Missions in Korea, August, 1906), p. 182. Also quoted by Paik, p. 344.

[30] William Newton Blair, *Gold in Korea,* third edition, 1957, p. 61.

[31] Sharp, Letter to the Board of Foreign Missions of the Presbyterian Church U. S. A. (Seoul, Korea: January 10, 1906).

[32] Baird, Letter to the Board (Pyongyang, Korea: January 3, 1907).

areas, were influential in the life of the Church. The Rev. Mr. W. N. Blair says that more than anything else, Bible classes accounted for the rapid growth and revival condition of the Korean Church in those early times.[33] The Bible training class system began in 1890 in Dr. Underwood's study in Seoul, with seven men attending. In 1891 it was written into the mission by-laws that each missionary should "work out a course of Scripture instruction for each sub-station according to the general plan approved by the mission."[34] The number of these Scripture instruction classes grew along with the Church.

On the nature of Bible training classes, the Rev. Mr. W. B. Hunt has written:

> The education of the whole church, all its membership, young and old, literate and illiterate, is being undertaken systematically, and largely by the Training Classes in which *the* textbook is the Bible. Some of these are representative in character, the attendance coming from every part of the field; others are local, meant only for the members of particular groups. Some are attended only by men, others only by women, but in most of the country classes both men and women are taught, though in separate divisions. Sometimes these classes are taught entirely by the missionaries, or by the missionary and several helpers, but more often by the helpers alone. Bible study is the object of the class, but prayer, conferences, and practical evangelistic effort are prominent parts of the work.[35]

In 1904 it was reported that sixty percent of the members and catachumens attended one or more of these classes. By 1909, in the area of the Northern Presbyterian Mission, there were about eight hundred classes held with an aggregate attendance of 50,000 or twice the number of communicant membership. The effect of this intensive and extensive study of the Bible cannot be overemphasized.

The most famous Bible class was held in Pyongyang and

[33] Blair, *op. cit.*, p. 73.

[34] "Jubilee Papers," The Fiftieth Anniversary Celebration of the Korea Mission of the Presbyterian Church U. S. A. (Seoul, Korea: June 30-July 3, 1934), p. 108.

[35] William B. Hunt, Annual Report of the Board of Foreign Missions of the Presbyterian Church U. S. A. (New York: 1910).

grew so large that it had to be held in several sections, dividing the men and women, and having separate meetings for those from the city and from the country.

Did the Revival Cause Church Growth? The great Revival of 1907 started in a Bible class and spread all over the nation, as leaders who had experienced it first in Pyongyang (described in Chapter Four) were invited to come to various places in the country and conduct revival meetings. In each meeting the results were similar, with a great outpouring of the Holy Spirit evidenced by a characteristic confession period. But if, as it has sometimes been alleged, the growth of the Church in Korea was caused by the Revival of 1907, we would expect to find a small rate of church growth until we came to the year 1907. Then we would expect the graph to take a sharp, upward swing. It is a great surprise, then, to notice on Figure 3 that the revival does not start a period of great church growth; rather it is set in the center of a period of amazing church growth. The revival actually stands in the latter half of nineteen years of increasing growth, and can be seen on Figure 3.

The explosive growth prior to the revival clearly indicates that the Revival of 1907 was not the *cause* of the growth of the Church in Korea. The revival did not even cause a large increase of professions of faith from the evangelistic campaigns held in Pyongyang. Instead, its results were of a different nature. Dr. Paik says that this great awakening marks the spiritual rebirth of the Church, resulting in better understanding and fellowship between Koreans and missionaries, in an improved moral tone of the Christian community, and in the establishment of religious habits. It is clear also that "the revival was a spiritual revivification of Christian believers rather than a movement to convert non-Christians."[36] A revival, by its very nature, is not a time when great ingathering is expected, although, when filled with the Holy Spirit, churches are naturally concerned with those about them who are lost.

A revival is, by definition, the working of the Holy Spirit in the Church for its cleansing and rededication. In Korea,

[36] Paik, *op. cit.,* p. 364.

the Holy Spirit revived the people inside the Church, convicting them of sin and giving them forgiveness rather than a great ingathering. We must make clear the distinction between a revival, an evangelistic campaign and church growth. While all of these are inter-related, we must be accurate as to whether church growth proceeded out of the revival or the revival proceeded out of great church growth (as it did in Korea in 1907).

The Evangelistic Campaign. In the wake of this great revival there was a 1910-1911 campaign carried on vigorously by all the Protestant Churches and missions in Korea for a "Million Souls for Christ." In Chairyung of north Korea, for instance, 10,000 days of preaching were subscribed by the Christian men. Again, in Pyongyang an audience of one thousand people promised over 22,000 days spent entirely in personal evangelism. Altogether, about 100,000 days of preaching were given. Many millions of tracts and 700,000 copies of the Gospel of Mark were purchased by Koreans. Thousands of Christians were praying daily for this great movement.

The Rev. James E. Adams gives us an example of a typical evangelistic meeting held in Taegu during this campaign:

> Every preparation was made along the most approved lines of the Western world revival meetings, and during and subsequent to the meetings no pains were spared. Every night the church building was practically filled with an audience of approximately one thousand, the majority of whom were non-Christians. There was an aggregate of between four and five hundred who professed conversion, came forward and gave their names and addresses and were assigned to the charge of some old Christian. Yet after the meetings were over, we were unable to get hold of more than forty or fifty and only a portion of those now remain. It seems manifest to me that the method indigenous to the Korean Christian, that of constant, individual personal work is vastly superior [to] our Western method of public evangelistic meetings, and that the product of it is much more permanent.[37]

[37] James E. Adams, Annual Personal Report to the Board of Foreign Missions of the Presbyterian Church U. S. A. (Taegu, Korea: 1910-1911).

Adams called individual personal work "vastly superior" because that is the way he felt the Church gained its great growth up to that time.

The "Million Souls for Christ" campaign, while it may have had its effect on the spiritual life of the Protestant churches, did not produce great church growth. Dr. Harry A. Rhodes says regarding the movement that the campaign slogan of "A Million Souls" may have been a mistake, for within a year following the campaign, many of the new converts had lapsed.[38]

The Korean Church Becomes Independent of the Mission. Coincidentally, September 17 of the year of the Revival — 1907 — saw another important event in the life of the Church in Korea. On this day, after complete negotiations with the general assemblies of four Presbyterian missions working in Korea, the Presbytery of the Presbyterian Church in Korea was brought into being. It was a solemn occasion, significantly held in Pyongyang, the site of the first great growth of the Church. Pyongyang Central Church was scarcely fourteen years old herself, but had in these years mothered three large city churches and scores of country churches.

The first moderator elected was a missionary, Mr. Moffett, but there was from the beginning a majority of national leaders. Mr. Rhodes records that there were thirty-eight missionaries and forty Korean elders in this first presbytery.[39] The Korean delegates were in the majority and have retained that majority in the church judicatories ever since. The presbytery met annually for several years and in 1911 decided to organize a General Assembly the following year.

Again in Pyongyang, in September of 1912, the Assembly divided into seven presbyteries, and Mr. Underwood was elected moderator of this first General Assembly. From 1907 there has been a truly independent Korean Church, and only once since 1915 was a moderator of the General Assembly again a missionary, and then only because in 1919 there was a possibility of persecution by the Japanese if a national were elected moderator.

[38] Rhodes, *op. cit.,* p. 287.
[39] *Ibid.,* p. 386.

In 1903 the Presbyterian Council, composed of the four participating Presbyterian Missions in Korea, established a seminary in Pyongyang, and, at the time of the formation of the Presbytery in 1907, seven graduates of the seminary were ordained as pastors. "These first graduates did not have a modern education but nearly all of them were educated in Chinese classics and were recognized leaders in their communities. They were well grounded in the Scriptures and had the spiritual qualifications that are necessary for capable church leaders." That the seminary had well prepared these men for their positions is shown by the fact that five of these orginial seven rose to be prominent leaders of the Church.[40]

One of the seven, Pastor Kil of the Central Church in Pyongyang, conducted the first baptismal service held by a national pastor on March 1, 1908. At the two services that Sunday, assisted by Dr. Moffett, Pastor Kil baptized two hundred one persons. Imagine a minister, the first time he conducts a baptismal service, being permitted to baptize in one day the number of persons that would be considered in many places a bountiful harvest for a year's work.

IV. ANNEXATION AND EMIGRATION
1910-1919

The year 1910 marks the year Japan formally annexed Korea to herself. Then, beginning in 1911, according to Dr. Alfred Wasson, "in both the Methodist-Episcopal and Presbyterian Churches there [was] an increase in the number of missionaries and Korean workers and a falling-off of the number of baptisms per year and in both [Churches] the total number of *members and probationers* [italics mine —R.S.] in 1919 is less than 1911."[41] Although Dr. Wasson's figures for this period are correct, his conclusion that this is a time of arrested growth is based on the statistics for members and probationers. A more accurate indicator of the growth of

---

[40] *Ibid.*, pp. 404-405.
[41] Alfred W. Wasson, *Church Growth in Korea,* p. 78.

any Church is the solid core of baptized Christians, who are full members of the Church: the communicants.

Using only communicant membership figures for the Presbyterian Church, Figure 3 shows us that there is good growth for the period from 1911 to 1919. In 1911 there were 46,934 communicants and in 1919 there were 69,047 communicant members. Although the number of probationers declined, the communicant membership rose. It is possible that a different Methodist definition of the term "probationer" led Methodist Wasson to include members and probationers together. However, the best picture of Presbyterian Church growth will be seen in the consistent use of communicant membership data, which I have used throughout this writing.

Poverty Stimulates Emigration to Manchuria. Following the annexation of Korea to Japan in 1910 came the 1911 "Conspiracy Case," a political persecution of Christians described in Chapter Four. This political pressure put on the Church by Japan is often said to have affected church growth but, in truth, it was not as important to church growth figures as the economic pressure. The Seoul Station evangelistic report for 1912 states that "the new political conditions of the country have had no effect to speak of on the country work this year, but new economic conditions have." Japan took some of the best farm land by purchasing it from Koreans who were in debt. There was a slow, definite take-over of the economy by the Japanese, and oppressed Koreans began to look for greener pastures in Manchuria.

The northward migration became rapid in 1910, the year of the annexation, and continued until World War II. At the height of the emigration there were one million Koreans living in Manchuria. In the south, Pusan missionaries reported in 1913 that "in a few instances, nearly all the members of a church have emigrated, leaving only the bare building."[42] All areas of the nation reported the same exodus of Christians to Manchuria; people were moving north to seek a better life.

From the growth figures of the Church in Manchuria, many

[42] Annual Report of the Board (from the annual report of Pusan Station; New York: 1913).

Christians were apparently lost in the move north. The Church in Korea sent workers and financial aid to help establish churches in Manchuria for the refugee Koreans. The missionaries from the border towns, Sunchun and Kangkei, had been giving as much time as they could in Manchuria since 1902. Finally in 1914 a station was established at Sinpin in Manchuria. However, the emigrants settled in widely separated places, and because of travel difficulties confronting Christian workers and constant upset political conditions, the Manchurian presbytery did not grow in proportion to the number of Korean Christians who moved there. There was always the threat of bandit raids, and one missionary was killed in 1932, either by Chinese bandits or by the Japanese police who said they were protecting the missionary.

Opportunity for evangelism among these displaced Koreans living in Manchuria certainly existed, but the missions and boards judged the opportunity in Korea proper to be greater. With limited resources, they first decided not to send permanent workers to Manchuria. "The first thought of the Boards and Missions was the kingdom of Korea where the mass of the Korean people were, rather than the Koreans, few or many, who were scattered among the Chinese in Manchuria."[43] Rather than spread their forces too thin, the Korea Missions were interested in concentrating their efforts on planting churches where they knew the opportunity was greatest. By 1921 there were only 1,566 communicant members reported in Manchuria, but by 1941 there had been growth to 10,503 communicant members.

Education Controversy. Soon after its annexation of Korea in 1910, the Japanese government put stringent regulations on the schools, and in 1915 gave them ten years to conform to the revised educational ordinance, which included a shift from the use of Korean to the Japanese language in the classroom. Even more tyrannically, it excluded religious instruction from the schools. This ordinance the mission could neither ignore nor pass over lightly. The new ordinance added fuel to the current fiery controversy raging over the mission's place in education. This problem had been

[43] Rhodes, *op. cit.,* p. 367.

plaguing the mission for some time in the form of whether or not to begin a new Union College in Seoul when a college in Pyongyang was already in existence.

Miss Harriet Pollard, a Northern Presbyterian missionary from Taegu, felt that the controversy, which raged in the mission from 1912 to 1920, decidedly affected the morale of both the mission and national Church. She said:

> So much time and thought were given to this question and so much vitality was consumed that spiritual loss to the native Church was inevitable. The mental strain undoubtedly shortened the lives of some of the most devoted men in the Mission and injured the health of others as the number of deaths and resignations of this period indicate.[44]

That this controversy came at the same time as a slowing down of church growth could be coincidental (see Figure 3: 1914-1920), but it seems reasonable to believe that it adversely affected the morale and hence the growth of the Church.

Exhibition of 1915. In 1915 at the exhibition in Seoul, held on the anniversary of the Japanese annexation of Korea, an exhibition site was given to the Protestant Churches for use as an evangelistic hall. This site was located on the wide avenue leading to the palace grounds where the exhibition was held. The Churches made the most of this opportunity and missionary and national alike worked during the fifty days of the exhibition, showing stereoptican pictures of the Bible stories and preaching. Of the 100,000 people attending these services, over 11,000 signed cards indicating that they wished to know more about the Gospel.[45] However, the percentage of these inquirers who finally became communicant members of the Church can be understood to be very small if one looks at the statistical increase in church membership seen on Figure 3.

Still, the government was not openly forbidding the preaching of the Gospel, and 11,000 people in fifty days expressed an interest in the Christian good news. Compared to the

[44] Harriet E. Pollard, *The History of the Missionary Enterprise of the Presbyterian Church U. S. A. in Korea with Special Emphasis on the Personnel,* p. 111.

[45] Annual Report of the Board (New York: 1917).

previous period of tremendous growth from 1895 to 1910 in Korea, this decade shows few converts, but the Korean people did remain basically receptive.

V. IMPRISONMENT AND POVERTY
1919-1928

At this time it was a question in the mind of Koreans whether the Church stood loyal to the Korean people or to the conquering Japanese. Most of the missionaries associated with the Church came from the United States, which as a nation stood idly by while Korea was being eaten up. This refusal of the U.S. to intervene raised doubts in the hearts of at least some Korean intellectuals. While the missionaries remained politically neutral, they were happy to see the early reforms that Japan brought to its backward neighbor. These reforms, coupled with the large volume of promises by the Japanese government, held hopes for a better Korea through the assistance of her progressive neighbor, Japan. When the missionary, wisely, did not become involved in any revolutionary movement to throw out conquering Japan, the common people of Korea had some question as to whether the missionaries had the Koreans' best interests at heart.

Demonstrations for Political Independence. On March 1, 1919 Korean Christians themselves erased any doubts as to the loyalty of Christians to their fatherland. The Church became a rallying point for the oppressed Korean people, and the new status of the Church is amply shown by the upturned growth of Figure 3. Missionaries had no part in planning this "Independence Movement," and the official mission board reports denied that it had any religious character, lest their missionaries be implicated in Korean politics and receive further pressure from Japan.[46] The missionaries felt that even indirect association of the Church with the independence movement could only harm church growth.

Yet the fact remains that the thirty-three Korean signers of the Declaration of Independence were religious leaders. Three were Buddhists, fifteen were Chundokyo believers,

[46] *Ibid.,* 1920.

and fifteen were Christians, some of whom were prominent Protestant ministers. Furthermore, the Japanese government held the Christians responsible for starting and aiding this movement. That association of Christianity and the independence movement would be detrimental to the Church was a mistaken idea. Actually, Christians and missionaries were seen in a new light, formerly as slightly suspect, now as associates in a patriotic movement.

The thirty-three leaders met in Seoul on March 1, 1919, in the Bright Moon Restaurant. They then informed the Japanese police that they were the signers of the declaration that was being read simultaneously all over Korea that day. This Declaration of Independence called for peaceful, non-violent demonstrations demanding independence from the Japanese government. The police came quickly and put these men in jail. Inspiration for this movement came from President Wilson's "Fourteen Points," which included in Point Five the right of small nations to self-determination:

> A free, open-minded and absolutely impartial adjustment of all colonial claims based upon strict observance of the principle that in determining all such questions of sovereignty the interests of the populations concerned must have equal weight with the equitable claims of the government whose title is to be determined.[47]

The Korean people were given hope that a peaceful move for independence would bring the force of world opinion to bear on Japan, giving Korea her freedom. Although no direct relation had been established, that same year in India, Gandhi was beginning his movement of passive resistance.

The secrecy with which preparations for this nationwide mass demonstration were carried out, vividly speaks of the united desire of all Korea to be free from the yoke of Japan. No missionaries knew in advance of the demonstrations. No Korean informed the police of the preparations. The nation as a whole took Japan by surprise. This surprise may explain, in part, the brutal and swift reaction of the Japanese police to the crowds of Koreans in the streets yelling "Mansei!"

[47] *Encyclopedia Britannica,* Vol. 9, pp. 565-566.

("ten thousand generations" or "Long Live Korea!") No demonstrator was armed, yet many were killed. Within a few days the jails were jammed. Many Christian leaders were thrown into jail, and not a few churches were burned.

It seemed a black day for the Church. Many churches stood almost empty, like the two reported by the Rev. Mr. A. A. Pieters, a missionary in Chairyung. "Almost all the men of these two churches took part in the demonstrations and fight. Those who were not arrested fled so that now the congregation consists only of women."[48] Christian schools had to be closed, and the country itineration of missionaries stopped temporarily. Colporteurs could not sell literature anymore, and it looked as if the year 1919 would go down as a black year for the Church in Korea. Yet within the space of a year it was evident that 1919 was not to be black, but instead the bright mark of a new era for the kingdom of God in Korea. The fears of Christian association with the Independence Movement proved to be quite unfounded.

Most of the mission station reports for 1920 read, "Perhaps the work of no year ever began under such adverse circumstances or closed with such bright prospects as the year 1919-1920."[49] The membership rose from 69,025 reported in 1920 to 72,138 reported in 1921. An increase of four and one-half percent is notable for a Church which registered a slight loss for the previous year (1919). (The statistics correspond with the report because of a year's statistical lag.)

As an independence movement, the March 1 uprisings failed, but the authorities in Japan were not unaffected by the demonstrations. The military government which had been in power in Korea was changed to a civil government. Prison terms were reduced so that within a few years many of the church leaders were back serving their churches. The Christians were not idle in prison either; they did not miss the opportunity to witness to their fellow prison-mates who were not Christian. Witnessing under difficulty is not hard

---

[48] A. A. Pieters, Annual Personal Report to the Board of Foreign Missions of the Presbyterian Church U. S. A. (Chairyung, Korea: 1919).

[49] Annual Report of the Board (New York: 1922).

to understand, but strange was the response of the people to the Gospel under prison hardships.

The Pyongyang station report of 1920 says:

> Many of the converts have thus come out of prison with the joy of the Lord in their hearts and have gone back to their homes to bear witness to the Gospel. They tell of catechumens received and baptisms administered behind prison walls. One of the pastors reports having received many letters since his return, asking for letters of transfer from the prison church to the ones in their home towns. This same pastor was moved about seven times from prison to prison during his fourteen months. Each time he found himself with a larger company of men.

This pastor could never have traveled on his own to various parts of Korea to preach, but the Japanese government moved him to different prisons, unwittingly giving him new opportunities to persuade men to accept Christ. In each place prisoners were led to Christ by this man's ministry, and letters of transfer given later bore the address of: the Presbyterian Church, Westgate Prison, Seoul.

The fact that Korean people came to Christ under prison conditions gives us a hint of the nation's great receptivity to the Gospel and a clue to the rapid growth of the Church for the next seven years. The reasons for this receptivity are not easy to see when one reflects that Christians, who took a major part in the Independence Movement, easily could have been blamed for its failure. Also the insistence of missionaries on a position of political neutrality would not commend itself to a loyal Korean as reason for associating himself with the Christian Church.

However, missionaries were not entirely neutral. In the face of human suffering from imprisonment, torture, and death, they adopted a policy of "no neutrality for brutality" and they let the world know what was going on in Korea.[50] Letters got to America and England despite Japanese watchfulness, so that pressure was brought to bear on Japan, resulting in the change of government noted above.

Evangelistic Campaigns Again Organized. At this time

[50] Pollard, *op. cit.*, p. 96.

of renewed receptivity of the Korean people, there were also organized efforts by the Church to expand in both the Methodist and Presbyterian denominations. The Methodists called their movement "The Centenary Advance," and the Presbyterians called theirs "The Forward Movement." Dr. William N. Blair was made chairman by the General Assembly of the Presbyterian Forward Movement. Its goals were to put "new life into the activities of the Korean churches . . . to increase its evangelistic efforts and . . . to give new stimulus to Sunday School work."[51] Dr. Blair prepared ten tracts for a special campaign and traveled to all the Presbyterian mission stations, holding meetings.

In almost all of the four thousand Presbyterian churches in Korea, special Forward Movement revival meetings were held, and during this year of 1920, 5,603 persons were added to the Church by confession of faith.[52] This is in strong contrast to the slight loss in membership reported the previous year.

Along with the Forward Movement growth came the advent of the Sunday-school movement in Korea. Up to this time, Bible study had been for adults and no special work was done with the children of the Church. The only place children could study was in the adult classes, and the Church had no special material written for children. It is significant that until this time there had been no emphasis on the evangelization of children or on Bible training for them.[53] In spite of this, the Church was growing. Perhaps this indicates that for church growth, the Western emphasis on educational evangelism and the producing of intelligent Christians through well-organized Church schools was not important in the Korea of days gone by, when the Korean family was a solid unit. The children learned about the Bible at home through their parents' example and through family worship that was common in Korean Christian homes.

In 1920 the Japanese government in Korea made it pos-

---

[51] Annual Report of the Board (New York: 1923).
[52] *Ibid.*
[53] Blair, *op. cit.*, p. 82.

sible for schools to receive recognition even though they taught Bible in the curriculum, thereby allowing graduates of the mission schools to attend higher institutions (if the mission schools met all educational and property standards required by the government). In 1923 the Presbyterian boys' high school in Seoul, John D. Wells School, became the first mission school to be "designated" by the government and was given the equivalent status of a high school.

"*A Sense of Doom.*" The oppression of Christianity by Japan became more widespread and increased in strength until the day of liberation in 1945. The first inkling of this oppression is seen in the report of spies in Miss Hallie Covington's Bible class, held in 1922 at Tungchun in North Pyongan Province. The spies were trying to make trouble for her and the church. Also in this year there are reports of church buildings left empty because of raids by the Tongnip Army (the Korean Independence Army) against the Japanese government. The Tongnip were actually bandits, plundering whatever they could lay their hands on.

In addition, 1920 brought devastating floods, especially in the northern part of Korea. The town of Kangkei in North Pyongan Province experienced famine. In fact, there was large-scale famine in the entire country. Dr. Blair's report in 1925 gives the picture of economic conditions in Pyongyang:

> The general tone of the Church has been depressing. Financial distress has very largely sapped the life of the people. They have the very hardest struggles to feed their families. In many of the churches the officers have been on the verge of starvation. A sense of doom seems to hover over the people — a hopelessness such as we have never seen before. A few city churches have grown phenomenally but it has largely been at the cost of the weak country groups.[54]

In spite of these real difficulties, some places report a definite growth, and the Church as a whole shows good growth around 1925. In 1926 Kangkei reports several new Christian groups established and many new believers. Still

[54] Blair, Annual Personal Report to the Board of Foreign Missions of the Presbyterian Church U. S. A. (Pyongyang, Korea: 1925).

others report losses from lax discipline in the churches. On his spring itineration, the Rev. Mr. Roscoe Coen of the Northern Presbyterian Mission baptized twenty-two. He says:

> While we were receiving these new ones by baptism it was necessary to suspend nineteen from the church privileges for various offenses, Sabbath breaking, drinking, etc. The churches are really badly in need of discipline. If all were suspended who really should be, we should have to import members to carry on in many places.[55]

The need for discipline described by Mr. Coen can be explained by lack of leadership, since in the past few years many church leaders had been in jail. Mr. Harry Rhodes ascribes the slower growth of the Korean Church in this time to another cause, which also could be a reason for lax discipline: "One reason why there has been a let up in the growth of the Korean Church the last few years is because the missionaries have more and more been withdrawn from direct evangelistic work into institutional and other forms of work. I am one of those who have been so withdrawn."[56]

Even in the face of all these troubles: government oppression, imprisonment and poor church leadership, internal strife and immorality, floods and bandits and famine and poverty, the fact remains that the churches grew and grew well between 1920 and 1925. The rate of growth was about thirty percent for these five years. The increase from 69,000 to 89,000 communicants is *good growth*. Those who were involved with the daily problems of the Church saw those problems and could not see the growth as we can from our perspective of history.

VI. SHINTOISM AND OPPRESSION
1928-1938

Although not steadily, the Presbyterian Church grew from 1928 until 1938. We can discount the drop in communicant

---

[55] Roscoe C. Coen, Annual Personal Report to the Board of Foreign Missions of the Presbyterian Church U. S. A. (Seoul, Korea: 1926).

[56] Rhodes, Annual Personal Report to the Board of Foreign Missions of the Presbyterian Church U. S. A. (Seoul, Korea: 1926).

membership in the year 1928, visible on Figure 3, as a statistical redefinition. Three years previous to 1928 the General Assembly of the Korean Presbyterian Church levied a per-communicant-member tax to pay for General Assembly expenses. According to the mission statistician, local churches then began to see the economic advantage of cleaning their rolls of "dead wood." This is a statistical redefinition and accounts for the sharp drop in 1928 seen in Figure 3.

The 1930 board report states the position of Korean church growth at that time:

> For some years past the growth of the Church in Chosen has not been as spectacular as it was during the second and third decade of the mission's history. Baptisms have been fewer, new believers have not been coming in large numbers and churches have not been springing up all over the country as of yore.
>
> This, however, does not mean the progress of the Church has slowed up to any marked degree; rather has the development been in a different direction, namely along the line of organization, self-support and knowledge of the truth. As more and more men have been graduated from the theological seminary the churches have been passing from the leadership of helpers and missionaries to completely ecclesiastical organization with their own ministers and elders. And where formerly a foreign missionary was at the head of a large number of churches which he could visit only about twice a year, there are now resident native pastors in charge of individual churches. This has naturally tended toward a better instruction of the Christians and fuller development of the church activities.[57]

Resistance of Presbyterian Schools to Shinto Shrine Worship. About 1930 the government began to press obeisance to the Shinto shrine upon the Church and mission. Students and teachers of all Korean schools, including Christian schools, were required to go and bow before a state Shinto shrine. Since Shinto had been divided into two distinct institutions, religious and state, the Japanese rulers declared that bowing to the state shrine was not a religious act. "A

[57] Annual Report of the Board (New York: 1930).

Japanese out of his duty as a subject must honor the ancestors of the Emperor. This cannot be a matter of choice. It is a duty. Therefore, this cannot be regarded as a religion. It is a ritual. It is the ceremony of gratitude to ancestors."[58] If this had been a simple patriotic act, as the Japanese insisted it was, there would have been no problem. But many Korean Christians and Western missionaries could not see the division of shrines; they saw more than patriotic expression in the ceremony at the state shrine.

Because religious elements could be seen even in the ritual at the state shrines, confusion and controversy arose. Bowing before the shrine that the Japanese claimed contained the spirits of the departed, seemed to be a religious act to many. So the Korean Church, which for fifty years had preached and practiced the worship of one God, even resisting its own deep temptation to continue ancestor worship, was now faced with the problem of doing obeisance to another god or paying the consequences.

For Christian schools the consequence of noncompliance was their loss of government recognition. The Northern Presbyterian Mission in Korea chose to close its schools rather than to "compromise" its religion. In the fall of 1935 Dr. George S. McCune, President of Union Christian College in Pyongyang, was called in by the governor of South Pyongan Province and informed that he would be expected to attend the shrine ceremony that day. He refused, so the governor told him to go home and think about it for sixty days. At the end of sixty days, on the advice of the Korean pastors in the city, he still refused, and his educational qualifications were revoked. This was just the beginning.

By mission meeting time in June 1936, the issues were well fixed in missionaries' minds, and the problem had been discussed thoroughly in private. So when the executive committee of the mission was called in by the police and informed that there was to be no discussion of the shrine issue at the annual meeting, it actually worked for the mis-

[58] D. C. Holton, *The National Faith of Japan*, A study in modern Shinto, p. 69. (Quoting Nagao Ariga, "Shinto Kokkyo Ron [Shinto as a State Religion]" in *Philosophical Magazine*, Vol. 25, No. 280, June 1910, p. 702.)

sion's benefit "since it obviated cluttering the session with lengthy discussions that would have arrived at nowhere and resulted only in hard feelings."[59] The vote taken at mission meeting, without discussion, is described as follows:

> Dr. Rogers wrote later that he would never forget the solemn hush that came over the assembly as the action was read. The Mission bowed in prayer for guidance and the vote was taken. It was passed by a large majority. The most important sentence of this reads: . . . "Recognizing the increasing difficulties of maintaining our Mission schools and also of preserving in them the full purposes and ideals with which they were founded, we recommend that the Mission approve a policy of retiring from the field of secular education."[60]

The language of this action may be vague but its meaning is clear. The mission felt it could not maintain the Christian character of its schools with any type of compromise.

In the spring of 1937 mission schools of Pyongyang city did not admit new classes. Since the government refused to excuse Christian schools from worship at the Shinto shrine, the mission executive committee received permission from the board in New York to close the school doors in Pyongyang and temporarily rent some buildings to the government while it was constructing new school buildings.[61]

The Southern Presbyterian Mission dealt with the "shrine issue" in the same way as the Northern Presbyterian Mission had done, but even more firmly. Dr. C. Darby Fulton, who prior to becoming executive secretary of the Southern Presbyterian Mission Board was a second-generation missionary to Japan, came to Korea in 1937, authorized to close schools rather than have the students and faculty bow at the shrines, if that seemed the best thing to do. He met privately with the missionaries of his denomination because the police prohibited open discussion of the issue. He found that the majority of these missionaries were in favor of closing the

59 Allen D. Clark, *A Study of Religion and the State in the Japanese Empire with Particular Reference to the Shrine Problem in Korea*, p. 50.

60 *Ibid.*, pp. 50-51.

61 *Ibid.*, p. 58.

schools rather than having their witness "compromised." However, Dr. Fulton's decision to shut them down met with opposition both from the Japanese government and from the Korean Christians who wanted to keep their children going to school. He speaks of this opposition from the Korean Christians:

> While each group presented some request or petition, usually in written form, and there was considerable variety of approach to the subject, the gist of all the petitions was the same — that somehow the schools should be kept going. For them all this was the one imperative, the schools *must* go on. Even those who took a strong stand against the shrines, declaring them to be unquestionably religious and wholly incompatible with Christianity, said, "Nevertheless we *must* educate our children. Attendance at the shrines is against our principles but we shall have to submit to this rather than deny our sons and daughters an opportunity for schooling."[62]

Even in the face of this conviction of some Korean Christians, the mission and Dr. Fulton finally decided that if further pressure to attend the shrines was placed upon the faculties, they should definitely close the schools. After the fall terms opened in September of 1937, both faculty and students were ordered to the shrines of the Sun Goddess to pray for the victory of the Japanese armies in China. When this happened, the Southern Presbyterian Mission sent the students home and locked the school doors.[63]

Japanese Police Move to Control the Church. The Japanese police worked methodically to break down the whole Church. They began with individual churches, then the presbyteries, and finally put pressure on the General Assembly. "The authorities commenced to sponsor 'voluntary' action in favor of the Shrines . . . using every means of persuasion and indirection to get individual churches and church leaders to go on record as favoring the Shrine ceremonies."[64]

Newspaper articles began to appear, such as the one stat-

---

[62] C. Darby Fulton, *Star in the East*, p. 190.
[63] George Thompson Brown, *Mission to Korea*, p. 156.
[64] Clark, *op. cit.*, p. 64.

ing that a deacon of the First Presbyterian Church of Chungju had "finally seen the error of his way and given up his
faith in Christianity."[65]   Dr. Allen D. Clark points out that
as a matter of fact this man was neither a deacon nor a
baptized member. But still the effects of this article and
others like it were felt throughout the Church.

The police put pressure on presbyteries by calling delegates in before the meetings and threatening them if they
would not approve a motion of consent to attending the
shrine ceremonies. In some presbyteries the leaders were
imprisoned, but most presbyteries were forced by the police
to approve this motion.

The 1938 General Assembly, which met September 10,
received a final blow in this organized program of stripping
the Korean Church of its power. During the summer previous to the meeting, the police had contacted each delegate.
Just as they had coerced presbytery delegates, they now told
general assembly delegates to approve the passage of a
motion sanctioning worship at the Shinto shrines. Those who
opposed shrine worship were put in jail and kept from attending the General Assembly. When the call for the vote on the
motion approving shrine attendance came, only the 'yeas'
were called for. The moderator did not call for the negative
vote. A missionary stood up to protest but was shouted down
by the police, who were in almost as great a number as
delegates. Finally several missionaries were allowed to speak,
but to no avail. The police now had a powerful weapon in
their hands; the morale of the Church had been broken.

Worship services were limited and many churches were
closed. Missionaries could no longer itinerate into the country. Some of them scheduled rural Bible classes only to have
them cancelled at the last minute by the police. The few
churches a missionary was able to visit were always subject to police questioning after he had gone. However,
many Christians not permitted to attend church services kept
the faith alive in their own homes.

Except for large city churches, church doors were largely
closed to the missionary. He then did the only thing possible

[65] *Ibid.*

and held tent meetings in places where there were no Christians to be persecuted. These meetings were attended only in comparatively small numbers, as Dr. Edward Adams reveals in his personal report of 1938:

> Five years ago my tent meetings had an evening attendance from 300 to 1,000. Now we rarely go over 300. Five years ago a week of meetings would bring in 100 to 200 decisions, but today our decisions seldom go over 50. In the place where we are now working there are many wild rumors as to what will happen if one becomes a Christian.[66]

Fifty decisions may seem like a good response, but not in this land of Korea.

The Dilemma of the Missions. The question, "Was it wise to close the schools during this time?" will still provoke a variety of answers. For a few years, certain children were denied a Christian education, but because the Northern and Southern Presbyterian Missions did not use their schools as evangelistic tools, they were able to close them without essential damage to their evangelistic outreach. Because they were closed, the schools did not have to bear the stigma of having compromised with their Christian faith. But lest there be any righteous self-satisfaction with this decision to withdraw from education, it must be clear that it was only temporary. The schools were not allowed to be in the hands of the Japanese for a long period of time because, fortunately, they were brought back to their former position after Japan's defeat in 1945. Schools that closed their doors because of the "shrine issue" lost financial advantage in buildings and equipment but were able to reopen with some former faculty members.

The Methodist Missions and the Canadian Presbyterian Mission took the general position that there was no religious significance to the attendance at a shrine and kept their schools running. Schools remaining open during the shrine controversy period were able to open again after World War II on a more firm financial footing. Today there is no great difference in economic strength nor in Chris-

[66] Edward Adams, Annual Personal Report to the Board of Foreign Missions of the Presbyterian Church U. S. A. (Taegu, Korea: 1938).

tian fervor between the schools of all the missions, but if the
Japanese occupation had continued over a long period of
time, those schools which had closed their doors would have
lost all influence as well as the original investment put into
them.

I am convinced that one reason some can say in retrospect
that it was good to have closed the schools over the shrine
issue is that the schools were all opened again in a short
time. To say that under the circumstances it was the right
action to close the schools is only telling part of the story.
Any application of the closing of Korean schools to present-
day situations must be tempered with the consideration
that, even if these schools had been the last bulwark of
Christian witness, as in some countries, they were only
temporarily silenced.

No statistical changes in the growth of the Church can be
directly attributed to the effect of the shrine issue and shut-
down of the mission schools. This problem did not affect
immediate numerical growth but spiritual growth of the
Church years later. The full effect of the shrine issue on
the Church itself will not be known for many years, because the tension from either guilt feelings or pride of those
who bowed or did not bow at the shrines was so strong that
while the problem passed with the demise of the Japanese
Empire, the emotional response remains within the Church
today.

Fanaticism. In other ways also, the Church was showing
signs of the pressure being put upon it. Fanatical elements
seemed to appear in the Church. There is no doubt these
aberrations sprang up partly as a reaction to the pressure
exerted on Korea by the Japanese government. We read:

> The Church is passing through a time of testing and trial.
> There is a large number of so-called evangelists who really
> have no church connections, going about the country teaching
> all sorts of strange doctrines and disturbing the faith of
> many.[67]

[67] C. F. Bernheisel, Annual Personal Report to the Board of Foreign
Missions of the Presbyterian Church U. S. A. (Pyongyang, Korea:
1933).

> There has come into Korea a new fanaticism, a kind of Holy-Roller type of religion which is doing in our churches a great deal of damage . . . The greatest danger of the Korean Church today is within the body itself. We are likely to lose great numbers who will be deceived by these so-called spirit-filled folk who will go off from our fellowship and will form new groups with a queer kind of carrying-on in their prayers and worship.[68]

These aberrations were probably caused by the persecution and by the background of Shamanistic religion of the masses in Korea. One of these aberrations, a syncretism of Shamanism and Christianity, was strong in South Korea in 1965. This movement, led by Tae Sun Pak, its founder, had its real roots during the 1928-1938 period, though it actually was founded after World War II.

VII. MISSIONARY DEPARTURE AND WORLD WAR II
1938-1942

By 1939 most of the evangelistic missionaries either had resigned or were relieved from their moderatorships of the sessions of various churches. They could not in good conscience conduct the Lord's Supper in a church that had gone out en masse to worship at the Japanese Shinto Shrine. Dr. Francis Kinsler, in 1940, reports being invited to preach in four different mountaintop worship services held outdoors in the springtime. He says:

> At one church I was enjoying a chicken dinner prepared for me in a Christian officer's home until I discovered that in his and every other home in the district had been placed a shrine designated in Chinese characters by the caption, "The Palace of the Great Spirit of the Heavenly Ruler," which is the Sun Goddess of Japanese mythology.[69]

[68] Charles L. Phillips, Annual Personal Report to the Board of Foreign Missions of the Presbyterian Church U. S. A. (Pyongyang, Korea: 1933).

[69] Francis Kinsler, Annual Personal Report to the Board of Foreign Missions of the Presbyterian Church U. S. A. (Pyongyang, Korea: 1940).

Many church leaders were thrown into prison for their resistance to the Japanese government on the shrine issue. Other church leaders paid lip service to the Japanese government but retained their Christian faith. A few no doubt capitulated and lost their faith. One cannot be harsh or overly critical of these leaders; we can only pray that such pressure, such oppression, coming in a subtle, inch-by-inch take-over of the Church, will never happen again. The effects of Japanese domination of the Church are to be found in it today, because they were the seeds of church division. Men who in 1938 had not bowed to the government pointed an accusing finger in 1948 at those leaders who had capitulated.

Figure 3 shows a huge drop after 1941, in the communicant membership of the Korean Presbyterian Church. This is the only indication of heavy loss during the history of the Church. In all other years, the people who came into the Church knew their Savior, knew why they were there, and for the most part stayed in the Church and won those around them to Christ. The 1941 drop, however, is a reflection of the pressure of Japan; it does not mean the Korean Christians renounced Christianity. After the 1938 General Assembly, the Church in Korea was under the strict rule of Japan, and the 1942 General Assembly minutes were written in Japanese. Churches were closed during this time and continued oppression drove the Christians underground. Had there been large-scale reversions, the Church would not have grown as it did after World War II.

The missionaries stayed as long as they were able to under the increasing, darkening war clouds. Those who were on regular furlough in 1940 were urged by the American government not to return to Korea that year. Many missionaries left Korea on the *Mariposa* in November 1941. Remaining mothers with young children and single lady missionaries were compelled to leave in September 1941, and several, including the Rev. Mr. Herbert E. Blair, were imprisoned for participating in the World Day of Prayer in which one item in the program was "Pray for the peace of the world." By coincidence this program had been prepared in Shanghai, and the World Day of Prayer fell on March 1, the very day commemorating the independence movement against Japan. Japan charged that this was a plot to alienate the Korean people from supporting the Holy War in China, but the case was soon dropped.

Japan demanded that the missionaries leave, so some went through Shanghai and directly to America. A few missionaries were on the high seas at the time of Pearl Harbor; these were interned in the Philippines, where some of the older missionaries died. When World War II began there were forty Presbyterian missionaries who remained in Korea. On December 8, 1941, they were all put into prison. It was June of 1942 before they were finally allowed to return to the United States on the neutral ship, *Gripsholm,* in exchange for Japanese civilians. Eventually all of the missionaries were able to leave Korea safely. Behind them the Korean Church had gone underground. Ahead of them was yet another period of great growth following the war, which period will be examined in Chapter Ten.

Chapter IV. Comparison of Geographical Sections of Korean Presbyterian Church Growth

MISSIONARY LITERATURE IS FULL OF PROFFERED REASONS FOR the great growth of the Korean Presbyterian Church. Perhaps the Presbyterians' use of the "Nevius Method" has been mentioned most often. I have outlined the environmental and political factors that have influenced the growth of the Church.

We must now ask, "Was the church growth the same in all areas?" There are hints in promotional literature of varying rates of growth in different areas of Korea, but from the sweeping statements most often given as reasons for the growth of this Church, one might assume that the Church in Korea grew rapidly and evenly in all sections.

The question of equal growth in all sections becomes pertinent when we look at Figure 5, which pictures the rates of Presbyterian church growth in nine geographical areas. Figure 5 and its corresponding detailed graphs, appearing later in Figures 7 through 15, were all derived from statistics of the General Assembly of the Presbyterian Church in Korea and of the Northern Presbyterian Mission. They were made by using mission station records prior to 1907 and by combining post-1907 records of presbyteries within the national political boundaries. The presbyteries included in each of the province areas are as follows:

Province	Presbyteries
A North Pyongan	Pyongbook, Yungchun, Weesan, Sansuh, Samsan, and Pyongdong.
B South Pyongan	Pyongnam, Pyongyang, Pyongsuh, and Anjoo.
C Whanghai	Whanghai and Whangdong.
D Kyunggi and North Choongchung	Seoul, Kyunggi, and, later, Choongchung.

80

E	North Kyungsang	Kyungbook, Kyungan, and Kyung-dong.
F	Hamgyung	Hambook, Hamjoong, and Hamnam.
G	South Kyungsang	Kyungnam.
H	North Chulla	Chunbook and Koonsan.
J	South Chulla and Cheju Island	Chunnam, Soonchun, and Cheju.

We see from Figure 5 not only minor differences in rate of growth of the nine areas compared, but quite slow-growing areas compared to very fast-growing areas. These differences in the growth rate are significant enough to call for a study of the growth of the Church not just as a whole, but area by area. Any sweeping generalization for the cause of growth, therefore, must be modified by the factors unique to particular provinces.

Missionaries and national workers were not oblivious to the fact that different parts of Korea saw different rates of church growth. Because comparisons are odious and because of attempts to keep down sectional rivalry, they did not feel free to illuminate the question of unequal growth. It is important to real understanding of church growth to find out how and why each area grew as it did. If someone were to say the Presbyterian Church in North Pyongan Province grew because of the methods used by the Northern Presbyterian Mission, then one would immediately have to ask why, when these same methods were used by the same mission in Kyunggi Province, was there so little growth registered there? A glance at the lower right-hand corner figures in each graph of Figure 5 shows that growth was not related to the number of ordained missionaries working in the area. Missionaries were approximately in equal distribution to all areas, but the growth was vastly different.

In order to discover answers to the question of unequal growth, from the nine areas in Figure 5, I have chosen five areas served by the same mission, using the same policies and yet having the most striking variance of growth. We will look in detail at these five areas: first Kyunggi and North Choongchung Provinces, which have been grouped

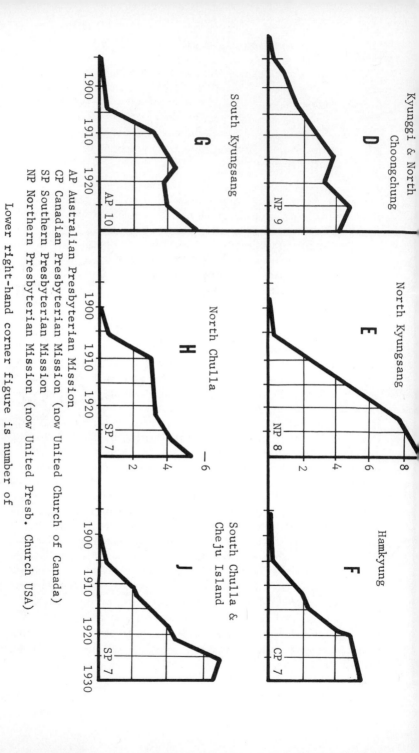

Kyunggi & North Choongchung — D (NP 9)
North Kyungsang — E (NP 8)
Hamkyung — F (CP 7)
South Kyungsang — G (AP 10)
North Chulla — H (SP 7)
South Chulla & Cheju Island — J (SP 7)

AP Australian Presbyterian Mission
CP Canadian Presbyterian Mission (now United Church of Canada)
SP Southern Presbyterian Mission
NP Northern Presbyterian Mission (now United Presb. Church USA)

Lower right-hand corner figure is number of
ordained missionaries in each area in 1911.

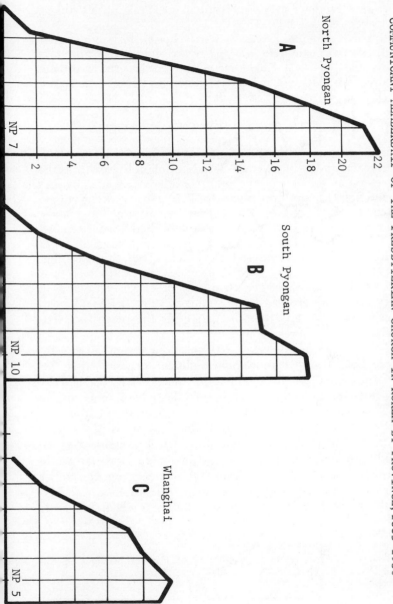

FIGURE 5

COMMUNICANT MEMBERSHIP OF THE PRESBYTERIAN CHURCH IN KOREA BY PROVINCE, 1885-1930

together as D, second North Kyungsang Province (E), third
Whanghai Province (C), and finally North and South Pyongan
Provinces (A and B).

The five province areas I have chosen for comparative
study do not comprise the entire Presbyterian Church of
Korea but are only those areas served by the Northern
Presbyterian Mission, whose territory by agreement prior
to 1935 is shown on Figure 6.[1]

I.   CENTRAL AND SOUTHEAST KOREA

Kyunggi and North Choongchung Provinces (D). It is
appropriate to begin a detailed study of church growth in the
provinces by looking at the area considered by missionaries
as the most important place to live and work: Kyunggi
Province. Kyunggi includes the national capital city, Seoul,
where the first mission station was established. Seoul seemed
so important that even later, when the opening of other
stations was being considered, the opinion was expressed that
"Seoul ought to have a large missionary force because it is
two or three times larger than any other place, being in
every sense the center of the country. It is visited by men
from every place and it is pre-eminently the place for seed-
sowing."[2]

It was true. Seoul was a city most important as a communication, transportation, and political center. Even today some areas in the country are more easily reached by
traveling through the capital and then back out to the
adjacent country area again, because the direct route is
devoid of roads and thus impassible. Seoul is the center
of transportation, government and even thought, and so
Seoul was chosen as the center for beginning Christian work.

In examining the period from 1885 to 1895, we remember
from the previous chapter that some Korean men, touched
by the work of John Ross in Manchuria, traveled hundreds

[1] Harry A. Rhodes, *History of the Korea Mission Presbyterian
Church U. S. A. 1884-1934*, frontispiece.

[2] D. L. Gifford, Letter to the Board of Foreign Missions of the
Presbyterian Church U. S. A. (Seoul, Korea: June 2, 1893).

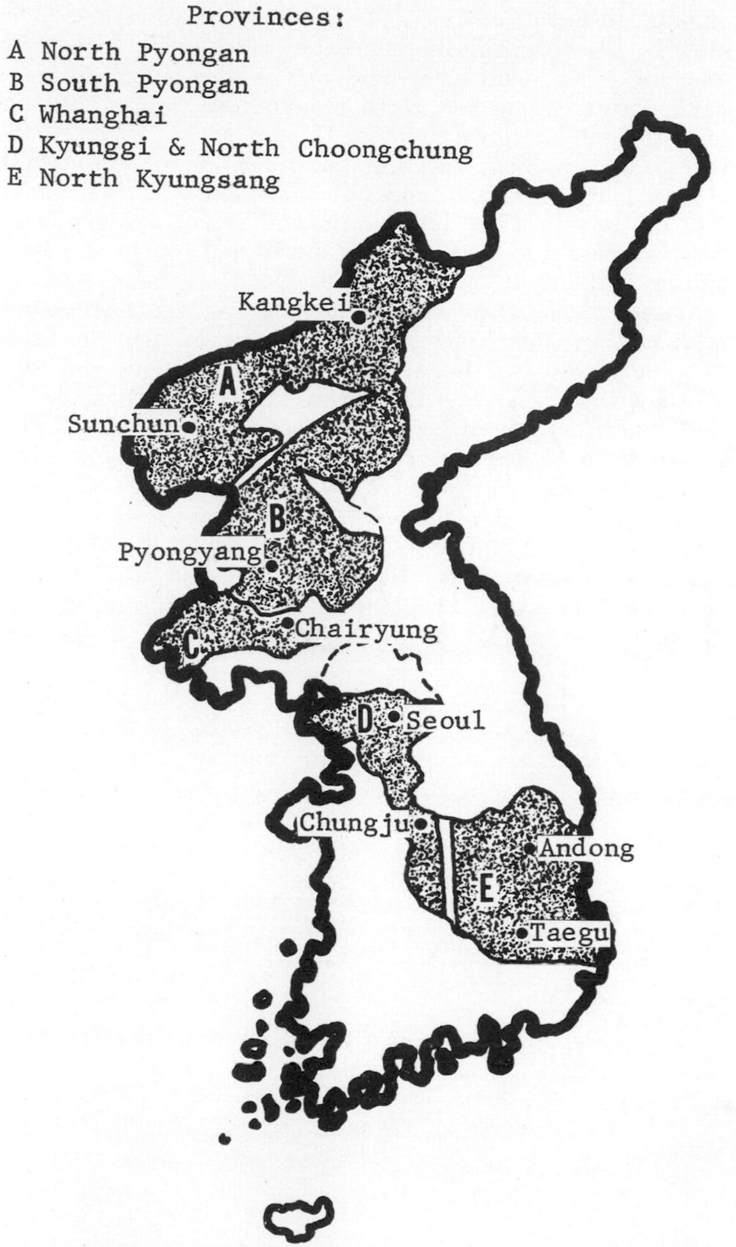
Provinces:
A North Pyongan
B South Pyongan
C Whanghai
D Kyunggi & North Choongchung
E North Kyungsang
Kangkei
A
Sunchun
B
Pyongyang
C
Chairyung
D
Seoul
Chungju
Andong
E
Taegu

AREAS SERVED BY THE NORTHERN PRESBYTERIAN MISSION

FIGURE 6

of miles to Seoul on foot and visited the missionaries. This mobility was particularly noticeable among the "yangban," or gentry class, who were used to traveling great distances to the great capital city. The mountainous terrain did not seem to prohibit travel as these Korean people followed the valleys and walked, carrying an indication of the length of their journey in the number of straw shoes on their backs. And the new missionaries in turn, with Seoul as their home base, traveled thousands of miles during the course of a year, visiting outlying areas.

Among the fourteen charter members of the first church organized by the Northern Presbyterian Mission in Seoul were men who had been taught by a Christian converted in Manchuria, who traveled down to Seoul with copies of the Chinese Scriptures.[3] This first Seoul Presbyterian Church, as yet the only one of its kind in Korea, was organized in 1887 and called the "Seh Moon Ahn Presbyterian Church." It was placed under the care of the three ordained missionaries of Seoul Station — Underwood, Gifford, and Moffett — who together exercised the functions of a session. All converts for a time were brought under this church, even from the outstations as far north as Pyongyang and Euiju near the Yalu River.

The Seh Moon Ahn Church gave assistance in winning men to Christ in these areas. In the second year of its existence, Underwood reports several baptisms in the town of Songdo (now Kaesung) in the northwest, that were a result of the evangelistic labor of Seoul Christians.[4] Until 1893 all of the communicant membership of the Presbyterian Church in Korea was reported from Seoul. In spite of the all-inclusiveness of these Seoul statistics, which embraced the Christians of outlying villages to the north, as seen on Figure 7, they indicate very little growth before the year 1893.

The missionaries, eyes open to the opportunities for evan-

[3] Horace Grant Underwood, Letter to the Board of Foreign Missions of the Presbyterian Church U. S. A. (Seoul, Korea: January 2, 1887).
[4] *Ibid.*, April 22, 1888.

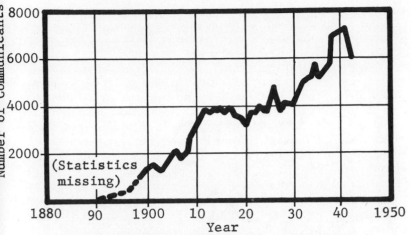

PRESBYTERIAN COMMUNICANT MEMBERSHIP
IN KYUNGGI AND NORTH CHOONGCHUNG PROVINCES (D)
FIGURE 7

gelism around them, visited these outstations surrounding
and to the north of Seoul as often as possible and attempted
to place unpaid national Christians in charge of them.[5]
However, there were five mission-paid colporteur-evangelists
at this time, two of whom were also working with the British
and Foreign Bible Society. Feeling the insufficiency of
workers, Mr. Horace G. Underwood wrote a letter in May
of 1890 pleading for reinforcements, telling of the much-
needed work in Seoul and the totally untouched areas in
the country. He wrote that there was plenty of room to work
in the "free treaty port" area and that there should be no
difficulty about passports.[6] The mission board and the American Church responded to this call. In 1891 two ordained
missionary men were listed in Seoul Station along with three
native evangelists, besides the colporteurs working with the
British and Foreign Bible Society. In 1903 Seoul Station

[5] Korea Northern Presbyterian Mission, Minutes of Annual Meeting (Seoul, Korea: October 21, 1890).
[6] Underwood, Letter to the Board (Seoul, Korea: May 29, 1890).

had increased to six ordained missionaries with ten national helpers, four of whom were on mission salary. Some of the eleven new missionaries who came in 1890 and 1891 were later transferred to new stations.

It is definite that the mission saw the opportunity, especially in the country, and was able to take it. It is no mere coincidence that, as these new missionaries were able to work, the Church started to grow. As we note on Figure 7, 1895 marks the beginning of growth. It is evident from their behavior that even at this early date, the missionaries saw that opportunities for planting churches were greater in the rural area. Mr. D. L. Gifford remarks that Seoul Station was barely manned because Moffett was in the country for four months, Underwood was off to Pusan, and Baird was out looking for a new station site. Gifford himself felt the pressure of the routine work of the station.[7] Almost two years later, Mr. Gifford is able to see that the hope of Korean Christianity in the future is in the country, for he says:

> When the new missionaries are able to take part in the work in Korea, we shall see hundreds and thousands of Koreans converted to Christ. On what can be done among the residents of Seoul, I reserve judgment. But among the visitors to Seoul and the people in the country, I certainly expect to see great spiritual results. I must add, however, that I do not expect to see these results this year or next year because your missionaries are either new men or shackled with routine cares.[8]

This is an accurate prophecy of what did actually happen, for in a few years, as can be seen in the graph of the whole Church (Figure 4), as well as in the graph of the Seoul area (Figure 7), the Church broke out in a great growth beginning about 1895.

In 1893 the second church in the capital was established. This new one (the Kongdangkol Church) is particularly interesting for the social class of people that made up its congregation. In the first year it had a membership of forty-

[7] Gifford, Personal Report to the Board (Seoul, Korea: February 27, 1891).

[8] Gifford, Letter to the Board (Seoul, Korea: November 2, 1892).

three, but a year later, when a butcher by the name of Pak was converted and came to church, several of the gentry or *yangban* class of people left the church and refused to worship. Their position was that they had endured the presence of servants and other lower-class people in the church but that the admission of butchers was just a little too much for them.[9] The butchers were the out-casts of Korea because of the Buddhist teaching against killing animals. This stigma had also extended to the people who handled slaughtered animals, and for five hundred years butchers had been oppressed by custom and were forbidden to wear hats, which were a symbol of status. The Rev. Mr. S. F. Moore, the missionary connected with Kongdangkol Church, was very much interested in the butchers and wanted to raise their position to the level of the ordinary Korean working people. Mr. Moore, with the help of Dr. Avison, appealed to the Korean King and as a result the government sent out an order to all communities declaring the removal of dress restrictions (such as that which forbade butchers to wear hats) and admitting butchers to the same protection of the law as that afforded other classes.[10]

We see that the church did not grow, however, as Moore reports in 1896: "The Kongdangkol Church has not increased much in members and the loss by removals and backsliding has about equaled the gain. The work among the butchers has not come up to expectation." The Kongdangkol Church actually stood by itself only four years and was then united with another to form the Seung Dong Presbyterian Church in Seoul. Miss Harriet Pollard judges that Moore's special interest in these butchers limited his converts in the city of Seoul almost entirely to this caste. She writes, "The Seung Dong Church in Seoul was for years under a stigma because

[9] Samuel F. Moore, Evangelistic Report to the Board of Foreign Missions of the Presbyterian Church U. S. A. (Seoul, Korea: 1895). Also found in Rhodes, *History, op. cit.,* p. 101.

[10] Harriet E. Pollard, *The History of the Missionary Enterprise of the Presbyterian Church U. S. A. in Korea with Special Emphasis on Personnel* (Northwestern University, Chicago: Master's thesis, 1927), p. 30.

of the large number of butchers in its membership."[11] During the first four years of its existence as Kongdangkol Church, one hundred eight adults were baptized in the church, thirty of whom belonged to the butcher caste.

The decade from 1890 to 1900 shows a growth increase from one hundred to fourteen hundred Presbyterian church members in Kyunggi Province. One can see in Figure 7 that most of the growth came in the latter half of the decade. The growth percentage in this period is over one thousand percent. This figure is exaggerated by the low starting base, but even at that the numerical growth was great. All three ordained missionaries assigned to Seoul in 1890 — Underwood, Moore, and Gifford — reported a steady growth. The greater part of this growth came not from the city but from the adjacent country area. In 1899 Seoul's three self-supporting churches had a total membership of 510, while the nineteen country churches totaled 689 members. In 1926 the baptized membership was divided into 1700 in the city and 1300 in the country, but the city members were in fourteen strong churches, while the 1300 baptized members in the rural area were in eighty-seven small churches averaging about fifteen communicants per group.[12] The decade from 1900 to 1910 shows more numerical growth than the previous decade but indicates only one hundred percent growth as compared with the thousand percent growth just mentioned.

In 1905 a new station at Chungju was opened. The statistics of that station, situated in North Choongchung Province, were not separated from Seoul and Kyunggi Province statistics until 1925. Because the growth pattern was quite similar and because they are adjacent territories, I have included both provinces in Figure 7. It is interesting to note that the Pyongyang Christians felt the need of evangelizing the people in Chungju. In 1906 the Rev. F. S. Miller from Chungju speaks of these Pyongyang Christians: "They realized the importance of winning these *gentlemen* [italics mine —R.S.] provinces to Christ that Korea as a whole may be

[11] *Ibid.*
[12] Seoul Station, Report to the Board of Foreign Missions of the Presbyterian Church U. S. A. (Seoul, Korea: 1926).

His."[13] The social distinctions between these areas will be discussed later on.

Growth continued for a few years, partly due to "a change of attitude of the non-Christians toward the Church, as the results of vigorous evangelistic campaign."[14] By 1914, however, Underwood sadly reported that the growth around Seoul stopped because "the political and social changes have been affecting the country, and brought about no small amount of migrating among the populace, and no small number of our Christian communicant members and catechumens have emigrated to Manchuria and other parts."[15] The response to the Church from the Seoul area and southward had been the landless tenant farmers, who are always the first to migrate when times become difficult. It will be recalled that the year 1914 marks the leveling off of nationwide church growth, apparent on Figure 3.

The rate of church growth in Kyunggi and North Choongchung Provinces for the twenty-five years following 1914 must be stated with all charity toward those working in the Church, but it must be stated clearly. To put it simply, the growth in this area and during the years from 1914 to 1939 was virtually nil. The net gain of 2900 communicant members meant a gain of two and nine-tenths percent a year, which was not even keeping up with the normal population increase. To say it another way, the Church in Kyunggi and Choongchung Provinces stopped growing, while in the adjacent areas it grew steadily.

As early as 1898 the Rev. Mr. Horace G. Underwood felt the difference in growth between the Seoul area in which he was working and the area of the northwest. He said in 1898:

> It is a matter of great rejoicing to us all to see how well the work comes on and it is my firm belief that the only reason why we do not see like results in the south and east is that we have not put forth the effort there that we have

[13] F. S. Miller, Letter to the Board of Foreign Missions of the Presbyterian Church U. S. A. (Chungju, Korea: 1906).

[14] Underwood, Personal Report to the Board (Seoul, Korea: 1911).

[15] Underwood, Evangelistic Report to the Board (Seoul, Korea: 1914).

in other places and *I have seen that wherever we have put
forth the effort, like results have always followed* [italics in the
original]. We should not think for a moment that the north
and west are the only places where work can be done with
success. The whole of this land is ready for the Gospel, and
oh, that we were ready to give it to them.[16]

But at this point, Underwood was mistaken. For listen to
the Rev. Mr. Harry A. Rhodes writing about the same territory thirty-six years later — in 1934:

> Anyone who goes into the country districts around Seoul
> will be impressed with the appalling need, even after fifty
> years of Protestant Missions and one hundred and fifty years
> of Catholic Missions in those parts, where more missionaries
> have resided, *more effort* [italics mine —R.S.] has been put
> forth, and more money spent than any other section of Korea.
> In the evangelization of the country districts around the
> capital . . . the results have been somewhat disappointing.
> During the [last] fifteen years at least thirteen men and five
> women workers of the station have had their major assign-
> ment for a term of years to country work, while many others
> gave as much time as they could.[17]

These two quotations are not from armchair missiologists
making judgments from the outside. Both of these men were
not only interested in making the Church grow, but were
daily spending their energies for that cause. They lived in
the same geographical area, but in two different periods of
the Church's history in Korea. Underwood was looking
forward, trying to make sure that the evangelistic witness
in the slow-growing area in which he worked would not
be overlooked, and so he called for *more effort*. Rhodes,
while he had the same commitment to evangelism in the
Seoul area, was forced by the overwhelming evidence of
thirty-six years of history to take a hard look at the results
of the tremendous effort that had been put forward through
the years. The results can be seen on Figure 7. The reason
commonly given for nongrowth in this area is the large con-

[16] Underwood, Letter to the Board (Seoul, Korea: August 5, 1898).
[17] Rhodes, Personal Report to the Board of Foreign Missions of the
Presbyterian Church U. S. A. (Seoul, Korea: 1934).

centration of the conservative *yangban* or gentlemen class, who wanted no change. This reason is the best offered yet, but it is obvious that tremendous effort, evangelistic zeal, and the proper methods are not always sufficient to break down barriers and cause the Church to grow. What other answers are there? Let us look for these answers in a study of the next four areas.

North Kyungsang Province (E). The center for missionary activity in the thickly-populated North Kyungsang Province in the southeastern part of Korea is the capital city of the province, Taegu. Visits were made to the province and Taegu early in the Northern Presbyterian Mission's history. The Rev. Mr. J. S. Gale visited there in 1889, and the Rev. Mr. William M. Baird, while living in Pusan, traveled north several times in 1892 and 1893. During these early itinerations through the province, all of the missionaries reported that wherever they traveled the people observed with interest these odd-looking foreigners and gave them a courteous hearing. The Board Report of 1892 puts it this way: "The Koreans of that province [Kyungsang, which had not yet been divided into north and south] are said to receive the truth readily but like the seed on stony ground it soon withers away. There are many listeners but few believers."[18] The interest of the people flagged when they found the missionaries were there merely to preach this strange Jesus doctrine. These Koreans did not exhibit the persistent inquiry which could be seen in other parts of the country.

North Kyungsang Province was another center of the conservative *yangban* class, which was steeped in Confucian ethics. The Northern Presbyterian mission board got the impression from field reports that these people would make good Christians. In writing of the Andong district in the province, they report that "the evangelistic aspect of the field is exceptional. The wealthiest, most conservative and aristocratic country gentlemen of Korea live in this district."[19] But the fact was that these people at that time were not

---

[18] Annual Report of the Board of Foreign Missions of the Presbyterian Church U. S. A. (New York: 1892), p. 175.

[19] *Ibid.*, 1911.

winnable. A later report affirms, "the wealthier people stand aloof and are very hard to reach."[20] The *yangban* seemed to want nothing to do with the new Western religion. In fact, through their economic control over the tenant farmers, the *yangban* were often able to keep these farmers from becoming Christians.

This obvious lack of response, coupled with the remoteness of the territory from the ports, probably provides the reason why the mission occupied this area later than other areas. Land was purchased in 1895, and after some difficulty, Mr. and Mrs. James E. Adams were permanently located in Taegu in 1897. The missionaries did not carry on evangelistic work in this area by dealing with a group of inquirers, answering questions and teaching them the Scriptures, as was the procedure in other stations. Here the inquirers were few. Rather, the missionaries worked by street preaching and by wide distribution of literature, which was sold rather than given, to make sure it would be read. The method of teaching inquirers as they came to the *sahrang* room — the method which worked so well in Seoul and northern Korea — did not work in this southern area, and it gave only slight results even after months of continued effort using the *sahrang* room as an evangelistic base.[21]

Scattered here and there were isolated converts, won by the method of "broadcast seed-sowing" as reported by Adams: "I have heard of two or three men who bought books from us in our itineration . . . and who from reading them have declared their purpose to be Christians."[22] A few scattered groups of Christians began to meet, some groups started by missionaries, others started by people who moved from the north, and still others started by traveling Christian traders.[23] But conversions were few, and even though the missionaries and two Christians from Pyongyang joined for

[20] *Ibid.*, 1919.
[21] James E. Adams, Letter to the Board of Foreign Missions of the Presbyterian Church U. S. A. (Taegu, Korea: March 6, 1899).
[22] *Ibid.*, February 20, 1899.
[23] Adams, Personal Report to the Board (Taegu, Korea: March 3, 1899).

a month's evangelistic campaign in the city of Taegu in 1899, the record for that year shows only two baptized communicant members. The following year, 1900, shows only four communicant members for the whole area. This can be seen on Figure 8.

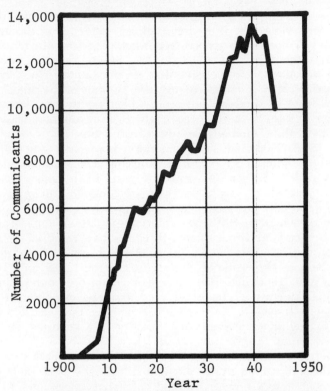

PRESBYTERIAN COMMUNICANT MEMBERSHIP
IN NORTH KYUNGSANG PROVINCE   (E)
FIGURE 8

The missionaries were concerned about the lack of growth in the Church, and they attributed this to "the house-building operations which [they had] been attempting."[24] The necessity of building a home for themselves kept the missionaries in the city and prohibited their travel to the country, where they felt there were opportunities for growth.

For fifteen years after the 1889 visits of the missionaries, and for seven years after they took up residence in the area, there was no church growth recorded. The use of literature limited those first contacts to the literate gentry, people who remained unresponsive for a long time. The street preaching, even in later years, is said by some of the preachers themselves to produce few countable results, but, because whatever results there were came from wide broadcasting methods, these methods cannot be condemned.

In 1905, 1906, and 1907 something happened. About this time the Church in North Kyungsang Province began to grow rapidly, as can be seen on Figure 8. In each of those three years there was a doubling of communicant membership from the previous year. The growth occurred in the country, where in 1904 the adherents in Dr. Adams' district alone increased from twenty-three to two hundred thirty-seven.[25] The sharp increase could not be missed by those involved in the work of evangelism. From 1905 and 1906 came statements like this: "Our work is on the bound. Since Annual Meeting we have received as many catachumens as we have received since the station was opened. Groups are springing up everywhere. Last year I reported 79 believers in my territory; this year I have 219."[26]

Until this upward swing of growth the missionaries of the northern fast-growing areas adamantly expressed their belief that it was unwise to send missionary personnel to an obviously unresponsive area like Taegu, because the present staff of northern missionaries was hardly able to keep up

[24] Taegu Station, Evangelistic Report to the Board (Taegu, Korea: 1900).

[25] Adams, Letter to the Board (Taegu, Korea: August 1, 1904).

[26] W. M. Barrett, Letters to the Board of Foreign Missions of the Presbyterian Church U. S. A. (Taegu, Korea: January 15, 1905 and July 20, 1906).

with the growth there. Then suddenly there came this period of growth in the Taegu area that did not abate (it can be seen on Figure 8). Why the sudden growth at the rate of four hundred forty percent per decade between 1909 and 1915? We can answer positively that the growth was given by God, but through what human means did it occur?

Factors causing the Church to grow elsewhere in Korea were also at work in the North Kyungsang area. Japan's take-over of Korea took away the security of the aristocratic, conservative *yangban,* who did not fit the progressive policies of Japan. There is no evidence of a sudden turning to the Church by the *yangban,* but their grip on the tenant farmers was evidently loosened, allowing the farmers a measure of freedom to become Christian.

The conservative town of Andong is just sixty miles north of Taegu in this same province. A station was opened in Andong in 1910. In this area, which had been visited only on itinerating trips but now had resident missionaries, a strong Church was established, and it grew rapidly. In the fourth year of the Andong city church's existence — 1913 — there were eighty-two communicants, forty-one of whom had been received into full church membership in the year 1913.[27] Churches were started in the villages surrounding Andong. One church, established earlier in 1902 in Kukkok, soon made a clean sweep of the village. Even today this village is practically one hundred percent Christian. The people of North Kyungsang Province obviously had turned receptive to the message of Christ. After fifteen years, the work of the missionaries in this province was beginning to pay off. The people were announcing this Gospel among themselves, and those who professed a belief in Christ were gathered into churches with the assistance of the missionaries, who were now spread out into two areas and were better able to assist the country churches.

The spurt of growth, however, begins to level off in 1915 and continues to abate until 1919. This leveling has been attributed in part to too few trained leaders who could not

[27] A. G. Welbon, Personal Report to the Board of Foreign Missions of the Presbyterian Church U. S. A. (Andong, Korea: May 31, 1913).

manage the follow-up of the large numbers taken into the Church. Some Korean church workers had as many as sixteen places under their care, so pastoral visits were rare and hurried. In some of the groups during a period of five and one-half years, the visits were made by five different men.[28] But this is only one reason for the slowing of church growth in 1915.

Another important reason for this slower growth is the increased Japanese invasion into this farming area. The Japanese took over choice farmland, and, even though there was increased rice production, the Korean people did not benefit from it. Also, the psychological effects of the Conspiracy Case, with the Japanese government's anti-Christian pressure, may have been felt in adjacent areas. This is possibly true because local Japanese pressure was more severe upon the farmers of the south than upon those in the north. An exact statement of all the reasons for slower growth during these years is difficult to make. The North Kyungsang area is one in which church growth certainly needs further research.

Until 1921 the statistics for the Andong area were included in the one North Kyungsang Presbytery, but in that year a new presbytery of 2400 communicants was formed from this larger parent presbytery. The new one included Andong and its surrounding territory. It must be noted that churches around Andong, after their initial spurt of growth, grew much slower than did the rest of North Kyungsang Province. The presbytery formed in 1921 did not even double its initial 2400 communicants until after the Korean War broke out in 1950, when the old Confucian traditions of the *yangban,* so strong in North Kyungsang, broke down in the Andong area.

The missionaries of Taegu felt that the inrush of Japanese civilization, which they claim affected the south of Korea more than any other place, had mixed effects on the growth of the Church. It turned people's minds to materialism on the one hand, but on the other: "our country church buildings are better; the church yards are neater . . . a substantial improvement has been made in raising of endowment for

[28] "More About Taegu," narrative presented to Chairyung Station on December 28, 1911, *Korea Mission Field,* February, 1912, p. 43.

churches and especially for church schools in the shape of wood tracts and fields."[29] The trials of the Conspiracy Case (yet to be examined in this book) were depressing, but the missionaries reported that the Church was purged and strengthened by these trials. Mr. W. N. Blair in 1914 says: "The [church] officers, especially, who stood so faithfully at their posts in the time of danger, have grown in strength and ability to lead their churches."[30] In a few years, beginning in 1919, we see on Figure 8 the fruits of strong leadership in a growth from 1919 to 1926 that almost equalled the rate of growth in the earlier period.

A comparison between the church growth in the Seoul area and that in North Kyungsang Province is instructive. After twenty years of mission work the Seoul area (Kyunggi and North Choongchung Provinces), with many missionaries and much money, shows a communicant membership of 2000, and North Kyungsang Province, with far fewer men and much less money, shows a communicant membership of 7500. Both figures are infinitesimal percentages of the population, and it is to be noted that the churches in Kyunggi and North Choongchung Provinces never even reached 7000 communicants until after World War II.

Since there was little response to early missionary efforts and also since North Kyungsang Province was noted for its extremely conservative, Confucianist *yangban* class, it would seem likely for the growth shown on Figure 8 to begin leveling off after 1920. In the territory around Seoul, after an initial spurt of growth, as Figure 7 shows, there was a leveling off. However, one can see that the Church in North Kyungsang, with the exception of several one-year drops which are probably incomplete statistics or statistical redefinition, shows on Figure 8 a continuous growth from 1921 to 1938. I believe this was due partly to the judicious use of foreign funds. This usage was not in accord with the Nevius principles but was approved by the mission and

[29] Taegu Station, Evangelistic Report to the Board (Taegu, Korea: 1912).

[30] William N. Blair, Personal Report to the Board of Foreign Missions of the Presbyterian Church U. S. A. (1914).

mission board at home. It was called the Adams Evangelistic Fund.

Adams Evangelistic Fund. Because the Rev. Mr. James E. Adams saw opportunities for evangelism in North Kyung-sang Province wasted for lack of personnel, a private fund was secured to bring new evangelistic missionaries to Korea for the sole purpose of planting churches. The mission board in its 1922 report paints a picture of the opportunity in this area:

> There is a population of about two million in the Taegu-Andong field, two-fifths of all that the entire mission has assumed evangelistic responsibility for: while there are only about eight Christians to every 1,000, and one church in every 30 square miles. It is time for the mission and the church at home to come face to face with the fact that the great mass of North Kyungsang's population has been left to plunge on down to perdition unchecked. Despite the shortage of workers the established work has prospered.[31]

Two new missionaries supported by the Adams Fund arrived from the United States, but, as it happened, one was taken ill and had to resign, as did Dr. Adams within a few years of setting up the fund. The other new missionary was transferred to Chairyung and became a regular member of the mission. The plan did not work as originally envisaged — with foreign missionaries supported by the fund — but the need for evangelism was still there, and so after Dr. Adam's departure, his two sons, the Rev. Mr. Edward Adams and the Rev. Mr. B. N. Adams, were assigned as trustees of the fund. Instead of supporting foreign missionaries, the fund was used to support Korean evangelists for a limited period of time, to support ordained Korean ministers for a maximum of two years, and to support preaching bands from the Boy's Academy, who did evangelistic work among the students of Taegu.[32]

The fund produced results. In the ten years preceding 1930, seventy-three churches were established by means of this fund, which is roughly fifteen percent of the entire num-

31 Annual Report of the Board (New York: 1922).
32 Rhodes, *op. cit.*, p. 186.

ber of churches in the province, and twenty-five percent of the total churches in Kyungbook Presbytery, which includes Taegu.[33] This careful and effective use of foreign funds for planting and developing churches is described in the Taegu Station Report of 1928:

> The most intensive evangelistic work for this province is conducted by the Adams Evangelistic Fund. This year about ten new churches were established. In sending the workers to a village, sometimes a Bible-woman is sent first and sometimes an evangelist, but generally the latter precede the former. The first month is spent in intensive personal work. They do not limit their efforts to the particular village in which they are located but work out in the neighboring villages for the radius of ten li or three miles. Usually, by the end of the month, if there has been any success to their efforts at all, night schools are started in which those who have some education are given instruction in the Bible. The more ignorant are taught to read their Bibles and all are drilled to sing the church hymns. As the work grows, less time is given to the house-to-house preaching and more time to nurturing those who have already decided to accept Christianity. Usually by the end of the month the worker knows his field pretty well and those who are likely prospects for becoming Christians.
>
> Each worker is required to make monthly reports. Every two or three months all the workers are called to a conference at Taegu. The missionary visits each locality where they are at work . . . at least once, and sometimes two or three times a year. In this way those directing the work are kept in pretty close touch with it. Constant pressure is kept on the evangelists to speed up and finish one location as soon as possible. No absolute time limit is set though it is pretty generally understood that the situation must be very special to run over six months. A few have taken eight months, none over. Some have finished it in two months. The average [time taken to plant a church] for 1925-1926 was a little over five months. The one thing that is emphasized the most as a standard of leaving a work well-finished is the securing of a meeting-house. It is considered quite a disgrace for the

[33] *Ibid.* Also found in *Korea Mission Field,* January, 1960, pp. 19-20.

workers not to get a church building erected before they leave.[34]

The financial problems of the people and the churches were real. Tenant farmers of the south were barely able to feed their families. Reports of hardship are numerous. It was in this situation that the careful use of foreign funds paid off in church growth.

The previous sentence is not to be taken lightly. It would be constitutionally rejected by a young missionary to Korea soaked in the Nevius principles, but the fact is that a quarter of the churches in the Taegu area had been planted through the use of the fund. There was good, continuous growth in this area from 1920 to 1935, while there was small growth in other areas. One wonders if the use of foreign funds specifically for church growth could not have helped the Church through a desperate time of strife in other areas also.

In 1930, with few environmental factors favoring growth, the Taegu Station reports that the Church is wide open for the preaching of the Gospel, and the only reason the Church is not able to keep up with the demands of the population is that there is a lack of leaders. "If there were a well-trained leader for each group, small as they are, we would grow and do well."[35] Weak churches would grow and new churches could be planted if there were leaders. Then, in 1931, from the foundations laid in the previous three decades, the Church began to grow at an astounding rate (observe Figure 8 from 1931 to 1938).

Until sufficient evidence to the contrary is found, I believe the growth increase during this time must be regarded as due to expansion of those churches planted by the Adams Evangelistic Fund. They were planted with foreign money but were soon set free to reproduce themselves, not being limited in their growth by foreign funds. Other factors not known to me may have had profound effects upon the Church in this time and area, but until they are unearthed, it would

[34] Taegu Station, Annual Report to the Board (Taegu, Korea: 1928).
[35] *Ibid.*, 1930.

seem that here a judicious disregard of Nevius principles produced great growth.

II. NORTHWEST KOREA

That the Presbyterian Church in Korea grew rapidly is an idea which thoroughly pervades missionary literature, but the reality is that chiefly *one section of the Presbyterian Church in Korea grew rapidly.* Just as the brilliant light from a welder's arc lights up the entire night sky, so the great growth in northwest Korea lit up the writing about the Presbyterian Church in Korea. Much of the promotional material fastened on this brilliant story of success and told it as if the entire Church were producing this glorious light. Even though missionaries wrote as if the whole Presbyterian Church in Korea were growing fast, the fact remains that an unspectacular picture of a relatively slow-growing Church, struggling and battling against great odds, is found in the intimate non-promotional writing from all of Korea except the north-western section. Even the growth just recorded in North Kyungsang Province seems small when compared with this really fast-growing section of the Church in Korea.

The hidden, exciting fact is that Christianity in northwest Korea was a growing and vital force in the society. From the statistical differences in church growth, no one should conclude that the missionaries of the northwest were more dedicated or energetic than those in discouraging, slow-growing areas. Although comparisons may seem at first sight odious, we must try to understand how it came about that, in this nation of one people and in this Church of one Presbyterian theology, such a great proportion of the members were concentrated in the limited area of the northwest with its small population of only three million.

First let us clarify terms. In this book, "northwest Korea" refers specifically to the northern part of Whanghai Province (C and Figure 9) and to Pyongan Province which was divided in 1896 into North Pyongan Province (A and Figure 11) and South Pyongan Province (B and Figure 10). The word "Pyongan" always refers to the province. Not to be confused with Pyongan is its largest city, called "Pyongyang." Because this city was the first place of missionary residence in the northwest area, it may also be referred to as Pyongyang Station. Other Northern Presbyterian mission stations of northwest Korea are Sunchun, Chairyung and Kangkei.

Whanghai Province (*C*). Church growth in Whanghai Province is an enigma to me. This province contains the village of Sorai mentioned before as the "cradle of Protestant Christianity in Korea." Most of the missionaries of the Northern Presbyterian Mission visited this church in Sorai as they traveled from Seoul to Pyongyang or to the far north. Also the entire Whanghai Province was frequently visited by missionaries from Pyongyang and Seoul. Yet it did not have its own resident missionaries until 1906. Up to that time the statistics had all been reported partly by Seoul Station and partly by Pyongyang Station.[36]

Seeing the early response to Christianity in Whanghai Province, we should expect the Church there to grow rapidly. Missionary trips through the territory indicated that the people were responsive. Mr. Graham Lee and Mr. Samuel A. Moffett made a trip in 1898 during which they received one thousand catechumens and baptized three hundred in Whanghai Province.[37] Other reports before 1900 show the same type of response, but in 1900, Mr. William B. Hunt, a missionary assigned to the Whanghai district from Pyongyang Station, says that a major problem there was the loss of members to the Roman Catholic Church. He attributes this loss to lack of missionary oversight and to the unfortunate choice of a native worker paid by the Korean Church.[38]

Losses to the Roman Catholic Church were not from the communicant membership but from inquirers and catechumens. Writing about a visit to Whanghai Province, Mr. Graham Lee says:

[36] In the years 1907-1908, South Pyongan Province (Figure 10) reflects a change in statistical reporting of the General Assembly so that the church membership in Whanghai Province all appears under Whanghai Presbytery rather than Pyongyang Presbytery in South Pyongan Province.

[37] Mrs. Graham Lee, Letter to the Board of Foreign Missions of the Presbyterian Church U. S. A. (May 31, 1898).

[38] William B. Hunt, Personal Report to the Board of Foreign Missions of the Presbyterian Church U. S. A. (1900).

On this last trip, I dropped about 100 catechumens. Very many of them have gone over to the Romanists. Our baptized people remain firm and few of them go over. In my district I have one baptized man who has gone over. The cause of his going was because I would not interfere in a case which he had with the magistrate.[39]

Christians who had been trained and instructed in the faith by missionaries and national workers stayed with their churches and were not looking for greener pastures, but those who had not committed themselves to the Presbyterian Church were tempted to become allied with the Roman Catholic Church, which was rising in civil power in the province at that time. The Roman Catholic priests and leaders used this power to their own advantage, not only persecuting Protestants, but at times mistreating government officials.

In 1903 Horace N. Allen, then of the American Legation in Seoul, requested that Underwood and Moffett travel to Haiju in Whanghai Province and attend the trials of the Korean government versus some Roman Catholics.[40] Fifteen of these Catholics were convicted and given sentences of beatings or prison terms.[41] The result was that overt persecution of the Protestants ceased. Several missionaries wrote that because of these trials the Protestant Church actually gained, as "Christian and non-Christian alike have learned to know something at least of the character of that institution [The Roman Catholic Church]."[42]

If Whanghai Province had had resident missionaries assigned to it as early as the North Kyungsang area, the growth might have been greater. Poor growth of the Church in the early days could have been caused by lack of missionary oversight, which left the new Christians not bound to the church in which they were converted. Whatever the cause,

[39] Graham Lee, Letter to the Board of Foreign Missions of the Presbyterian Church, U. S. A. (Pyongyang, Korea: January 11, 1900).

[40] Samuel A. Moffett, Letter to the Board of Foreign Missions of the Presbyterian Church U. S. A. (Haiju, Korea: February 26, 1903).

[41] Rhodes, *op. cit.,* p. 227.

[42] W. L. Swallen, Pyongyang Station Letter to the Board of Foreign Missions of the Presbyterian Church U. S. A. (Pyongyang, Korea: July 3, 1903).

when in 1907 the statistics for the area were first recorded
separately, Whanghai Province showed significantly less
growth than one would expect from the early strong response noted by missionaries who traveled in this area. Two
thousand communicant members by 1907 seems like poor
growth when we remember that on one trip in 1898 Mr.
Lee and Mr. Moffett reported they had baptized three hundred Christians in Whanghai.

From the time the mission station in Chairyung was opened
in 1906 until the Independence Movement in 1919, Whanghai Province shows a rapid rate of growth. The aggregate
attendance of the Bible classes that had been established all
through the countryside totalled more than the entire Christian
community, indicating that most Whanghai Presbyterians attended these Bible classes at least once, and some more than
once. Even during this time of great growth, there were
discouraging reports of reversions and churches that went
out of existence. Mr. A. A. Pieters, also assigned to the area,
tells of several valleys where there were no churches and
gives, as an example of the difficulty in planting them in
these valleys, the story of a Korean evangelist who spent
six months in a district without one convert. Mr. Pieters
says that one possible reason for the hardness of heart in this
one section is that the mountains of the area had been for
many years a rendezvous for outlaws, who came into the
churches for supposed protection from the authorities but
soon left the Church.[43] The outlaw valleys were only a
small part of the province, however, and there was rapid
growth in the rest of Whanghai.

This growth between 1906 and 1919, which can be seen on
Figure 9, comes at a time when there was slow growth in
adjacent areas of the Church to the south and east. In fact,
it comes when there were political factors like the conspiracy trials, that would seem to hinder church growth. Why
the churches in this area grew rapidly while other areas
around were not growing is not clear and no particular reasons have been offered by missionaries in the official reports

[43] Alex A. Pieters, *Personal Report to the Board of Foreign Missions
of the Presbyterian Church U. S. A.* (Chairyung, Korea: 1914).

or letters. It seems that this must remain a mystery until new facts are uncovered.

Even more a mystery is the following fifteen-year (1919-1934) period of nongrowth in a time when nearby areas in the north and areas to the southeast were growing fast. Nongrowth like this in a place where the Church was first planted and first had a period of rapid growth, certainly could not have gone unnoticed. It is strange that official board reports and personal reports I have searched neither acknowledge this fact nor try to explain the lack of growth. It does seem that Whanghai churches received severe persecution from local police following the 1919 Independence Movement. Several churches were reduced to membership of women only, because the men were sent to jail. Examples are given of church officers who met with death as a result of the 1919 demonstrations. Also, a famine is reported in 1920 by Mr. Pieters, who describes the condition of the Church: "Owing to the famine and political disturbances of last year the number of men fallen away has been large."[44] Even though there are reports of police brutality aimed at anti-Japanese church leaders, as late as three years after the Independence Movement, this type of persecution did not continue through the total period of nongrowth noted on Figure 9. The question remains: why did the Church stop growing during the time when churches around it were growing?

I do not believe the growth stoppage was due to a lack of responsiveness. The principal fact leading me to say this is the very line of the graph (Figure 9), showing as it does a sharp upswing of growth, with an abrupt halt in 1919. Then again in 1934, after fifteen years of stoppage, growth begins just as quickly as it stopped.

I know of no environmental factors that would seem to change the people's responsiveness to this great an extent. In a description of the use of tent evangelism and market preaching, a missionary, at the end of his report, is only able to say that he cannot cite any churches or any direct results from his work. Without further evidence, I can only conclude that either there were internal problems in the

[44] *Ibid.*, 1920.

Church or mission station in that area or else policies adverse to church growth were followed — policies which naturally were not recorded but which severely affected the growth of the Whanghai churches at this time. I have been told by people who know the situation that there were personnel problems in Chairyung Station and that the mission station, involved in its own institutional work, was sealed off from the Church.

In considering the period from 1934 to 1942, we return to Figure 9 and note what happens beginning in 1934: the Church began to expand as never before. This resurgence of growth after the period of nongrowth is startling, but the records are silent as to why it occurred. I have been told that the Chairyung missionaries were quite startled when they suddenly realized that the Church around them was growing rapidly.

We can be thankful, though, that the Church did grow until 1941 at a rapid rate, reaching in 1941 above 18,000 communicants. Between 1931 and 1939 the Church increased more than one and one-half times in membership. It grew from 9,000 to 15,000. Other areas in the Church were growing during this time when the Korean people increasingly lost their freedom, but in no area of the Church was the upsurge of growth so sudden nor the rate of growth so high. No other area in the Church during this period had a rate of increase of seventy-two percent a decade as did Whanghai. It is as if some mysterious force had been holding the Church back during those fifteen years, and then, when the Church was able to grow, it burst out with the force of an unleashed giant, too long held in bondage.

North and South Pyongan Provinces (A & B). In the area that was in 1896 to become *South* Pyongan Province, three baptized communicants were recorded in 1890, all being in Pyongyang city, though there were no regular church meetings. By 1893 a church had been organized, and in 1894 fifty-two communicants were recorded. If we turn to Figure 10, we see that these small beginnings from 1889 to 1895 have no comparison with later growth; they even look like a slow start, common all over Korea. Only in 1895 did the Church

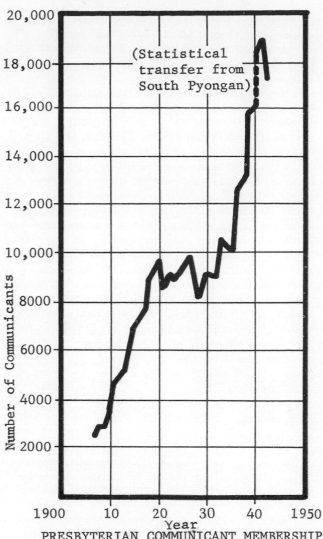

PRESBYTERIAN COMMUNICANT MEMBERSHIP
IN WHANGHAI PROVINCE (C)
FIGURE 9

start its rapid growth in this province and continue its astounding ascent until 1938.

In the area that was in 1896 to become *North* Pyongan Province, the twenty-five communicants in 1889 grew to two hundred two communicants within a decade. So we see that in 1899, with two hundred two communicants (see Figure 11), the Church begins its upward swing and continues at a rate of growth that produces more Christians by 1940 than does the Church, earlier, in South Pyongan Province. Great growth in North Pyongan Province began in 1900; it began in 1895 in its sister province to the south.

In Figures 10 and 11 there are no plateaus, i.e., no periods of retarded growth, but continuous great growth throughout the forty-five years. The jags in the line are either new presbyteries begun or statistical redefinition made; they are not membership losses. They are only for one or two years, and growth following these jags continues at a high rate. The details of these jags can be found in the Appendix.

Inspection of Figures 10 and 11 will show us several interesting things. For instance, notice the prerevival growth from 1895 to 1906. Not only was there considerable growth preceding the revival, but the rate of growth before and after this revival in 1907 is quite the same. It was not suddenly accelerated by the famous coming of the Spirit in Pyongyang. Also, the graphs show us that the Church refused to slow down during the period from 1912 to 1919, a period called static by Alfred Wasson. From 1921 to 1926 also, in spite of the economic and political difficulties of this period, the Church increased greatly with continued, amazing, steady growth. The members in the presbyteries of northwest Korea formed the following percentage of total Presbyterian membership in all Korea: in the year 1905, sixty-six percent; in 1915, sixty percent; 1925, fifty-six percent; and in 1935, fifty-five percent.

Early Responsiveness of the People, 1887-1894. Soon after arriving in Korea, the first missionaries made trips to the north. The Rev. Mr. H. G. Appenzeller, a Northern Methodist, visited there in 1887. The Rev. Mr. H. G. Underwood made his first trip to Pyongyang and Euiju, a town on the northern border, in 1888, partly because of the news of con-

verts there, gained through the work of John Ross in Manchuria. After this 1888 trip, Underwood concluded that
Pyongyang was a good place for a new station, and he hoped
to have permission to start it the summer or fall of that same
year.[45] Even at that early date, he noticed an obvious responsiveness of the people. Underwood records on his brief
visit that there were twenty-two applicants for baptism in
Pyongyang City alone, while in Seoul, where missionaries
had resided for four years, there was a communicant membership of only sixty-five.

These first trips of the Underwoods (Mrs. Underwood went
along on their honeymoon in 1889) were meant to explore
the north, but in addition to exploring they obtained aston-
ishing evangelistic results. In Euiju, which is located on the
border of China in North Pyongan Province, Mr. Underwood
baptized twenty-five men, saying that there were over one
hundred others who desired baptism.[46] Mrs. Underwood
writes of the anxiety of leaving thirty-four newly baptized
Christians in Pyongyang. She says the wives of these thirty-
four men all wanted to be baptized, but since they did not
even know what prayer was or who Jesus was, they were not
ready for baptism yet. Mrs. Underwood longed to stay there
and teach them for they were eager to learn.[47]

The year 1890 marks the year the Rev. Mr. Samuel A.
Moffett arrived in Korea. Six months later he made his first
trip to Pyongyang, which was to be his home and field of
labor for the next forty years. On this trip, Moffett traveled
with Mr. Appenzeller, the Methodist missionary, and Mr.
Hulbert, who was trying to secure coal for the foreign community in Seoul. After Appenzeller went farther north and
Hulbert returned to Seoul, Moffett, with only six months'
language study behind him, spent fifteen days in an inn in
Pyongyang, trying with the help of his teacher to tell the
Gospel of Christ to the many who sought him out. Moffett's
accounts of those first visits to that city are most charming,

[45] Underwood, Letter to the Board (Seoul, Korea: March 11, 1888).
[46] *Ibid.*, Euiju, Korea: April 1889.
[47] Mrs. Horace G. Underwood, Letter to the Board of Foreign Missions of the Presbyterian Church U. S. A. (May 5, 1889).

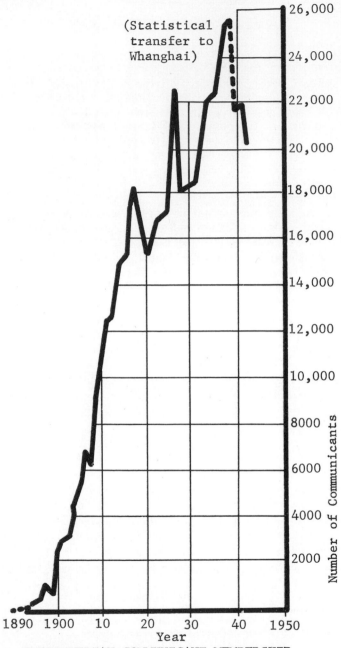

(Statistical
transfer to
Whanghai)

PRESBYTERIAN COMMUNICANT MEMBERSHIP
IN SOUTH PYONGAN PROVINCE (B)
FIGURE 10

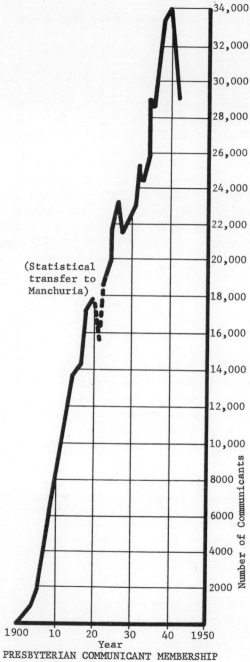

(Statistical
transfer to
Manchuria)

PRESBYTERIAN COMMUNICANT MEMBERSHIP
IN NORTH PYONGAN PROVINCE (A)
FIGURE 11

because it is obvious that he loved the people he had gone to live with.

He was concerned also that they hear and believe in the Gospel, and he took every chance to present it. In 1893, on an extended trip from Seoul, he made an attempt to buy property in Pyongyang, but the local magistrate blocked the sale and ordered people to drive him out. A mob of about three hundred shouting, angry men gathered where he was staying. Moffett stepped out in front of the crowd and asked them what they wanted. They told him they had been ordered to drive him out, so Moffett invited several of the elders to come in and talk it over. The leaders explained that they were under the magistrate's orders to drive Moffett out and that their lives were in danger unless he left. Even though he had a perfect right to stay, Moffett respected the judgment of the elders and wanted no harm to come to them, so he promised to leave the next day. Then, he says, "That won their friendship and the mob dispersed after hearing an explanation of the gospel."[48]   Moffett took the opportunity of a hostile crowd gathered to drive him out, to tell the story of Christian salvation.

At one time Moffett thought it advantageous to delay work in Pyongyang in order to begin intensive work in the town of Euiju farther north, where Underwood had previously found men so eager for baptism. Moffett also saw in Euiju much response that was created by the work of Ross just across the border. In 1891 there were more baptized members in Euiju than in Seoul. Moffett says of his 1891 trip north through Euiju to Manchuria:

> We were able to preach in cities, towns, villages, to hundreds of groups of people who had never heard of the gospel. We found them ready to listen and time and again we found men eager to know more, and with the Chinese Bible and our evangelists, the pure gospel was taught to many. The far north is open for successful work, the people in no way being opposed to the teaching of Christianity.[49]

[48] Moffett, *Korea Mission Field,* March, 1925, p. 53.
[49] Moffett, Letter to the Board (May 21, 1891).

In spite of all this, he and the mission later decided to open the station in Pyongyang, not Euiju.

Moffett goes on to say that it is his impression that prejudice against the foreigner is much greater in the south. Recall that in the Taegu area, early missionary work in 1892 had to be limited to market preaching and the giving of tracts. Moffett found the people much more responsive in the north, and he properly used different methods. He was able to plant a church in Pyongyang without open air preaching because there was a constant stream of visitors who came to his room, where he presented the Gospel in a personal encounter. Even when he tried to take a rest by walking the streets, men would gather and talk with him.[50]

Tremendous Growth and Village Evangelism, 1894-1906. The amazing response Moffett found in northerners soon became an amazing growth of church membership. Turning back to figures 10 and 11, let us examine the crucial ten years of stupendous growth in the Pyongan provinces from the year 1894 to 1906, prior to the revival. In these years are revealed some important secrets of church growth, not only valuable with respect to Korea, but also applicable in many lands.

Two outstanding events of 1894 left their mark on the young Church of northwest Korea. In the spring, while Moffett was in Seoul, a presecution led by the governor of the province broke out against the Christians in the city of Pyongyang. Hearing of the trouble, Moffett appealed to the British and American consulates and immediately set out from Seoul for Pyongyang. Through his influence the persecution was halted, but only just before another cataclysmic event took place in the city — the Sino-Japanese War.

The war began that summer. Instead of returning to Seoul for protection, Moffett says that he "stayed in Pyongyang in order to strengthen our little flock, to protect them and . . . to stay with them unless the Lord showed me plainly it was right for me to leave."[51] Moffett stayed in Pyongyang even

50 *Ibid.*, September 6, 1892.
51 *Ibid.*, August 27, 1894.

after the Chinese troops had arrived, but, because Americans and Japanese both wear dark clothes while the Korean people wore white clothes, he could not venture out into the streets for fear of being shot. Finally, on the advice of the little band of Christians, Moffett left Pyongyang in August for Seoul.

The war came closer, and a battle was fought in Pyongyang itself. In two days, September 15-17, 1894, the town of Pyongyang was nearly destroyed, and the population was reduced from about 60,000 to 15,000. The Japanese won, and the Chinese fled, leaving the place in a terrible state. Bodies of Chinese soldiers were piled deep in the streets and remained there for days. The mission property was destroyed. The Christians were scattered out in the country, and, as in New Testament times, these refugee believers gave witness to those around them. Less than a month later, in October, Moffett and his colleague, the Rev. Mr. Graham Lee, returned to Pyongyang and gathered the little flock of Christians who returned to the city, ministering to them by what spiritual and physical means they could. This service and devotion no doubt influenced the people of that war-torn city, stimulating interest in the Church.

After the Chinese beat a hasty retreat from Pyongyang, they rushed through Euiju, plundering it as they went. With them departed the old, conservative ways and hopes of the conservative, pro-Chinese Confucian leaders. Now was a time for the small church in that area to grow. Moffett says of the effects of the Sino-Japanese War in 1894: "The whole nation was shaken from its lethargy and extreme conservatism. The Church *with solid foundations laid* [italics mine — R.S.] was in a position to take advantage of the situation, so that from this time on there has been both steady and rapid growth with no retrogression."[52] The Sino-Japanese War was an important factor in the growth of the Church, but we must also acknowledge that the mission could take advantage of the vacuum left in the society by the defeat of China, only because a core of believers and workers were ready to act.

[52] Moffett, "Some Evangelistic Work," Quarto-Centennial Papers before Annual Meeting (August 27, 1909), p. 25.

These were the "solid foundations" Moffett refers to. The sudden receptivity of the people of Pyongyang in the autumn of 1894 could have passed unclaimed but for the church of fifty-two members who had been courageously baptized by Underwood and Moffett during the preceding six years. Again, Christians might have been lost if Moffett had not returned to a still dangerous situation to help build the young Pyongyang church. But Moffett, with his single-minded goal of planting churches, seized the opportunity.

The early church growth came about through Christians moving out among their friends and neighbors and winning them to Christ. Moffett writes: "More than a score of men have taken books and visited other cities and villages, preached Christ, gathered *groups of inquirers* [italics mine— R.S.] and started them to assemble on the Sabbath and instructed them as far as they could."[53] From these *groups started by ordinary Christians,* requests came for missionary instruction. The Church began to multiply ahead of the missionaries. A man, newly converted, could not remain silent about his faith and so told his friends and relatives about it. But in the northwest, there was more than just the telling of his new-found faith; the man's friends and relatives were ready to receive the Gospel and believe in it themselves. There were no overwhelming hindrances to becoming Christian and many people did believe. The missionaries spent all the time they could in the country, teaching groups of new believers more about the principles of the faith and accepting them for baptism after a thorough examination of that same faith. In this fast-growing area, using a principle of self-support that freed the flow of the Gospel from limitations of mission budgets, missionaries were not able to keep up as well as they would have liked with the enormous task of teaching the Bible and making sure that these new converts had a fair understanding of their Christian faith.

By 1896 the membership in the churches had trebled from the previous year and quadrupled again two years later, i.e., from *73* in 1895 to *1058* in 1898! These members were com-

[53] Moffett, Pyongyang Station Report to the Board (Pyongyang, Korea: 1895).

municants. The total Christian community by 1898 may
have numbered three thousand or more. This tremendous
growth is one thousand percent in only three years. By contrast, it took Seoul ten years to grow one thousand percent.
Observe again in Figure 4 the sharp upswing of the Korean
Church as a whole. The dynamism which caused this sharp
rise came almost entirely from Pyongan Province and particularly from the area in and around its large city, Pyongyang.
Other areas were not beginning to approach the same numerical growth as the northwest was granted.

This spontaneous, early growth affected the nature of
the Church itself. A man converted in one of these growing
congregations was inevitably interested in growth, for he
saw conversions on every hand, constantly heard about them,
and very naturally told others about them. Not only did
men travel to other towns to preach and tell this conversion
story, but a Christian who moved his place of residence
often started a new congregation in his new village home.
His old kin group had become Christian; why should not his
new group? We read of a Mr. Kim who moved twelve miles
from the city of Pyongyang and for a time frequently came
to his Pyongyang city church, but soon he so interested the
people of his new village in the Gospel that they began to
worship every Sunday. Mr. Kim was their teacher, and together they erected a church building.[54]

This, according to my conversations with several Korean
pastors of today (1965), is the way many churches originated
in the country. By 1896 the missionary letters from Pyongyang are full of accounts of church plantings all over the
area. Three new "substations" here; thirty new catechumens
enrolled there; sixty new converts in that village — and
almost all of them were heads of families.[55] The missionaries
did not do the planting; the local Christians did. In Korean
society, when the patriarch received Christian baptism, he
quite naturally brought his whole family into the Church in
the New Testament pattern.

[54] Moffett, Personal Report to the Board (Pyongyang, Korea: 1895).
[55] Moffett, Letter to the Board (Pyongyang, Korea: February 18,
1896).

The Pyongyang city church was growing so fast that in the one year — 1896 — the church building had to be enlarged three times. New members were taken in almost every Sunday, and an average Sunday attendance was about five hundred people. Certainly the large gathering of new Christians, five hundred strong and worshiping together, gave each of the individuals power and courage. The individual in that large congregation could look around and see friends and relatives joining with him in worship. Persecution by the family of members who became Christian was infrequent. In Pyongyang a Christian was not ostracized from the rest of society, because the church, by its sheer size, became a part of the society. As early as 1896 a new missionary writes: "In Pyongyang one could easily forget that he is in a heathen land."[56]

Until 1901, missionaries working in both North and South Pyongan Provinces lived in Pyongyang. It was from there that they sallied out on foot and horseback to visit the multiplying village churches. However, it soon became obvious, in view of the large number of Christians in North Pyongan Province, that it would be more efficient to have missionaries living up there. So they began to consider opening a new mission station.

Since 1887, the northern part of Pyongan Province had been repeatedly visited by missionaries. On those early visits they were particularly interested in Euiju on the border. A town called Sunchun, a little farther south, did not draw their attention, for it was only a wide spot in the road, with no Christians in the early years. Mission historian Rhodes says of the town simply: "Sunchun is an unwalled town without any known history."[57] This, in an Oriental setting, speaks volumes for this little town of three thousand ordinary, uncultured people.

In 1896, the same year that the northern part of Pyongan was declared a separate province, the Rev. Mr. Norman C. Whittemore, recently arrived in Korea, was sent to the North

[56] Norman C. Whittemore, Letter to the Board of Foreign Missions of the Presbyterian Church U. S. A. (December 26, 1896).

[57] Rhodes, *op. cit.,* p. 198.

Pyongan Province to open a station there. As he traveled the country, he decided — and the mission concurred — that the best place for the station was in Sunchun, not because of anything this little town had to offer, but because it was in the geographical center of the constellation of new congregations in the southern counties of the new province.[58] The site was picked, not in hopes of "reaching the leaders of the land," but for convenience in caring for the many churches and encouraging their further growth and spread. The Sunchun Station was actually established in 1901 and then Kangkei Station, still farther north, was similarly located in 1908 with a single eye toward church growth in the northern part of North Pyongan Province.

In 1897 the Christians of Sunchun purchased a Korean house which was used as the first church sanctuary. It was remodeled and would hold about four hundred fifty people. But the congregation in this little, out-of-the-way, unpromising town grew so fast that by 1901 the church was already too small for the congregation, and by 1903, two years after the station opened and four years before the revival, on any given Sunday morning ten percent of the population of five thousand in the town could be found in church. Truly this was a remarkable growth in comparison with other sections of Korea.

The church built on this firm, growing foundation in small-town Sunchun, soon received an opportunity to grow even more and reproduce itself across the countryside in a way that was not foreseen when Sunchun was picked as a mission site. The Japanese built a "Pusan to Manchuria" railroad in 1905, following the Russo-Japanese War, and put it right through Sunchun. With the railroad, the town became a communication center and grew in population. Hundreds of examples around the world can be given of this: the town that gets the railroad grows and influences the countryside around it, while nearby towns sometimes disappear entirely. The church in boomtown Sunchun, already greatly growing, became a "boomtown church" and inspired the worshiping groups in the adjoining rural areas to grow along with it.

[58] *Ibid.*, p. 199.

As waves crash on a lonely island and produce no sound unless there is an ear to hear it, so there could have been no growth of the church in Sunchun after the railroad boom unless a church had already been planted there. Yet the Church was there; it was concerned with its own extension, and it grew and reproduced to amazing numbers. Churches proliferated so fast in this area around Sunchun that the mission and board really did not realize what was going on there; it was so unbelievable. The little town of Sunchun had an enrollment and average Sunday attendance greater than the three churches in Seoul added together.

Effect of Tremendous Growth on Mission Policy in the Northwest. The growth of churches in and around the northern stations came before the missionaries were really settled and before any institutions had been established. This was true even of the first station, Pyongyang. Great and early growth determined the policies of Pyongyang Station missionaries, and these methods were such as to favor continued, rapid growth. For instance, "self-support" is more readily achieved in a greatly growing Church; it becomes an easier and, indeed, the only feasible method to follow. Self-support can be defined as the encouragement of a young Church to support its own organization wherever possible. Imagine a mission trying to erect buildings for these rapidly multiplying congregations! Had the mission tried to finance new church buildings, a new congregation would ask, "Is there any money from America for another building?" Growth would have been stunted. Provision of buildings for the large numbers professing the Christian faith was both unnecessary and impossible. Fortunately, self-support principles were followed by these northern missionaries and these principles naturally suited the situation.

In 1896, Pyongyang Station reported twenty-two congregations in its territory of the northwest. One year later the Gospel had been preached in all but one of the fifty-four counties in its territory, and there were fifty-three groups meeting regularly for worship. Twenty-five of these fifty-three groups had church buildings used only for religious purposes.[59] By the next year there were 126 congregations with sixty-nine church buildings in northwest Korea. During that one year, forty-four new church buildings had been erected. In the face of growth like this, self-support was both natural and inevitable. To offer to build churches for congregations already putting up their own would have been sheer folly and an insult.

Some have wondered if, in a growing area like this, the principle of self-support was not a result of the growth rather than its cause, as had been so often claimed. In point of time, self-support principles were set down in 1890 by Nevius, whole-heartedly accepted as part of the mission policy and rigidly followed by men like •Moffett in 1890, which was before great growth in any section. So it could be said that self-support principles caused growth. However, as we have just seen, great growth not only made possible but even demanded rigorous self-support.

An important issue connected with self-support is self-government. A self-government policy made it possible for the Church to adapt itself to the social and family structure of Korea, where the elder person was the leader. At first, the missionaries appointed leaders, hoping to choose those who had leadership qualities, but as the Church grew spontaneously, the guidance of the numerous churches went naturally to the leaders of the communities. This was sound psychology. Those who received the responsibilities of leadership in their congregations were pleased to be able to exert their influence and to gain additional respect. The effect of this psychology on church growth in 1895 to 1910 is described in 1929 by Dr. L. George Paik:

> There was . . . a desire for recognition. When a man brought in more believers and increased the membership of a church, he soon became a leader, and from that an elder or a local preacher.[60]

[59] Pyongyang Station, Report to the Board (Pyongyang, Korea: 1897).

[60] L. George Paik, *The History of Protestant Missions in Korea* 1832-1910, p. 284.

He no doubt enjoyed being a ruler of his people and enjoyed the feeling of power.

Handing control of new churches over to their indigenous leaders was no mere academic question with the Pyongyang missionaries just before the turn of the century; it was a practical necessity. The vast numerical increase of members forced the missionaries to turn control over to both local churches and the national Church as quickly as possible. It was unthinkable to try to keep control over this large Church. It was also absurd to think that out of this large number of Christians, some would not be qualified for leadership. As scores of churches led by their own able leaders arose, the ability of Koreans was easily seen by missionaries who found churches functioning well — churches that had had few or no previous visits from a missionary. Turning over to these men the entire control of the Church seemed sensible. Samuel Moffett even in 1898 writes:

> One of the most important steps before us [is] the gradual and judicious transferral of the government and management of the native Church to those Koreans whom we have been training to meet the responsibilities of leadership.[61]

Thus we see that the principles of self-support — that congregations erect their own church buildings, choose their own sessions[62] from among their own recently converted, "un-Westernized" members, and control their own governments — were made necessary by the great numerical growth of church members. Perhaps the adoption of these principles also helped produce further growth.

Medical policy in the northwest of Korea was also affected by the amazing church growth. Read what a doctor writes about his own medical work:

> One thing about evangelistic work here in Pyongyang — they don't need a hospital to draw or attract converts. Indirectly hospitals and dispensaries are strong features of missionary effort but directly, I'm afraid that they are often over-rated. I write simply from my own experience of our

[61] Moffett, Letter to the Board (June 27, 1898).
[62] Presbyterian term for local church governing committee.

10,000 patients seen within the time I've been in Korea [twenty-one months] and from reading, conversation and observation. I feel, therefore, that to do my duty as a medical missionary, I must have some other work and I'm glad to report the Sunday-school I have been in charge of is prosperous and growing.[63]

In addition, the missionaries' educational policy was affected because the multiplying churches began building schools faster than the missionaries could even think about acquiring new school locations. These missionaries did not have to fall back on educational institutions as evangelistic tools, because the churches were blossoming and multiplying by other means.

Great growth also affected actual missionary method. For instance, the missionary traveled widely. Recall that Underwood, seeing the response of people outside of Seoul, undertook his first itineration to the north. The travel he began was continued by Moffett at an even greater pace. The purpose of later itineration in the northwest, unlike that in many mission fields and in much of south Korea, was not primarily for distributing literature or "wide seed-sowing." Its two purposes were: one, to teach and examine those who had decided to become Christians and wanted to become catechumens or to be baptized, and two, to conduct the sacraments of baptism and the Lord's Supper.

Mr. Whittemore writes that, consumed with care of the numerous Christian churches, he had not much time left for the unevangelized.[64] As an example, in the 1899 fall itineration alone, Pyongyang Station added a thousand new persons to the rolls of the Church: 630 as catechumens and 370 as baptized members. This represented tremendous travel by five missionaries during October and bitterly cold November and December.[65]

[63] J. H. Wells, M.D., Letter to the Board of Foreign Missions of the Presbyterian Church U. S. A. (Pyongyang, Korea: March 1, 1897).
[64] Whittemore, Letter to the Board (Pyongyang, Korea: March 29, 1900).
[65] Wells, Letter to the Board (Pyongyang, Korea: December 30, 1899).

These were not quick trips with the missionary just saying a greeting and then passing on to another church. Beside the time and labor it took to get to the churches, all candidates were examined carefully regarding their faith and their knowledge of the Scriptures. It was standard practice during this time for an evangelistic missionary to be in the country at least one hundred days out of the year and often more. I stress this point lest anyone think a growing Church just grows by itself. Had the northwest missionaries not poured themselves out in ceaseless church planting, had their sweat not fallen on thousands of miles of road, had they spent their time in institutional work in their stations, the responsiveness of northwest Korea might very well have come and gone to no great increase of the Church.

Yet the Church did increase. The missionaries met the problem of huge numbers of new Christians by ceaseless itineration into the villages along the roads, and spent months trudging from one village church to another, constantly talking in this foreign tongue to people who wanted to learn more about the Gospel of Christ. The northwest missionary found the greatest demand upon him was for his teaching ministry.

Particularly where conversions are few and far between, men are often suspicious of great numbers of people coming into the Church. Pyongyang Station received its share of such suspicion from missionaries in the slower growing sections of the Church. A Seoul missionary, whom I shall not name, wrote that converts in *his* area were thoroughly trained and examined before they were admitted into the Church, but that in the "north" all one had to do was confess Christ and he was in. It is particularly revealing that this criticism had no basis in fact. The Pyongyang missionaries were unusually careful and, with very large numbers of catechumens, could well afford to be. Many statements like the following are found in the letters and reports:

> In no cases are all who apply being received as catechumens or baptized, but it seems to us a slow, steady and solid growth.[66]

[66] *Ibid.*, January 4, 1897.

Out of forty-seven candidates for baptism in one area, twenty were not received because they lacked adequate knowledge of the fundamentals of the Christian faith.[67]

If the workers in this area had been simply shooting for numbers, bringing in large masses of actually undiscipled people, Figures 10 and 11 would have broken, showing a great outflow of the disillusioned; or perhaps the Church would have become corrupt. Neither of these events happened. Instead, there was continued, tremendous growth.

Again, contemplating such growth, missionaries and national church leaders from little-growing Churches asked: do the people coming into the Church really know what they are doing? Are the converts intelligently Christian? Are we not taking them in too fast? In the midst of huge increase of Christians, Pyongyang missionaries were asking these same questions. Yet, facing the responsive multitudes, what else could they do but take them in? The apostles on the Day of Pentecost must have experienced a similar tension. A Pyongyang missionary was quoted in the 1900 Northern Presbyterian Board Report as saying that when people are responding, it is impossible to tell them to go slowly.

The missionaries met this problem in several ways, the first of which was a strictly followed catechumenate. Serious inquirers were enrolled as catechumens. Not wanting inquirers to go uninstructed to baptism, the missionaries spent the largest share of their time teaching the catechumens. They also met this problem by regularly training leaders through the Bible classes held in the country. In addition, they held month-long winter Bible schools in the cities for all who would come. Hundreds of lay leaders from scores of little churches did come, since their rice paddies required no work in that season. Eventually those who had been trained in these classes taught classes of their own throughout the country and city churches.

Task of Educating Christians in Northwest Korea. As hundreds and thousands poured into the churches, leaders had to be trained. This need for trained Christian leaders

[67] Hunt, Letter to the Board (December 1, 1897).

could not be disregarded by the missionaries in Pyongyang. Moffett says of missionary workers:

> Think of two men within a month trying to visit over sixty churches, carefully examine over four hundred candidates for baptism, hold services in one or more of these places, baptize three hundred people and meet and receive nearly a thousand catechumens besides discussing all the other various phases of church work.[68]

Just walking to two churches a day would be a difficult task for some of us missionaries of more recent vintage. Training leaders was not an academic exercise but a desperately vital affair. No one asked about the validity of spending much time and energy in conducting Bible classes for prospective church leaders. Conducting them was necessary for survival; the people who had come to Christ needed training in the rudiments of the faith, otherwise the Church would dry up and come to nothing. Many would revert to former religious practices or become nominally Christian without any intelligent understanding of their faith. The people would soon lose interest and church doors would have to be shut.

Not only did leaders have to be trained but they themselves demanded training. The first classes in Pyongyang were scheduled for January of 1898. The missionaries invited twenty-five Korean Christians to attend, and so prepared for that many. In a response typical of the northwest at that time, the twenty-five came bringing with them more than seventy-five friends and relatives who brought their own rice, some coming a distance of one hundred miles to get all of the instruction that could be had.

Just after the turn of the century the winter Bible classes which started with such unexpected response in 1898 expanded and grew to the overwhelming proportions so characteristic of this Pyongan area. Reports from various towns indicate attendance of two hundred here, three hundred there, and four hundred fifty yonder. In the city of Pyongyang, classes of fifteen hundred in attendance were recorded.

[68] Moffett, Letter to the Board (June 27, 1898).

In the villages winter Bible classes were smaller, but hundreds of them were held. The following Table, made from information in missionary letters and board reports, clearly shows the growth of the Men's Winter Bible Class held in Pyongyang.

Year:	1898	1899	1900	1901	1902	1903	1904	1905	1906	1907
Enrolled Students:	100	150	250	360	600	713	610	800	----	940

GROWTH IN ENROLLMENT OF MEN'S WINTER BIBLE CLASS
PYONGYANG, KOREA, 1898 - 1907
TABLE II

As in the growth of the Church itself, the sheer weight of numbers of Christians searching for knowledge of God had tremendous effects. First, it attracted non-Christian relatives and friends and helped the classes to grow even greater. Second, the large numbers also kept these classes rigidly focused on the Bible. There was no time to teach English, geography, or Western culture. No doubt many Koreans were attracted by the "big-nosed foreigners," but their teachers could only put first things first and center their teaching on the Bible and on little else. Third, there were just too many classes for missionaries to be present at all of them, and so there were many national teachers. A large part of the teaching *had* to be done by Koreans. To the multitudes assembled, Christianity often looked like, and was, a Korean faith. Fourth, these training classes gave a firm Biblical foundation to the great revival of 1907. And fifth, the Bible classes always were connected with an evangelistic campaign.

With the Bible classes in Pyongyang there was a careful,

organized evangelistic campaign where "mornings were given over to Bible study and the afternoons . . . to a systematic, house-to-house visitation. They went out two by two, preaching in practically every house in the city."[69] Tracts were printed, and each student attending the training class, as he was able to give time, participated in this visitation evangelism program.

The classes grew in size in the city. Most rural villages held their classes during the winter slack season, when the rice fields needed no care and when men and women from all of the churches around could attend. As churches multiplied the number of such classes increased. Bible lessons were also held in other sections of Korea, but none of them came close in size to those in the Pyongan Provinces. It would be easy to rationalize that these smaller classes were really a blessing in that they allowed for more intensive personal teaching, but an honest appraisal indicates that Christians who were swept along in the tremendous Bible study groups of fast-growing churches of the northwest were concerned about the growth of the Church in a way different from that of the churches in the south. Northerners saw great numbers of people responding earnestly to the Gospel and to intense study of the Word. They became deeply interested in spreading this message to their own families and to the rest of Korea too. Many northwest Christians were sent to other areas to hold Bible classes and to help in the perfecting of the Church, a perfecting which under these circumstances had powerful evangelistic results.

The great growth in the northwest had a pronounced effect on the revival. This revival began with missionaries in Wonsan in the year 1903. After that, minor revivals broke out here and there in other stations and churches in 1904, 1905 and 1906.

A description of this manifestation of the Holy Spirit on the eighth day of the Men's Bible Training Class on Monday, January 14, 1907, at Pyongyang has been given in several

---

[69] Swallen, "Revival in Pyongyang, Korea," an article on file at the Commission on Ecumenical Mission and Relations of the United Presbyterian Church U. S. A. (Pyongyang, Korea: February 16, 1906).

publications such as *Gold in Korea* by William Newton
Blair and needs only to be summarized here. The outward signs of this great Pentecost were the overpowering
conviction of sin among the Christians, both Korean and
American, and the power to make public confession of sin.
Graham Lee gives us one of many examples of the extreme
physical pain and agony connected with these confessions of
sin. In a mid-week prayer meeting in Pyongyang, Wednes-
day night, January 16, 1907:

> I noticed that Elder Chu was standing beside me on the
> platform, asking for an opportunity to confess. Then began
> a scene the like of which I never saw and which I am not
> anxious to see again very soon. He was trembling from head
> to foot and he fairly shrieked in agony as he told of the sins
> that he had committed. I have never seen a mortal in such
> agony of mind. He confessed to adultery and misappropria-
> tion of funds and at last he sank to the floor and fairly
> wilted and writhed in agony.[70]

In spite of this, there was no evidence given of mental
illness caused by the distress of this revival. Truly it was a
spiritual movement, and its results were momentous.

When in 1907, the fire of the Holy Spirit fell on that great
mass of assembled Christians in Pyongyang, the whole nation was affected as it had not been by earlier revivals. As
the power generated by touching a match to a drop of
gasoline is different than that generated when a spark ignites
a tankful, so was the power vastly greater when the revival
came to that huge congregation of men in Pyongyang. These
Koreans were free to travel all through Korea, and they did
so. Thus the Holy Spirit affected the Church as a whole
to an extent beyond that of His earlier manifestations, when
fewer men had been visited in other areas.

Beside the Bible classes, additional training for the new
Christians was begun on a higher level. In 1903 a theological
seminary was organized in Pyongyang with six students.
The huge church growth in the northwest demanded that

---

[70] Lee, Letter about the revival (Pyongyang, Korea: January 17,
1907). The letter was written on Thursday, the morning after the
experience cited in the text.

the seminary be located in Pyongyang, even though it was not the capital or the cultural center of the nation. In 1905, out of the twenty-two seminary students, only a few were from Seoul and two or three from the other southern sections. The bulk of the students were from the north. Until World War II, the Presbyterian Church of Korea and the four participating missions supported this one theological seminary for all of Korea.

The 1903 decision placing the seminary in the midst of the huge movement to Christ was sound. Had men from the Pyongan Provinces been sent off to Seoul to be trained by missionaries, not themselves getting much church growth and not experienced in the specific way multitudes were being added to the Lord in the northwest, the entire rate of advance might have been slowed. In addition, after three years in the capital, the northwest men would have been reluctant to return to remote country towns.

Many of the seminary students acquired direct experience in the growing churches, some of them taking a course that took five years to complete. They took one term a year in each of five years and spent the balance of the year working in country churches. Generally the students received support from their local churches during the three months of theological school, while these churches carried on with an unpaid lay worker as a preacher. Later, the course of study was modified to permit completion of the full theological course in three years' time. Even as late as 1931, only one-fourth of that year's graduates had been full-time students; the rest had been alternating between study at the seminary and service in their local churches.[71]

This type of theological education, which included practical experience in a fast-growing Church, affected the ministry of the Church all over Korea. It was an improvement over the Western tradition of training a student for three full years and then placing him in charge of a church. The Korean seminary educated leaders who in addition to taking theoretical courses were getting practical experience in a

[71] Federal Council of Missions in Korea, *Korea Missions Yearbook* (Seoul, Korea: Christian Literature Society, 1932), p. 39.

growing church, and at the same time it furnished part-time leadership for some of the churches. The program also had the good effect of weeding out students not committed to service in the Church. Any man who had less than the highest motives of service soon dropped out. On the other hand, any man who continued his education bit by bit over a period of five years, upon graduation could be considered not only soundly educated, but a dedicated minister, one who most likely had had the privilege of participating in the enthusiastic growth of the Church in northwest Korea.

Missionary Reinforcement of Responsive Area. Missionaries all over Korea saw that there was something special going on in the Pyongan Provinces. At the 1896 annual meeting of the Northern Presbyterian Mission, after the Pyongyang Station report was read aloud, the whole mission responded with the Doxology as a fitting praise of the work of God. The mission realized that the opportunity required human response too, and two additional ordained missionaries were sent to help part time with the work of nurturing young Christians and the young Church.

The growth of the young Church was so great that, even by using all their energies in teaching leaders and instructing new Christians, missionaries could not keep up with the movement. They pleaded with the board to send new missionaries to this fast-growing area. Mr. William B. Hunt and Mr. Samuel A. Moffett both were disappointed that, even with all their labors in this time of tremendous growth, some serious reversions took place, and some persons, having made a confession of faith in Christ, slid back. That reversions occur and people should fall away after the first glow of conviction is not pleasing to man or to God, but it seems inevitable that some will make a decision to become Christian and later change their minds. This is implied in the parable of the sower: where the seed fell on rocky ground there was a joyful response with a later rejection. Reversions happen under all conditions, whether people are converted one by one or whether they make their decisions in a large group. Some are lost whether we like it or not. Then, too, some are lost through lack of shepherding, as happened in the northwest. Moffett and Hunt, correctly, did not think this loss due to rapid growth but rather to "our inability to provide sufficient oversight and instruction."[72]

The missionaries in the northwest were hard at work trying to conserve the rapid growth that was going on about them, and they felt they had been dealt a bitter blow when in 1899 the mission assigned missionaries supposedly sent out for Pyongyang Station to the nongrowing Taegu Station. There were four or five times as many people in the Taegu area as there were in the Pyongyang area, and the mission doubtless hoped that a large Church would develop in the populous south also. To leave Taegu without a witness was unthinkable, and pressures built up to "give the Gospel to Taegu." Taegu missionaries maintained that growth was forthcoming.

The Pyongyang Station replied, "Growth is already upon us and in proportion to those seeking to become Christians the missionary staff is very slim." A Pyongyang missionary pointed out that in his area alone (Sunchun), one thousand believers were attending services and desiring instruction. These were gathered into twenty-three organized and twelve unorganized churches scattered over fourteen counties.[73] Mr. Whittemore, pleading for more missionaries, says: "I can barely swing the work now and at the end of the year before another worker has even one year's knowledge of the language I will be swamped."[74] Strong letters protested the mission action placing the new missionaries in Taegu. When in 1900 the dust of combat settled, vastly growing Pyongyang Station had six ordained missionaries and practically nongrowing Taegu had three.

Christian missions are constantly tempted to make this mistake. Instead of reinforcing on the edge of a growing movement, they begin stations in new places, sometimes with a reasonable hope that churches there will also spread, but often simply to be occupying some "great new territory." The clash of the two views of mission — one, to disciple the

[72] Moffett, Letter to the Board (July 10, 1899), and Hunt, Letter to the Board (April 6, 1899).
[73] Whittemore, Letter to the Board (Pyongyang, Korea: November 10, 1899).
[74] *Ibid.*

nations and two, to preach the Gospel everywhere — constantly prevents the reinforcing of fruitful fields. However, that Pyongyang was given six missionaries proves that, in view of its overpowering growth, the mission could to some extent forget its sectional rivalries and use its limited resources to help churches grow in the place where most church growth was possible.

This issue kept cropping up. Not only in the beginning, but throughout the next fifty years, areas of little growth were consistently and systematically favored. Dr. A. M. Sharrocks of Sunchun wrote in 1902 that one in seven of all the Presbyterian adherents *in Korea* were in the Sunchun mission station's area; yet only one of every thirty ordained missionaries was at work in this area, showing the great unbalance.[75]

The Rev. Mr. Carl Emerson Kearns also illustrates this imbalance. Making full allowance for bias as a northwest missionary from Sunchun, the facts he adduces are correct. He says that the south was greatly overmanned with missionary personnel in comparison with northern Korea. Kearns writes in 1906 that Sunchun Station, only one of four northern stations, was just a trifle behind the total of the four southern stations in extent of territory, but in developed "native work," by which he means churches, Sunchun Station was far ahead. The four southern stations he mentions are Seoul, Chungju, Taegu and Pusan. Kearns states that *any one* of the thirteen helpers under him is carrying on a larger work, that is, caring for more Christians and churches than is the work of Pusan Station. While there were two foreign ministers to each church in the city of Seoul, Mr. Kearns alone was in charge of nearly eighty churches for the year 1906. This missionary stated his case so firmly because he was in an undermanned station. In the area around Seoul, including the country churches, there was one missionary for every 160 communicants, while in the northwest there was only one missionary for every 880 communicants. Mr. Kearns caps his argument by saying,

[75] A. M. Sharrocks, M.D., Letter to the Board of Foreign Missions of the Presbyterian Church U. S. A. (Sunchun, Korea: June 21, 1902).

More than half of the work of the mission is at the ful-
crum, Pyongyang, and one-quarter in Sunchun, which is considerably heavier than the one-quarter in the Seoul, Chungju,
Taegu, Pusan end. But the ordained men of the mission are
distributed fourteen in Pyongyang and Sunchun [and sixteen
in the south]. The total missionary force stands twenty-four
for the northern three-quarters of the work and forty-four
for the southern one-quarter. I know it is the immemorial
policy of mission boards to pour men and money into unpro-
ductive fields and economize . . . in handling the harvest,
but I cannot refrain from saying that it looks to a superficial
observer like very poor agriculture.[76]

There is always the possibility that a large missionary
force sent into a slightly growing area would smother the
Church there. In a rapidly growing area where the huge,
expanding Church is moving out ahead of the missionaries
and is almost entirely self-supporting, the danger of smother-
ing is far less, but that of insufficient expansion is very much
greater. I wonder if God would not have granted even more
growth in northwest Korea if His mission had assigned
evangelistic missionary personnel in accordance with the
obvious responsiveness of the local people.

Continued, Rapid Northwest Church Growth, 1906-1928.
The Church in northwest Korea was growing very fast dur-
ing the years from 1906 to 1910, as was the whole Korean
Presbyterian Church. A Southern Methodist, Dr. Alfred
Wasson, in his study of church growth in Korea, feels that
factors affecting the growth of his Church similarly af-
fected all of the Korean Churches and in some sections of the
Presbyterian Church his conclusions seem to hold. The
period from 1906 to 1910 he labels "Five Years of Rapid
Growth."[77] Since many church-growth factors listed by
Wasson for these years may have affected northwest Korea
as well as the area occupied by the Southern Methodist
Church, we will examine them here.

[76] Carl Emerson Kearns, Letter to the Board of Foreign Missions of
the Presbyterian Church U. S. A. (Sunchun, Korea: April 10, 1906).
[77] Alfred W. Wasson, *Church Growth in Korea*, p. 51.

Wasson's first factor is the 1907 revival. It is true that in those areas of Korea where there had been little church growth, the rate of growth shows some increase directly following the revival. Though their growth does not match the people movement in the northwest, those churches were given a push by the power of the revival. However, the revival, which should have been a more important factor in the northwest because of its huge breakout there, was not. We have seen that, in Figure 3 of the total Presbyterian Church and in Figures 10 and 11 of the Pyongan Provinces, the Church shows significant growth *before* this revival and *very* little change of growth rate following the revival. Therefore, we must conclude that in the northwest also the revival was not the original cause of the growth of the Presbyterian Church and probably was not even a major cause.

Bible classes and Bible Institutes are named by Wasson as a second factor in the growth of the Korean Methodist Church. Certainly these factors were influential in northwest Korea, where these large Bible classes were centered, where people studied the Word of God, and where they rubbed shoulders with men who were both fellow countrymen and vitally interested in learning the basis for spreading the Good News.

Third, Wasson says that because the government had not yet developed medical and educational work in Korea, and because of an intense interest of the Korean people in Western education, the Southern Methodists' emphasis on educating children was a stimulus to church growth. In the light of church growth in the northwest, however, I think this was not an important factor in the Presbyterian Church. While not opposed to medicine and education, the Northern Presbyterian Mission as a matter of policy did not emphasize either. Yet its churches grew far more than those of the Southern Methodist Mission. It seems that formal education must be ruled out as a significant factor assisting northwest church growth.

Political and environmental factors stimulating the growth

of the Methodist Church are also spelled out by Wasson.[78] Certainly the loss of independence and oppression at the hands of Japan were felt all over Korea. Unsettled conditions allowing for the rise of robber bands and patriots in the "righteous army" gave the people a feeling of helplessness. There is much indication that the Korean people turned to the Church as a last resort during this troubled period. They also turned to the Church because it stood for Western strength and Western education. All these environmental factors had some bearing on the rapid growth of the Church, but they do not explain the variance in growth rates of different geographical and denominational areas, because these environmental factors were present throughout all of Korea.

Wasson's is an excellent study; his environmental and missionary factors are real insights; but the basic weakness of this study is that he takes Korea-wide totals for both Methodist and Presbyterian Churches, and so does not see the areas of great growth compared to areas of slow growth. The use of only nationwide totals has led him to dubious conclusions.

Referring to the years from 1911 to 1919, "Nine Lean Years" is the title of Dr. Wasson's next chapter, in which he names certain factors which he thinks responsible for the nongrowth of the Southern Methodist Church in these years, factors which were also influential in churches in the Presbyterian territory. He says much evangelistic work was carried on, church organization progressed and educational work increased, but church growth slowed due to (1) loss of security of life and property before Japanese law under Japan's conditional government, (2) the Conspiracy Case, and (3) heavy government regulations imposed upon the Korean people in all areas of life. These years saw government-run schools and medical services improved, lessening the demand for services of Western schools and hospitals. Also, this time was one of severe economic depression. If all these factors, felt throughout Korea, had been determinative, they would have halted growth in the northwest, but the Presbyterian Church in the northwest exhibited re-

[78] *Ibid.*, p. 62.

markable growth during these nine years, contrary to Wasson's indications. As can be seen from Figures 10 and 11 of the North and South Pyongan Provinces, there was steady, rapid growth in both these areas from 1911 to 1919. Although evangelistic methods remained the same as in previous years, these new environmental factors "slowed" church growth, in Wasson's opinion. However, we must conclude that if environment affected church growth as severely as stated by Wasson, the sections of Korea where growth stopped must have contained a Church more susceptible to external pressure from its environment. For example, the Church in Southern Methodist territory where Wasson worked (northern Kangwon province in middle-east Korea) may have been more susceptible to adverse conditions around it because of its relatively small membership base.

Let us examine in detail one of the environmental factors mentioned by Dr. Wasson — (2) the Conspiracy Case. In 1911 over one hundred fifty persons were arrested on the charge of conspiring to kill the Japanese governor-general Terauchi as he passed through remote Sunchun, a northwestern town close to the Yalu River, in December of 1910. Nearly all of those arrested were teachers and students of Christian schools, church officers and other Christian leaders. Several missionaries were also under suspicion, but none were arrested. A missionary reporting from Sunchun says that "there is no zeal in preaching and personal work and since the arrests, there has been some falling away among the catechumens and new believers. Full church members have been very little affected by the arrests."[79]

The long, drawn-out trials for one hundred twenty-three of these Christians, which began June 28, 1912, in Seoul, attracted much attention all over Korea and in Japan. The trial in district court ended in September of 1912 with one hundred five persons being sentenced to terms of imprisonment. These terms were really not commensurate with

[79] Henry W. Lampe, Annual Personal Report to the Board of Foreign Missions of the Presbyterian Church U. S. A. (Sunchun, Korea: 1911-1912).

convictions of the crime of treason. In the end, after a trial by appellate court on March 20, 1913, six of those arrested were finally sentenced from four to six years in prison, and, after serving two years of their sentences, they were pardoned by the emperor.[80] It is obvious that the Japanese government did not have a very strong case against these people and the missionaries are no doubt right in believing that all of these men were innocent. There is ample evidence that the "confessions" were extracted by torture. This kind of police action had at least temporary effects on the Church as Christians from all over the country were arrested.

> In the fall of 1911 the Japanese suspicion of the Churches began to find more open expression in the arrest of leading Korean Christians. While reports of harsh treatment came from several parts of Korea, the town of Sunchun . . . suffered the heaviest blow. The mission high school, the Hugh O'Neill, Jr. Industrial Academy with 158 students, is next to the church, the dominating institution of the whole region. October 12, 1911, three pupils were arrested and sent to Seoul. Other arrests followed until so many teachers and students were in jail that the Academy had to be closed. Pastors, elders, deacons and the other leading church members were also imprisoned and sent hand-cuffed to the capital, until the whole Christian population was in a panic.[81]

Despite this adverse publicity, the Church continued to grow, even though at a slower rate, as we can see on Figure 3. In the long run, this publicity may have had a good effect on the Church. This is seen in the board report for 1913: "All over Korea ingatherings have been *great*, but not so great as in some past years and the number of those who have come into the Church with ulterior motives has been the smallest in years, which means that those [who] have accepted Christ have accepted Him intelligently and earnestly." The growth was "great" in Korea in comparison to other fields, even during this time of trouble when many Korean congregations were without regular leaders due to imprisoned pastors. There was always some person with a little train-

[80] Arthur Judson Brown, *The Korean Conspiracy Case*, p. 17..
[81] *Ibid.*, p. 12.

ing who could step in and fill the gap left by an imprisoned pastor or helper. The Church grew in spite of "a lack of persistent inquiry that the first years witnessed."[82]

By 1914, even though the fear and oppression connected with the Conspiracy Case had subsided and new believers were coming into the Church, they came "not in great numbers, only in twos or threes."[83] The General Assembly instituted a new movement for evangelism where preaching bands composed of two or three workers and some other church officers went out to places where the Church was not yet established; they engaged in systematic preaching for a short time. Their house-to-house preaching was followed by evening meetings.[84] The Gospel was still preached openly, but there were fewer converts.

Notice that the center of the persecution was located in Sunchun of North Pyongan Province, where the Japanese governor-general was reportedly to have been assassinated. Had the Conspiracy Case been an important factor in the growth of the Church, one would expect that the area immediately affected with the harshest persecution would have slowed in its growth. But look at Figure 11 of North Pyongan Province. This is the area worked from the mission station of Sunchun. One searches in vain for any slowing of communicant membership growth attributable to the Conspiracy Case, unless it be a delayed reaction coming in 1916 that was only temporary.

In summary of the reasons Dr. Wasson gives for this period of "arrested" growth, he says: "The growth of the Church was arrested because the currents that had been bringing people in large numbers to its doors had ceased to flow."[85] The fact remains that the whole Korean Protestant Church was not in a period of arrested growth; some sections were growing very fast during 1911-1919, and the northwest was the chief of these. If the environment, policies and practices of the various missions were similar throughout the

---

[82] Annual Report of the Board (New York: 1913).
[83] *Ibid.*, 1916.
[84] *Ibid.*, 1914 (From the Annual Report of Seoul Station).
[85] Wasson, *op. cit.*, p. 97.

nation, they must have had different effects on church growth in different areas. If so, we still must look further to see how these factors affected growth. We must see how the Church grew before we can tell why it grew. In other words, we must discover what these currents were which brought people to the doors of the churches. Before looking into the question of how the Church grew in north Korea, we will examine two more periods from Wasson's study, one of rapid and one of arrested growth.

The period from 1920 to 1924 is entitled "The Second Period of Rapid Growth" by the Southern Methodist author.[86] That the 1919 independence movement had a profound effect upon the whole Church in Korea is unquestioned. It is interesting to realize that during this time of reforms, a new respect for Christianity followed in the wake of the independence movement and influenced church expansion in the whole of Korea. Look again at Figure 5. One of the fast-growing areas of the previous "nation-wide lean-year period," during this "period of rapid growth," shows a slight reduction in the rate of growth. The area is Pyongan Province, pictured in detail on Figures 10 and 11 from 1918 to 1924. The Church in North Pyongan Province grows in spite of poor environmental conditions and slows down when a climate favorable to growth is present! The area seems oblivious to its environment as regards the birth of new congregations.

The years 1924 to 1928 are called "arrested growth" by Wasson, who cites as the principle reason for lack of growth in the Southern Methodist Church the severe economic distress brought about by Japanese oppression and world-wide agricultural depression. The Japanese helped Koreans increase their agricultural output but, instead of leaving the produce in Korea, took much of it to Japan. Korea was hungry. Wasson also mentions a wave of unrest in the young people, who were dissatisfied with the Church. Another stated cause of nongrowth was the failure of the Church to deal with social problems.

[86] *Ibid.,* p. 98.

Missionary correspondence from the Presbyterian areas, including the northwest, is full of references to the economic stress upon both Korean people and their churches. Economic and political problems were similar all over Korea, but they simply did not stop the churches from multiplying in some areas. A look at the years 1924 to 1928 — in Figure 8 of North Kyungsang Province and Figure 11 of North Pyongan Province, two widely separated areas — reveals that both of them show remarkable growth. Figure 11 indicates a drop in communicant membership from 1927 to 1928, but a steady rise both before and after this one year drop. The mission statistician reports some changes in methods of keeping statistics during this year, so this again constitutes another statistical redefinition. There is steady growth all the way through this period save for that one year.

At this same time, since there were non-growing Northern Presbyterian areas, it would be invalid to conclude that Presbyterians were able to grow and Methodists were not. It is likewise incorrect to say that because of economic distress and unrest among the young people the entire Protestant Church was not able to grow. It was able to grow in the northwest, and it did, very rapidly.

The Church in the north grew so fast that on any Sunday morning in Pyongyang in 1930, ten percent of the entire city population would be worshiping in the eighteen Presbyterian Churches.[87] Sunchun, by then a population of 13,000, would have half of its population in the churches on Sunday.[88] In many rural areas of the northwest, practically entire hamlets or villages had become Christian. So many churches had been established that in a few places there was no ground to plant others. However, not all the people of all the villages had been won to Christ, so there was room for the Church to grow more, and it grew and grew.

[87] Pyongyang Station, Report to the Board (Pyongyang, Korea: 1930).
[88] Arch Campbell, *Christ of the Korean Heart,* p. 118.

Chapter V. How Did the Fire in the Northwest Spread?

SIMPLE EXPLANATIONS OF THE REASON FOR GREAT GROWTH in the northern section of Korea are not wanting. If we ask the question, "Why did the Church grow in the north?" we will get a cacophony of answers, but if we look at *how* the Church grew, we may find a clue as to why it grew. Evidence telling how the churches grew is slim, but, when clues from many sources are joined together, the real picture of how the Church grew emerges.

A Seoul missionary made this observation gained from a visit to Pyongyang:

> The Pyongyang men are bright, spirited and many of them are quite handsome. Yangbans are not numerous among them. The men do nothing by halves. In Christian work they are aggressive in their testimony. The work in the country has spread like wildfire.[1]

By work he means that the *Churches* spread like WILDFIRE. This missionary was keenly aware of the vast difference in the growth of the Church in Pyongyang as compared to that in his own area. He was witnessing the beginnings of a type of church growth different in the north from that in the south.

The definite cultural differences between the people of the north and those of the south, noted in Chapter One, seem to have affected church growth in various ways. First, the people of the north, easily attracted to the Church, were more literate than those of the south. In 1902, a missionary who had held Bible classes in both the north and south said that nearly all northerners had studied Chinese and knew how to study, while those in the south not only had dif-

---

[1] D. L. Gifford, Letter to the Board of Foreign Missions of the Presbyterian Church, U. S. A. (September 1, 1896).

143

ficulty in Chinese but could barely read the native Korean script, which is far easier to read than the Chinese characters.[2] A second obvious regional difference affecting church growth lay in the fact that the south was more conservative, holding strongly to Confucian ideals, while the north was open to change. This helps to explain why those in the south did not respond to Christianity in as great numbers as did those in the north.

Third, there is an obvious economic difference between the people of the north and those of the south, particularly evident after the Japanese occupation began. When the Japanese brought in industrialization, northern farmers, who were independent landowners, prospered by their mineral-rich land. An editorial in the January 1918 edition of the *Korea Mission Field* magazine notes that "a missionary from the north affirmed that Korean farmers in his district never had been possessed of so much money as now so that the salaries of the pastors and helpers all through his district were being raised."[3] For these reasons, then, northern people could afford to build churches and support pastors. However, in the more populous south the tenant farmers, held in an economic vice by their *yangban* landlords, were even further oppressed when resident Japanese crowded some of them off the land. These landless people, who at first had to defy the will of the landlord in order to become Christian, now under Japanese occupation were much less able to support the Church than were Christians in the north.

Fourth, there was a political difference between the north and south. Southerners held control of the central government. It has been suggested by missionaries and nationals alike that the Church as an organization was particularly attractive to northerners, who were not allowed much power in their civil government.

These special regional factors, coupled with those examined in Chapter One, can be summed up by saying that the northern people were in a psychological environment that produced

[2] F. S. Miller, Letter to the Board of Foreign Missions of the Presbyterian Church U. S. A. (Seoul, Korea: February 7, 1902).

[3] Editorial, *Korea Mission Field* (Seoul, Korea: Evangelical Missions in Korea, January 1918), p. 3.

an active response to the good news of Christ. Another missionary who confirms this point of view writes that the reason for the difference of church growth in north and south lies more in the receptiveness of the people than in any difference in method of work.[4] This difference in receptivity is illustrated by a conversation between two missionaries to Korea:

> I remember hearing a Pyongyang missionary say enthusiastically, "Oh, our people are just hungry for the gospel." And a Seoul missionary responded dully, "I've never seen a Korean that was hungry for anything but rice."[5]

No wonder the recorder of that conversation says that the north and south are different enough to be two separate nations as far as the Church was concerned. One blanket missionary policy for the whole nation would not be satisfactory, but policy would have to be flexible to fit local situations.

We have seen that missionary itineration was another factor helping to produce great growth. But how shall we account for churches springing up where no missionaries had even visited? Here is one example from among many:

> Away up in the mountains at the head of a little valley we found a whole family, consisting of a man 74 years of age, his four sons and their wives, and daughters, and her husband who were Christians. No missionary had ever visited them, and a helper but three times. The whole family of 11 persons except one son who was away from home passed a most creditable examination and we rejoiced to receive them as catechumens. The son-in-law had first heard the Gospel here in Pyongyang three years ago and was interested enough to buy some Christian books which he took home and which in turn led the whole family into believing.[6]

[4] E. H. Miller, Letter to the Board of Foreign Missions of the Presbyterian Church U. S. A. (Seoul, Korea: June 17, 1902).

[5] Carl Emerson Kearns, Letter to the Board of Foreign Missions of the Presbyterian Church U. S. A. (Sunchun, Korea: November 2, 1902).

[6] C. F. Bernheisel, Letter to the Christian Endeavors of Chicago Presbytery (December 19, 1901).

This example of a family tucked away in a valley indicates one way in which the churches grew. Jonathan Goforth, a missionary from China visiting Korea, gives us another example of this type of family conversion in 1907:

> There was a man who confessed his Savior in his native village, only to find that his clan turned him out of house and home. He did not go to law but by the grace of God remained sweet. He meekly bore with insult and wrong and lived and preached Christ until the whole clan was converted and his possessions restored.[7]

Another missionary, in his first visit to a Korean village, found that all of the village people were Christians and had regular family worship, even though a missionary had never visited them nor was there any organized church as yet.[8]

There are several examples of this type of growth along family lines around Andong in southeast Korea. One is the church at Kukkok, which began in 1902 and grew rapidly to include most of the members of the families in the village in its fellowship. I submit that the majority of Korean Christians were led to Christ in this same way, that is, brought to Him by their friends and relatives. A missionary, formerly of North Pyongan Province, writes in 1954 of all of Korea:

> The million that have come to the Savior and have received Him in their hearts have not been won by foreign missionaries. . . . Nearly all have heard the Good News from the lips of their own countrymen. The story goes from mouth to ear and from heart to heart.[9]

One most important factor governing how the Church grew is the structure of Korean society. In Korea we are dealing with a society based on the family, not tribe. This family unit is strong even today in 1965 and is the basic social unit in the country. The soundest way for a man to come to Christ is in the setting of his own family. Its members make the move as individuals, but still belong to the family. Sung

---

[7] Jonathan Goforth, *When the Spirit's Fire Swept Korea,* p. 30.
[8] *Ibid.*
[9] Arch Campbell, *Christ of the Korean Heart,* p. 12.

Chun Chun declares, "The family was the basic unit in society [so] it was not unusual for all the members of a family group to adopt Christianity at the same time."[10] He affirms that the great numbers who rushed into the Church came because whole family units moved together.

We read of Korean Christians engaged in intensive evangelism. Often they traveled away from home on evangelistic trips, but more often they led people to Christ from their own villages. Even today, after the turmoil of World War II and the Korean War, most of the people of most villages will be related to each other by marriage if not by blood. The Christians did not go out and "beat the bushes" talking to strangers about their faith, but they talked to people they knew and to people with whom they had strong family ties.

In a study of fifty years of development of the Church, the Rev. Mr. Herbert B. Blair concludes that while the Korean Christians went far and wide with their evangelism, the Gospel really flowed along family channels. It was in the intimate relationships of the home where firm belief was spoken from heart to heart and believers have been harvested. Strong men who became Christian went to their clan villages and convinced their relatives that they too should acquire this new life.

As an example, Mr. Herbert Blair tells of a church in Kyungsang Province that was started by a Mr. So. One day, young Mr. So went with a friend across the mountain for a visit to a nearby church; he obtained a Bible and became a believer. His father remained unconverted, but Mr. So soon won his uncle and several cousins, who began meeting in a home on Sundays. The whole village was aroused, discussing the new religion. The community resented the singing of the Christians, but when in early spring Mr. So, the priestly head of the clan, refused to prepare foods for ancestral worship at the shrine of their ancestor, the whole clan and community rose in rebellion. The wilder the furor, the wider the Gospel story was spread. Mr. So, his uncle, and his cousins went right on believing. They studied the Bible,

[10] Sung Chun Chun, *Schism and Unity in the Protestant Churches of Korea,* p. 16.

kept the Sabbath, preached, and endured persecution. Finally
after much community turmoil, Mr. So turned over the ancestral shrine and its endowed fields to another family. Grad-
ually the followers of Christ increased. The home they used
for meetings proved to be too small, so the family moved
out and interior walls were removed to make the house into
one long room. In a year, this space became too crowded;
the room was extended and a schoolroom added on the side.
Soon over a hundred people crowded into the little church,
and they again rebuilt it. The young men of Mr. So's clan
were thoroughly in earnest, living and preaching real Christianity. The church grew even larger and was divided, and
a new group sprang up three miles away in a village where
other cousins lived.[11]

In a study of Korean villages by the Japanese government-
general in 1933, more than half of the 14,672 villages studied
had in one village thirty or more families that were related
to each other through a common ancestor.[12] This is not a
mere statistic appearing on civil records. Common ancestry
was and still is a real clan linkage of village families.

This is the means by which the Korean Church multiplied
ahead of the missionaries. Because of the close-knit web of
family relationships and the interfamily relationship through
the clan, no one wished to make a great step in accepting
a new religion which would break down these family ties.
A person hearing of the Gospel of Christ, or reading of it
from a Bible sold to him, would go back to his own village,
talk it over with the members of his family and clan, and if
a positive decision was made, the entire group often quite
naturally became Christian, still holding fast to its family
relationships. As in the example cited by Blair, if all were
not immediately won, each family member in his own time

[11] Herbert E. Blair, "Fifty Years of Development of the Korean
Church," *Jubilee Papers* (Seoul, Korea: Korea Mission Fiftieth Anniversary, 1934).

[12] Won Yong Kang, *A Study on the Family System of Korea: The
Christian Approach to Its Changing Situation* (New York, Union Theological Seminary: S. T. M. Thesis, 1956). He is quoting N. S. Yoshi
Yama, *Korean Villages* (Figures from Korean Government-General,
1933), Vol. I, p. 12.

became Christian, until soon the whole family and sometimes the entire clan was won to Christ.

This great movement to Christ that we see in the Pyongan Provinces of the northwest was not a mass movement in the sense that mobs of unconverted people were taken into the churches. It was rather a response of faith to the Gospel, flowing unimpeded along the web of family relationships. A father became a Christian, led his wife, and then his sons and daughters and sons-in-law, into a conviction that Christ was their answer. This conversion was followed by a long period of training, and these new Christians then led others by the same method.

In answering the appraisal of Dr. Arthur J. Brown, that the Korean people "were simple-hearted and merely obeyed the instructions given by the missionaries" to join the Church, Dr. L. George Paik gives an excellent description of how the Church grew:

> A Korean village is generally composed of a number of closely related families. If the first man converted in the village happened to be influential, his conversion might result in the mass conversion of the village. On the contrary, when a less important member of the village became a Christian he faced a hostile environment. If he was to continue to live in the village, he had to win others to this religion. There are certain village undertakings, such as offering sacrifices to village gods, which are contrary to Christian teachings. When a man's conviction was strong enough, he made an effort to win others in the community so that he might avoid social ostracism. Again, when the majority of a village turned to the new religion, the minority either conformed or withdrew. There was a fellowship among converts that was attractive to an outsider. The Christians were sympathetic toward each other and stood together in sorrow and joy. When a man had a friend who was not a Christian, he exerted himself to win his friend into the fellowship of the Church. Thus self-propagation began within the family circle and with close friends. Not only was the fellowship an attractive feature, but by winning members of his own family and his friends a convert might do away with all possibility of persecution.[13]

[13] L. George Paik, *The History of Protestant Missions in Korea 1832-1910*, p. 284.

We in the West tended to forget how strong family ties were in our own past histories. We have not been aware of the fact that, in places where the younger Churches grew rapidly, men made their decisions to become Christian not as lone individuals, but as individuals in the context of a social unit, such as a tribe in New Guinea or a family in Korea. A multi-individual decision occurred so that a whole social unit moved over to Christianity with only slight dislocation. We call this a "people movement."

"People movement" is the term used in *Bridges of God* by Dr. Donald McGavran of the Institute of Church Growth. Note that, since Korea is not tribal, we are not talking about a tribal movement, nor are we speaking of a mass movement of a large horde of unconverted people coming into the Church. Here, in Korea, is a "people movement" in the sense that the Gospel flowed along the web of family relationships. This web is the transmission line for the current of the Holy Spirit that brought men and women into the Church. It is the dry grass which turned the fire into wildfire.

Of course, the northwest is not the only place where people movements have occurred. From previous examples cited, it is evident that there were movements of this type in the south of Korea also. Nowhere in Korea, however, was this great movement to Christ so dramatic as in the northwest. Even in areas of small growth, because of family solidarity, it is quite probable that believers came to Christ as families rather than as isolated individuals pulled outside their family relationships.

Wherever the Church grew rapidly, it grew through the family web. Since there is no evidence of a difference in family structure in the various areas of Korea, the cultural factors previously mentioned allowed the Gospel to flow along the web of the family relationships and must be considered influential. Even these cannot be the full explanation. The conclusion is pressed upon us that it was God's preparation of some of the people of Korea at a certain time which led them to Himself in great numbers. The exact reason why must remain unanswered, save in the mind of God. We can only stand in awe and testify that in some parts of Korea, God's Spirit moved and people responded.

There is *no* evidence that missionaries consciously opposed this large people movement to Christ. The absence of this kind of movement in areas of little growth is not explained by a deliberate decision of missionaries to limit accessions to Christianity to a slow, individualistic pace. Rather, it is explained by a difference in the types of people and perhaps environment.

The question has been raised: why, when the family pattern is thought to be similar throughout the Orient, did the Church grow so rapidly in Korea while Japan and China had slower church growth? An accurate comparison of church growth in these three countries, with study of the respective family patterns, will eventually be necessary if we are to understand fully the growth of the Church in Korea.

Chapter VI. Korean Presbyterian Church Growth in Other Presbyterian Mission Areas

THE POLICIES AND PRACTICES OF THE FOUR PRESBYTERIAN MIS-sions in Korea were similar in many points and different in others. Because the rates of growth were different, it would be very instructive to study in detail the growth of the Korean Church in each geographical and denominational section. I have not had the original sources to consider each section adequately, and so I will leave that to future students of church growth. Here, I will give only a brief outline and present the graphs of growth in the different sections of Korea where the Church was planted by the remaining Presbyterian Missions. I must leave for future study the conclusions as to how and why the Church grew in the Southern Presbyterian, Canadian Presbyterian (later the United Church of Canada), and Australian Presbyterian areas.

I. SOUTHERN PRESBYTERIAN MISSION AREA

The principal source for this study of the Southern Presbyterian Mission area is the recently published book by George Thompson Brown.[1] The Southern Presbyterian Mission area is that shown on the accompanying map. The Presbyterian Church in the United States (Southern Presbyterian Mission) first sent missionaries to Korea in 1892, partly because of the influence of Mr. Horace G. Underwood, who had spoken about the opportunities in Korea on his first furlough in 1891. The new missionaries arrived in 1892, took up residence in Seoul, and began work on the Korean language. They made trips with Northern Presbyterian missionaries as well as exploratory trips to the two Chulla Provinces in the southern part of Korea, pictured on the map. They were

[1] George Thompson Brown, *Mission to Korea.*

152

prevented by the Sino-Japanese War from opening a station in the Chulla Provinces until 1896, when conditions became more settled. Their first station was established in North Chulla Province, in the provincial capital of Chunju. Later a station was opened at Koonsan in the same province. In 1898, a station in South Chulla Province at Mokpo, a large port city, was opened. All of southwest Korea, including Cheju Island, was eventually served by the Southern Presbyterian Mission.

Let us turn to Figures 12 and 13, picturing the growth of the Presbyterian Church in the two Chulla Provinces, the Southern Presbyterian Mission area. The figures of these two provinces, which I have obtained from General Assembly sources, do not equal the total figures given by Dr. Brown for the Southern Presbyterian Mission. The difference between his figures, which are based primarily on mission records, and the total communicant membership of the two Chulla Provinces and Cheju Island, derived from Korean Church minutes, is small, but it increases proportionally

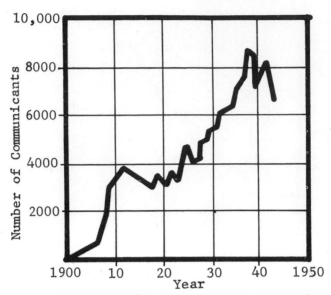

PRESBYTERIAN COMMUNICANT MEMBERSHIP
IN NORTH CHULLA PROVINCE (H)
FIGURE 12

to the increase in membership. At this writing, no satisfactory explanation has been found.

Culturally the people of the Chulla Provinces are slightly different from those around Seoul or in the northwest. A noticeable dialectical difference in their speech still exists. However, it seems that the Southern Presbyterian Mission, which also adopted the Nevius Method and was interested primarily in church planting, met a responsive population in the Chulla people.

During the years 1905-1911, after laying the foundation, the mission witnessed great church growth in both north and south Chulla, while churches were also growing in other areas of Korea. The general reasons given by Brown for this phenomenal growth are those inadequate ones we have already discussed: the 1904-1905 Russo-Japanese War that left Korea a pawn of Japan and the revival movement that

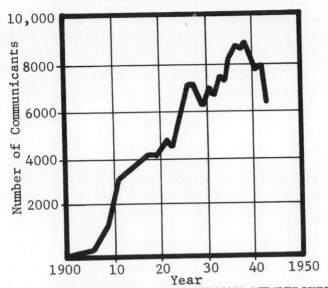

PRESBYTERIAN COMMUNICANT MEMBERSHIP
IN SOUTH CHULLA PROVINCE AND CHEJU ISLAND (J)
FIGURE 13

broke out in Pyongyang in 1907 affecting the whole Protestant Church in Korea.[2]

Southern Presbyterian missionaries noted, as did those in other areas of southern Korea, that churches grew faster in the country than in larger towns.[3] Here too, these missionaries were "left behind" watching a great movement to Christ as the Church spread spontaneously through people leading their friends and relatives to Christ. The missionaries spent a great deal of their time in intineration, preaching to churches, and organizing those who wanted to become Christians into the continuing fellowship of the Church.

Between the years 1911 and 1921 a plateau of relatively little church growth is seen on Figures 12 and 13 of the

[2] *Ibid.*, p. 55.
[3] *Ibid.*, p. 61.

Chulla Provinces. This plateau coincides with the experience of the Southern Methodists in Kangwon Province. Also, Dr. Brown gives reasons for the nongrowth in his area similar to those stated by Dr. Wasson for the Southern Methodist area: political unrest caused by the Conspiracy Case, increased Japanese pressure, particularly on the point of education, and extreme poverty.

While these factors of poverty and oppression were nationwide, it may be that both Southern Presbyterian and Southern Methodist area churches were more susceptible to them, for church growth stopped and did not begin again until the outbreak of the Independence movement in 1919, with its distinctive religious overtones. The plateau period is called one of "consolidation" by Dr. Brown because, though there was little church growth, the gains* of the preceding period were consummated. He also says: "Undoubtedly, the missionary enterprise and the indigenous Church were in stronger positions at the period's close than at the beginning."[4] This may be a correct judgment, but this same kind of statement has been used around the world to rationalize when there is no growth. It will be remembered that the Presbyterian Church as a whole made substantial gains during this same time, and that this growth occurred mainly in the northwest.

In the next period, 1920-1925, we see that South Chulla Province (Figure 13) grew faster than the northern province, gaining 2,700 communicant members while North Chulla Province gained only 800 (Figure 12). Numerical gains of the churches in the Southern Presbyterian Mission provinces began in 1920 and were more than just a relationship in time to the Independence Movement. This political movement gave impetus to the churches' growth in many areas. In the Chulla Provinces, the movement stood at a dramatic point of reversal — from being a nongrowing Church to becoming one whose congregations were growing quite rapidly.

The next period to consider is 1926-1942. South Chulla saw a slower rate of growth than North Chulla, particularly from 1926 to 1937, by increasing by only 1300 communicants

[4] *Ibid.,* p. 91.

while North Chulla increased by 4600 members, an increase of more than three times as many communicant members as the formerly rapidly growing South Chulla Province. A serious investigation of the church growth in the Southern Presbyterian area should be made from primary sources to tell us why these two adjacent areas, assisted by the same mission, showed such a variation in growth.

Brown records the appearance in the 1930's of a divisive movement in the Church: "On several occasions it looked as if a division of the General Assembly was imminent." The three issues stated as causing this threatened division of the Church in southwest Korea are described as follows:

> First, the majority of the Christian constituency lay in the far north, and among the southern presbyteries there was considerable feeling that northerners dominated the assembly. Political power cliques dating from the time of the Independence Movement were also influential in spreading disharmony. A third factor was the cleavage between some church leaders who had been trained abroad and the less educated pastors and lay members at home.[5]

This first reason indicates that the Presbyterian Church in southwest Korea was aware of the different growth rates in different geographical sections. Because the delegates to the General Assembly were sent on a membership basis, the north always had a much greater representation. Evidence indicates strong sectional feeling in Korea. The different sections were considered by the Korean people themselves as not mere geographic divisions but as actual cultural divisions. The south did not rejoice in the great strength of the Church in the north, but saw it as a threat to its own desires. The Church in the north no doubt used its numerical strength to elect its own men to the main offices and to pass motions favorable to the north. Naturally, the sections of the Church outside the northwest, whose total membership did not equal that of the northwest, were keenly aware of their status. In fact, this imbalance between the northwest and the rest of the land is the primary reason why writers

[5] *Ibid.,* pp. 147, 148.

have played down sectional differences of church growth
in Korea. The effect of the forced Shinto shrine worship on the
Southern Presbyterian Mission, discussed in Chapter Three,
was felt also during these years of threatened division.

II. AUSTRALIAN PRESBYTERIAN MISSION AREA

The Rev. Mr. J. Henry Davies and his sister arrived in
Korea from Australia in October 1889. However, on the trip
to Pusan, Mr. Davies contracted smallpox, and he died in
1890. The news of his death served as a challenge to the
Presbyterian Church in Australia to send new missionaries.
These Australians arrived in 1891 and began mission work
in Pusan in the same year that the Northern Presbyterian
Mission opened a station in that city. The two missions
worked side by side. The Northern Presbyterian Mission
never had many missionaries in Pusan, but the few they did
place there were reluctant to give up their foothold in this
great port city and did not withdraw until 1914.

Shown on the accompanying map is South Kyungsang
Province, the territory served by the Australian Presbyterian

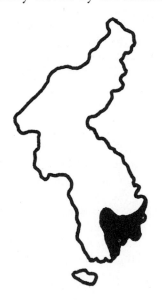

Mission, which includes the city of Pusan within its boundaries. Americans who traveled from Pusan to Taegu in 1889 with an eye to opening a Taegu Station (in North Kyungsang Province), encountered much hostility to foreigners and their Gospel. The Church in this area had a slow start, began its great growth about 1907, continued this growth until 1914, and then after six years of no growth from 1914 to 1920, the Church in South Kyungsang Province began to grow rapidly until 1938 (see Figure 14).

A comparison of Figure 13 and 14 shows that the periods of growth in southeast Korea coincide with those periods in the adjoining Southern Presbyterian Mission area, and were probably subject to the same influences. They saw similar growth until 1914 and a similar leveling off until 1919, and finally a resumption of growth from 1919 and the Independence Movement, until 1938.

A closer inspection of the lines of growth, however, reveals certain marked differences. The Church in South Kyungsang Province (Figure 14) continued to grow until 1914, but when its western neighbor, the Church in South Chulla Province (Figure 13) was growing rapidly, from 1922 to 1925, "Pusan Province" (South Kyungsang) was standing still. Between 1925 and 1926, when South Chulla (Figure 13) was standing still, Pusan Province, like North Chulla Province (Figures 14 & 12), was experiencing pentecostal growth. The South Kyungsang area is very like the North Chulla area in church growth and quite unlike South Chulla Province. At one period, from 1934 to 1938, we see a remarkable phenomenon: the Church in all three areas experienced rapid growth.

After 1938 South Kyungsang and South Chulla Provinces lost 2600 members and North Chulla lost 2000. The startling drop in South Kyungsang, because it was followed by a sharp rise, I believe to be a difference in definition of members. There are answers to the question about the periods of growth and nongrowth. These answers are locked in missionary correspondence and reports. Someday these must be opened fully to give a complete picture of the growth of the Korean Church.

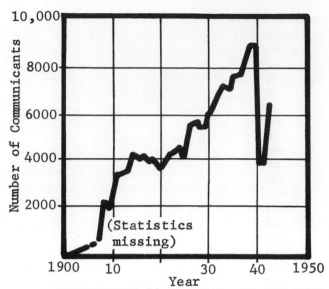

PRESBYTERIAN COMMUNICANT MEMBERSHIP
IN SOUTH KYUNGSANG PROVINCE   (G)
FIGURE 14

III. CANADIAN PRESBYTERIAN MISSION AREA

The final area of the Korean Presbyterian Church to be studied is that of North and South Hamkyung Provinces in the far northeast of Korea, as shown on the insert. The mountains are extremely high in these provinces, but there are some good harbors along the seacoast and the population is centered in these seacoast towns. In 1892 the Northern Presbyterian Mission opened a station in Wonsan, began evangelistic work, started a church there, and baptized the first members in 1894. In 1898 the Canadian Presbyterian Church sent missionaries to Korea, and after consultation the Northern Presbyterian Mission decided to move its two missionary families elsewhere and turn the work of planting churches in the two Hamkyung Provinces over to the Canadian Presbyterian Mission.

The city of Wonsan in South Hamkyung Province was used as a base for early missionary travel into the Hamkyung Provinces. One interesting fact written by the Rev. Mr. W. L. Swallen prior to his moving from Wonsan, is that fully eighty percent of the Wonsan Christians were not local people but emigrants from Pyongan and Whanghai Provinces. In the city of Hamheung, sixty percent of the Christian congregation originated not from South Hamkyung Province alone but also from these two northwest provinces. At Hongsoon (a small village) practically all of the Christians were from Pyongan Provinces.[6] This fact is significant and points up the responsiveness of the people of Pyongan and Whanghai Provinces, even when these people had migrated to an adjacent province. This also would seem to indicate a nonresponsiveness of the people of Hamkyung Province. As we see on Figure 15 there was a lack of growth during the early years of mission work there.

[6] W. L. Swallen, Evangelistic Report to the Board of Foreign Missions of the Presbyterian Church U. S. A. (Wonsan, Korea: 1898).

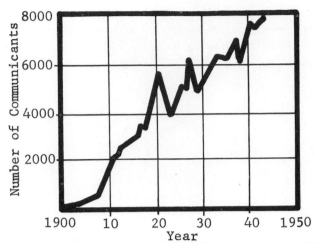

PRESBYTERIAN COMMUNICANT MEMBERSHIP
IN NORTH AND SOUTH HAMKYUNG PROVINCES   (F)
FIGURE 15

In 1908 growth in the Hamkyung Provinces (Figure 15) takes an upward swing. As expected, it grows during the period in which the rest of the Korean Church grew, but it does not stop growing in 1914. It continues on at a healthy rate until 1918 and at an even higher rate from 1918 to 1921. The churches in Hamkyung Province were growing rapidly at the same time economic and political pressures were slowing the growth of churches in the southern provinces. This may have been caused by emigration of Pyongan residents to Hamkyung, but I have no evidence that this is true.

Then in 1921, when much of the Presbyterian, Church in the rest of Korea began growing rapidly again, the Church in northeast Korea shows a serious setback and a period of loss. Why did the churches in this area grow when others were getting small growth? What caused the Hamkyung churches to show losses when other areas were showing gains? A partial explanation has been given that following the Independence Movement, Communism gained strength in these provinces, thus weakening the Christward movement.

Why was there a second peak in growth in 1927 and why no fall-off in growth beginning in 1938, as with all of the other Presbyterian areas (Figure 15)? These questions should be answered to give a complete picture of church growth in Korea. Having no data other than the General Assembly statistics with which to work, I will not venture a guess. Someone from the United Church of Canada should search the records and correspondence of the Canadian Presbyterian Mission to find answers for these questions. If possible, he should pursue these studies at the Institute of Church Growth in Eugene, Oregon.

Chapter VII. Growth of the Methodist Church In Korea

THE METHODIST AND THE PRESBYTERIAN CHURCHES IN KOREA were planted at the same time. Underwood, the first evangelistic missionary for the Northern Presbyterian Mission, and the Rev. Mr. H. G. Appenzeller, the first Northern Methodist evangelistic missionary, arrived in Korea on the same ship Easter day, 1885. From the beginning, cordial relations existed between the Presbyterians and Northern Methodists. There were also cordial relations between the Presbyterians and the second Methodist Mission to come to Korea in 1896, that of the American Southern Methodist Church. The two Methodist Missions together established their own seminary and cooperated in several schools. Each of these Methodist bodies established separate but cooperating Churches which were united into one strong Methodist Church in 1930. This denomination has weathered well the troubles of war and strife and still remains unified and operating today. While it did not have as great a numerical growth as the Presbyterian Church in Korea, Methodism brought its own peculiar gifts which have influenced tthe nation of Korea.

Because of the obvious difference in numerical growth (see Figure 17), both open and implied comparisons between the Presbyterian and Methodist Churches have been made frequently in attempts to show why there was great growth in the Presbyterian Church and moderate growth in the Methodist Church. Presbyterians said, "Our method caused us to grow." Methodists rejoined, "We may not have grown fast, but we have the quality." Answers like these are not instructive as to how the Churches grew or what can be done to increase church membership, but serious attempts at explanation also have been made, like those of A. W.

Wasson and Charles A. Clark, whose material we shall consider.

The geographical areas of Korea where Methodists worked were contiguous to and interspersed through the Presbyterian territories. Shown on this map are the areas of the Northern Methodist Mission. From the beginning, the methods and practices of Methodist missionaries in Korea were slightly different from those of the Presbyterians. There was also a difference in the number of missionaries assigned to active church planting. So it is not surprising that there is a difference in the rate of growth.

I am not convinced that the traditional Presbyterian answer for growth in Korea ("we used the Nevius Method") was correct. As I study the Methodist Mission, which did not conscientiously follow the Nevius methods, it is increasingly clear that any single answer is dangerously inaccurate. The reasons for growth in the Korean Church are complex. Some areas where the Methodists and Presbyterians worked side by side, each using slightly different methods,

achieved the same amount of church growth. As we found
it necessary to compare different areas of the Presbyterian
Church, we must now compare one denomination with another, trying to seek not substantiation for one position or another, but better ways to complete the unfinished task of evangelism in Korea.

Anyone studying Methodism in Korea must rely on Wasson's *Church Growth in Korea* and Ryang's *Southern Methodism in Korea.* Supplementing both is a valuable doctoral
thesis by Charles D. Stokes on the history of Methodist Missions in Korea from 1885 to 1930, written from the original
sources with sharp, accurate evaluations of the Methodist
Church.[1] Particularly full of insights are his comparisons of
the work and methods of the Presbyterians and Methodists.
This excellent thesis has the same high standards as Dr. L.
George Paik's *History of Protestant Missions in Korea* and
ought to be published.

Let us look then at the graphs of growth of the two Korean
Methodist Churches, shown on Figure 16. These two lines,
while quite different in appearance, have some similar characteristics.   Both show a rather slow church growth until
1905; then, from 1905 to 1912, rapid church growth. The
Northern Methodist area shot up to 12,600 membership, and
the Southern Methodist to 7,000. Then there is a slowing of
growth which occurs earlier in the Southern Methodist area,
followed by rapid growth again, beginning, of course, in
1919. This rapid growth lasts until 1925 in one and until
1926 in the other. Finally, the Methodist Church begins a
period of decline until 1930 when the two Churches combined.
There was a plateau from 1930 until 1937 and growth until
World War II. As we proceed with the study and examine
more closely the periods of growth and nongrowth in the
Korean Methodist Church, I will refer to Figure 16, which
records communicants only and not — as Dr. Wasson's information records — communicants and probationers.

[1] Charles Davis Stokes, *History of Methodist Missions in Korea,*
1885-1930 (Yale University: Doctoral thesis, 1947).

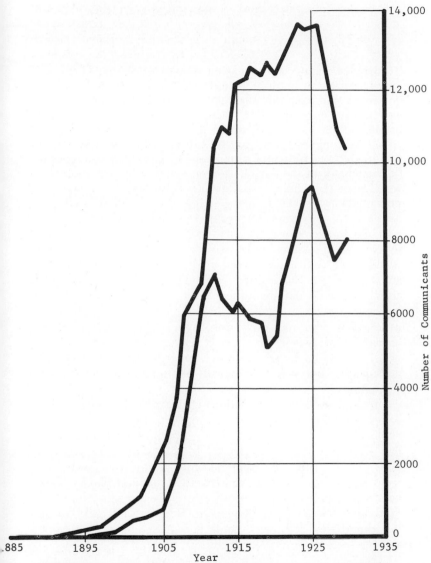

COMMUNICANT MEMBERSHIP OF THE METHODIST CHURCH IN KOREA
FIGURE 16

I. BEGINNING THE NORTHERN METHODIST
MISSION
1885-1896

Early Methodist missionaries who arrived in Korea co-incident with Presbyterians did not begin aggressive evangelism as early as the Presbyterians did. Dr. Stokes gives two reasons for this: first, there was the difficult language barrier which had to be sufficiently overcome to engage in effective evangelism; and second, Methodists were most sensitive to the governmental opposition to Christian evangelism: "The memory of the earlier Roman Catholic persecutions hovered over them like a shadow."[2]　However, there were no restrictions concerning evangelizing the Japanese living in Korea, so Mr. Appenzeller began work among them.

While the Korean laws against propagating the Christian religion were on the books, we have seen that they were a "dead letter" and not enforced at the time Protestant missionaries arrived in the country, although Presbyterian missionaries, too, were not unanimous in their readiness to launch out with direct evangelism. Indeed, Drs. Allen and Heron believed it was too early for preaching, and only stout-hearted Underwood proclaimed Christ and baptized converts. Perhaps a factor in church growth was the number of missionaries not willingly bound by unrealistic government regulations.

One and one-half years following the arrival of Mr. Appenzeller, the first advance in evangelism by the Methodists came about.[3]　On June 24, 1887, Appenzeller baptized the first Korean Methodist convert.　In that same year on April 3, Mr. T. H. Yun, who later became "Baron Yun," was baptized in Shanghai and there became a member of the Methodist-Episcopal Church South, years before the Southern Methodist Mission opened work in Korea. So strictly speaking, the Methodist Church South had a Korean convert before the Methodist Church North did.

　2 *Ibid.,* p. 81.
　3 *Ibid.*

Northern Methodist missionaries began early exploratory itineration as did the Presbyterians. In fact, Underwood and Appenzeller made a trip to Pyongyang together in 1888. In the early years, recorded communicant membership of both Presbyterian and Methodist Churches was similar, but several important differences are indicated by Stokes. Remember that Dr. Allen, the first Presbyterian missionary, won particular favor from the Korean King for his timely medical treatment of the young, wounded prince. He continued on good terms with the King and Queen who extended friendship to other members of the Presbyterian Mission. "The Methodists, on the other hand, began independently and received government recognition on the basis of merit."[4] Through the Rev. Mr. R. S. Maclay, Methodist missionaries had received permission from the King to engage in educational and medical work in Korea, but they received no special favors from him.

Dr. Stokes attributes the early success of the Presbyterian missionaries to the reaping of a harvest of converts of John Ross from Manchuria. The first communicants and leaders in the Presbyterian Church were men who had heard the Gospel in Manchuria, it is true. Methodism also profited by this work of Ross but to a lesser extent than did the Presbyterians.[5]

The Methodist Mission was far in advance of the Presbyterian Mission in the field of education. This difference remained significant throughout the course of the two missions. One might say that while other original differences between the missions passed away, the educational policies of both bodies grew farther and farther apart and became fixed with different goals. We need to investigate these goals at different points in the Churches' history to see how they affected growth. Simply stated: the Presbyterian Mission put its emphasis on evangelistic effort, using education only for the training of Christians, while the Methodist Mission laid strong stress on education in general for both Christians and non-Christians as an evangelistic tool. Just four

4 *Ibid.*, p. 90.
5 *Ibid.*, p. 91.

months after Appenzeller's arrival in Korea, he started a class with two students that was later to become the Paijai Boys' High school.[6]

Another difference pointed out by Dr. Stokes is that the Methodist Mission had more women missionaries and did more women's work than the Presbyterians. I was told by a Methodist missionary that this emphasis on women's work slowed church growth. The American women evangelists did not seem particularly involved in the numerical growth of Methodist churches. Their time was spent mostly in teaching country women, as the Korean society decreed a strong division of the sexes. Women missionaries were most valuable in that they taught these church women the fundamentals of the Christian faith from the Bible. Missionary writings tell of Korean men leading whole families into the churches, but these writings are devoid of instances in which women brought large numbers of people into the Church. This is because of the dominance of the Korean male. It is possible that no matter how much one trained Korean Christian women, their converts would be fewer than those of Korean men, not because of any lack of evangelistic zeal on the part of the lady missionary or the Korean woman evangelist, but simply because the woman's position in society prevented her from leading great numbers to Christ.

This is not the entire picture. From a search of original sources, a professor of anthropology and mission in the Institute of Church Growth said, concerning women's work, that Korean "Bible women" (women evangelists) were most effective in confronting Shamanism. Some Christian women were themselves converted *mudangs, shamans* who manipulated demons and knew well what it meant to wrestle against "principalities and powers." These Korean women drew a good deal of help from the women missionaries. It is probable that this indirect evangelistic value of women missionaries was greater than the direct effort they made through teaching and nursing in institutions. Quantitatively, conver-

[6] *Historical Sketch of the Korean Methodist Church,* Seventy-Fifth Anniversary (Seoul, Korea: Annual Conference of the Korean Methodist Church, 1960), p. 17.

sions made by women did not register on the graphs of growth, but the value of conversions made by former *mudangs* is high, in that they removed superstitious obstructions to the tremendous family conversions that followed. Bible women were effective in reducing the power of the *shaman* that had held families in the grip of fear; Bible women were agents of "ripening" rather than "reaping." The whole question of the role of the power encounter in conversion from the animist substructure in Korea, indeed in all of Asia, needs thorough investigation.[7]

As converts to Methodism grew in numbers, they began to lead their own people to Christ. By 1892 Methodist missionaries recorded a change in attitude among the Koreans toward Christianity. "The seekers come seeking us out and asking for instruction. . . . We do not need to hunt them but they come to us openly."[8] There had been earlier instances similar to this recorded by the Presbyterian Mission. In fact, the early trips of Underwood in 1887 had been in response to new Manchurian converts who desired instruction. While this seeking for instruction from both Presbyterian and then Methodist missionaries may have occurred earlier, Figure 16 shows an upward swing in 1895 and 1896, representing the resulting spontaneous expansion of the Methodist Church.

Methodists, like Presbyterians, were not achieving growth in the capital city but in the outlying districts. In the city of Inchon (twenty miles west of Seoul on the coast) twenty-two out of the mission's total of seventy communicants were recorded. There, in 1894, Inchon Christians constructed the first Methodist chapel. This was the banner church of the Korean Methodist Mission.[9] Along with this church, education was established as "the handmaiden of evangelism" in the Inchon district. A boys' school was opened there which enrolled "sons of both Christians and non-Christians, the parents of the latter fully understanding that religious in-

[7] Alan R. Tippett, Professor at the Institute of Church Growth in Eugene, Oregon. Interviewed July 13, 1963.

[8] Stokes, *op. cit.*, p. 111. Quoting W. B. Scranton, Letter written December 3, 1892 and printed in *Gospel in All Lands*, April, 1893, p. 191.

[9] *Ibid.*, p. 112.

struction would be given." The school thus became an evangelistic agency with the intention of reaching not only the boys themselves but their parents also.[10]

II. ENTRANCE OF SOUTHERN METHODIST MISSION

In 1896, when the mission of the Methodist-Episcopal Church South entered Korea, a more exact division of territory was imperative. And so by 1905 there was a firm agreement between the Northern Methodist and Presbyterian Missions and by 1907 with the Southern Methodist Mission. The matter was thoroughly studied by the missionaries. There is some indication that heat as well as light was involved in the negotiations, but the division of territory was carried out with as little dislocation of existing churches as possible. In 1909 two thousand Presbyterian adherents of Whanghai Province (including four hundred and sixty baptized members from forty-three churches) were transferred to the Methodist Church, while two hundred adherents were received by the Presbyterians from the Methodists in the same province. A look at Figure 9 will show that even though there was a numerical loss, the Presbyterian Church in Whanghai was growing fast and soon won new Christians, so that there is no loss shown in the communicant membership of the Presbyterian Church. The accompanying map shows the Southern Methodist Mission area by comity agreement.

When Southern Methodist missionaries arrived in Korea they began immediately with evangelistic work in Seoul. Within ten years they had firmly established the Methodist-Episcopal Church South in the cities of Seoul, Songdo (now Kaesung), and Wonsan, the territories to which they were assigned in the comity agreements. [11] The details of the growth of this denomination have been set down by Alfred W. Wasson in his book *Church Growth in Korea*. Reference has been made in the previous chapters to this work. His

[10] *Ibid.,* p. 113. Quoting George H. Jones, "Mission Work on the Chemulpo District" from *Gospel in All Lands,* September, 1894, p. 415.
[11] *Ibid.,* p. 145.

conclusions cannot be applied in their entirety to the Korean Presbyterian Church, because his stress of environmental factors affecting church growth is not borne out by significant changes in communicant membership in all areas. For instance, church growth in northwest Korea during times of strong economic and political upheavals was not changed as in other areas. On the other hand, since Wasson lived through a good share of the Southern Methodist Mission history and knew it first-hand, and also since the population where this mission was working evidently was not as responsive as in the northwest (the people in Southern Methodist territory were of a cultural strain different from that of northwest Koreans), these environmental factors may well have had more effect on the various growth periods of most sections of the Southern Methodist Church than they had on the rapid-growing areas of the northwest.

Because this Methodist Mission stressed education, an area which the government always wanted to influence, the Southern Methodist Church no doubt felt adverse Japanese governmental pressures more than Presbyterians who had a smaller stake in education. Thus, political disturbances also may have had more effect on this Methodist Church. The conclusions reached by Wasson in his study of church growth in Korea, stressing that environment greatly influenced church expansion, may be valid for the Southern Methodist Church. However, not because of a difference in denomination, but because of the dissimilar cultural environment of the two areas assigned by comity agreement, it is evident that some of the important factors which caused the people movement in northwest Korea were not present in Kangwon Province (Southern Methodist territory) nor in some Northern Methodist areas of work.

III. A RESPONSIVE TURNING TO CHRIST
1896-1905

During the period from 1896 to 1905, the line of Figure 16 begins to swing upward. Methodist Mission reports sound like the northwest Presbyterian reports, saying that people were rolling into the churches in great waves. Stokes quotes several Methodist missionaries, one saying:

> "There are groups of believers springing up all over the territory, even in places that have not been visited by a missionary but only by native helpers."[12]

With the defeat of conservative China came a willingness for change, which affected both Methodist Churches as it had Presbyterians. The churches began to grow out beyond missionary control because new Christians led their friends and neighbors to Christ. The Methodists used paid helpers and colporteurs who sometimes worked with missionaries but more often, with a minimum of training, were placed in charge of large districts in attempts to keep up with fast-growing churches.[13]

Until 1905 growth of Northern Methodist Mission territory was concentrated largely in two areas outside of Seoul. The Inchon district, under the able leadership of the Rev.

[12] *Ibid.*, p. 150. Quoting M.E.S. Report, 1901, p. 38.
[13] *Ibid.*, p. 153.

Mr. George H. Jones, increased from 94 members and probationers in 1896 to a membership of 2,625 in 1905. The north Korea district during this same period increased from 51 to 2,151 members in 1905. Dr. Stokes, quoting Mr. W. A. Noble, who wrote from the north in 1901, says the reason for no greater growth in the northwest was lack of missionary workers. The next best thing would have been to send national preachers, but even they were lacking.[14]

During the time of this responsive turning toward Christianity it was tragic that "the relations between the missionaries and the Board of Foreign Missions of the Methodist-Episcopal Church reached their lowest ebb."[15] Methodists, as did Presbyterians, realized the need for reinforcements and funds. These were needed desperately in the face of the increasing groups of converted people who wanted, as well as needed, to be instructed. Stokes says that while the mission itself had emphasized institutional work rather than evangelistic work, and while it cannot be completely absolved from the responsibility for the lack of evangelistic workers, still there was a rapid succession of different Methodist bishops who supervised the mission. These bishops changed every year or two before each was really familiar with the Church and its needs, and thus they were not able to represent to the home board the opportunities and responsibilities of the work in Korea.[16]

Between 1895 and 1905 the Northern Methodist Mission responded with three evangelistic missionaries. Southern Methodists also sent three evangelistic missionaries in that period, while the Northern Presbyterian Mission responded with twenty-one new evangelistic missionaries, ten of whom went to the northern stations of Pyongyang and Sunchun. To put it simply, the opportunity for growth rested in the northwest and was recognized by both Presbyterian and Methodist missionaries, but the Presbyterians got reinforcements and concentrated on church growth while the Metho-

[14] *Ibid.*, p. 147. Quoting "The North Korean District," *Gospel in All Lands*, February, 1902, p. 93.

[15] *Ibid.*, pp. 171, 172.

[16] *Ibid.*, p. 172.

dists could not. The result was that Presbyterians got the
growth and Methodists did not. By 1905 the Northern
Methodist Church in Korea had 2,457 communicant members
on its rolls, representing twenty years of mission work. This is
good growth compared with some other missions around the
world. However, the Korean Presbyterian Church in Northern Presbyterian Mission territory had 9,756 communicant
members by 1905.

IV. GROWTH PATTERN OF THE TWO METHODIST
CHURCHES
1905-1930

From 1905 to 1910 both Methodist Churches grew rapidly.
This was the time when all Protestant Churches demonstrated
a consistent, high rate of growth. The rate for the Southern
Methodists was 700 percent, for Northern Methodists, 180
percent, and Northern Presbyterians, 250 percent. The conclusions I have reached on the effect of the revival on Presbyterian church growth also hold true for the Methodist
churches in Korea. With the interesting exception of the
Northern Methodist Church, which for two years following the revival (between 1908 and 1910) showed a slowing of growth, Methodist Churches were growing rapidly
both before and after the revival. However, this exception
reads suspiciously like another statistical readjustment rather
than indicating a decrease in actual growth. I suspect this
because the rates of growth before and after this two-
year period are the same, as can be seen on Figure 16.

During this exciting period of fast growth and revival,
intensive Bible training was also stressed. In the Methodist
Church too, the fast growth made imperative the training of
lay leaders to fill the urgent need for teachers to instruct
new converts in the first principles of the faith. Methodists
also did this by holding Bible classes. In 1901 the first lay
preacher was ordained.[17]   Now there was even more need
for trained leaders.

The "Million Souls for Christ" movement, actually of

---

[17] *Historical Sketch of the Korean Methodist Church,* p. 20.

Methodist origin, was a mighty effort in the year 1910 to extend the Church, but it failed to increase church membership. The churches which had been growing, largely through the witness of converted friends and relatives, did not seem to respond to American methods of tract distribution or large evangelistic meetings.

Beginning in 1911, the Southern Methodist area shows a loss in communicant membership, while the Northern Methodist Mission area remains static (note Figure 16). It can be recalled that the Presbyterian Church was growing, but not rapidly, at this time. The pressures placed on the Korean people by Japan, prior to the eruption of pent-up feelings on March 1, 1919, were felt in the churches. That the Methodist Churches showed decline in one case and no growth in the other, while Presbyterians were still getting some growth, is due in part to the Methodist emphasis on education as an evangelistic tool.

The government of Japan, wanting to use its educational system to train the Korean people to become good Japanese citizens, built new government schools and placed restrictive measures on private schools. These measures were claimed to be an effort to elevate school standards. Because of increased government requirements and the new competition of government schools, the energies of Methodist educational missionaries were siphoned off into work which did not produce churches. Also, because a Western education was available through Japanese government schools, missionaries no longer stood as the sole source of Western learning. Methodist schools, therefore, may have been at that time even a hindrance to evangelism; they were, at least, a burden on the Methodist missionaries. The Presbyterian Church, without a heavy burden of school administration, merely slowed in its growth. In the Methodist Church, growth stopped.

Aside from the conditions faced in common by all missions, Dr. Stokes gives as the chief reason for the decline of members in the Southern Methodist Church "the fact that the growth of membership in the preceding years was too rapid to be firmly established."[18] It is commonly assumed by many who criticize from both within and without the Churches that this is a fault of any rapid-growing Church. Certainly a Church that brings in masses of undiscipled people who do not know the basic tenets of the Christian faith is only deceiving itself when it rejoices in statistics of great growth. But before we decide that "too rapid growth" causes decline, let us make sure we see the other side of the coin.

That the Southern Methodists had rapid growth from 1905 to 1912 cannot be called bad in itself. All of the missions watched their churches growing rapidly during this period. Some of the missions were able to take care of this increased desire for baptism and instruction, by extensive itineration, training, and teaching of the young Christians, but the Southern Methodists had a difficult time doing this. Their territory was sparsely populated and mountainous, making travel most difficult. Their stations were located on the fringes of the territory instead of in the center of it. Missionary residences were far removed from many of the new Christians, and missionary contact was not easily maintained.[19] Many of their missionaries were tied to the stations by institutions. Rapid growth did not cause the 1912-1914 decline in Southern Methodist Church membership but rather lack of aftercare. Here, as in case after case around the world, great growth followed by adequate care and training succeeds, while the lack of follow-up instruction is likely to end in losses.

From 1920 to 1925, Figure 16 makes clear that once again both Northern and Southern Methodist Churches began advancing in their church memberships at a rate of growth almost equalling the 1905-1910 rate. The Southern Methodist Church shows a greater rate of growth than the Northern. That the people all over Korea were responsive following the Independence Movement of 1919 is clarified by the general growth of all churches in all sections of the nation. Coincident with this responsiveness, the Southern Methodist Mission inaugurated its "Centenary Advance" campaign, dur-

[18] Stokes, *op. cit.*, p. 302.
[19] *Ibid.*

ing which the American Church, celebrating one hundred years of being, made funds for evangelistic work available. These funds accompanied an intensive campaign of evangelism in the Southern Methodist Church. At this time the principle of self-support, largely followed by the Southern Methodist Mission, was bypassed, and mission funds were used to aid in building churches. Funds were also used to begin new institutes for training of leaders.[20]   The result was that while there was considerable loss of new believers who had responded in the evangelistic campaigns, still during these five years the church membership increased 3,873, or at the rate of 115 percent per decade. The Northern Methodist Mission's three-year spurt of growth from 1920 to 1923 was not so high as that of the Southern Methodist Mission.

From 1925 in the Southern Methodist Mission and from 1923 in the Northern Methodist Mission, we see on Figure 16 a period of decline or an almost static church membership level until World War II. In trying to examine the causes for this drop in growth, Stokes gives the following table of the proportion of mission resources devoted to kinds of work in 1927:[21]

	Evangelism	Education	Medical	Other
Northern Methodists	32%	42%	23%	3%
Northern Presbyterians	54%	21%	21%	4%

STOKES' 1927 DISTRIBUTION OF MISSION RESOURCES
TABLE III

One can see that in 1927 the Northern Methodist Mission placed its emphasis on education rather than evangelism. In addition to having the low percentage, the Northern Methodist Mission was smaller and so had far fewer evangelistic missionaries than the Northern Presbyterian Mission. The distribution of personnel is reflected in the fact that

[20] Wasson, *op. cit.*, p. 113.
[21] Stokes, *op. cit.*, p. 356. Quoting Annual Meeting of Federal Council of Protestant Evangelical Missions in Korea, 1927, p. 32.

Northern Presbyterian communicants and catechumens were four and one-half times as large as those of the Northern Methodists. But the Presbyterians enrolled in their primary schools slightly fewer than twice as many boys as Methodists, and even fewer girls.[22] The decline in Methodist membership during the years of extreme Japanese pressure upon educational institutions may be because the Methodists tied their mission work, including evangelism, to their education work.

V. COMPARISON OF METHODIST AND PRESBYTERIAN POLICY

Here is an indication of the policy difference in education between Presbyterians and Methodists. Presbyterian missionaries, contrary to the views of some of the home board staff, did not feel that education was the handmaiden of evangelism. Their schools, as a matter of policy, were for enrolling children of Christians. Enrollment of non-Christian students and their subsequent religious instruction were not felt by the Presbyterians to be a good method of evangelism. Further, buttressing the Presbyterian position, Dr. Stokes remarks that:

> . . . in considering the rapid strides of advancement in the Inchon Church, it is significant to note this was the only place in the Methodist area to have a missionary assigned solely to evangelistic duties.[23]

In 1892 Dr. Hall, of the Northern Methodist Mission, visited Pyongyang in northwest Korea, traveling with Dr. Moffett. Finally in May of 1894, Hall took up residence there. He returned to Seoul during the Sino-Japanese War, but he and Moffett went back to Pyongyang, and Dr. Hall began to treat those of the city in need of medical care. As we realized from the Presbyterian account of the Church in the northwest, this field around Pyongyang was ripe for harvest. It was a great tragedy that Dr. Hall, while working with these people in need of both medical care and spiritual

[22] *Ibid.*, p. 356.
[23] *Ibid.*, p. 114.

conversion, was taken ill with typhus fever and died on November 24, 1894. Had Dr. Hall lived, the foundations of a Church able to reproduce itself rapidly in the Methodist areas of northwest Korea might have been built.

Policy differences, important as they are in the dissimilar growth of Methodist and Presbyterian Churches, do not account for this simple but often overlooked fact: the Presbyterian Church early established a large, vigorous, growing Church in the responsive northwest, while the Methodists did not. The Presbyterian Church started to grow rapidly about 1895, and its main strength came from the area around Pyongyang. To put it another way, take away Presbyterian growth in Pyongyang and the Korea-wide picture would have been quite similar to that of the Methodist Church.

Stokes remarks of the Methodist Mission that its "ambition had over-reached the mark in undertaking to include eight cities outside the capital in its bounds."[24] These Methodists simply could not man adequately all of the areas of ordinary response that they were attempting to work, and the highly responsive northwest did not receive the personnel it did in the Presbyterian Mission. The Methodists chose to reinforce less responsive areas. Through fortuitous circumstances, they chose two areas in which to labor — areas that at first showed promise, but later became static because economically and physically they were not growing.

The town of Yungbyun was an old cultural center in North Pyongan Province that influenced the surrounding territory. Methodists chose this town as their area, but, when the railroad was put through from Pusan to Manchuria in 1905 by the Japanese, it bypassed Yungbyun, leaving it high and dry, while going through the town of Sunchun, making it an influential center of transportation and commerce. The Presbyterian Church in and around Sunchun, with its citizens of lower social status, grew, assisted by the growing town, while the Methodist Church in Yungbyun was held back from growing by the cultural resistance to change and by the lack of economic growth.

A similar instance is the town of Inchon, which in the

[24] *Ibid.,* p. 117.

early days was the port for Seoul and which, before the railroad, was more important than it is now. All foreign travelers and foreign commerce came through this port of Chemulpo and the nearby city of Inchon, moving overland twenty miles to Seoul. Inchon was the center of coastal traffic for Songdo and Haiju, both of Whanghai Province. There were large hotels in the city, and it was prosperous, but when this same railroad was put from Pusan to Seoul, ships then could stop at Pusan, which has a better harbor for large ships. Thus freight and passengers came overland by rail from Pusan. Coastal shipping became less important, leaving Inchon to become a city of secondary importance. Even though George Heber Jones records great growth early in the Inchon area, later the church did not grow well in this city, partly because the city itself soon began to lose its influence and position as well as decreasing in population.

During this time the Methodist Mission was undergoing a change of policy. Its first emphasis had been on medical work, and as late as 1892 a request for new missionaries included the request for one-half of them to be doctors.[25] Later on, when the opportunities for unhampered evangelism were seen, this medical stress was changed to a call for evangelistic missionaries.[26]

At an early date, Methodists tended to stress institutional work. Five out of seven men of the mission in 1895 were giving most of their time to institutions, and only one man was entirely free for evangelism.[27] Again comparing Presbyterians with the Methodists during the early period, Stokes says the Presbyterians through their Nevius method stressed itineration and personal evangelism such as Moffett carried out in his *sahrang* room, and they had "fewer institutional establishments and paid less attention to this type of missionary activity." While the Methodists "laid plans for extensive evangelism . . . they refused to carry them out at the

[25] *Ibid.*, p. 125. Quoting W. B. Scranton, Letter to Dr. A. B. Leonard, May 6, 1893.
[26] *Ibid.*, p. 126. Quoting Methodist Episcopal Mission Minutes, 1895, p. 38.
[27] *Ibid.*, p. 126.

expense of the educational and medical departments of the mission. Since the missionaries on the field were so strongly concentrated in schools and hospitals, the evangelistic program was largely frustrated."

Dr. Stokes has compiled a table from missionary reports showing the distribution of missionary force in 1893, which is reproduced here.[28]

	Evangelistic	Educational	Medical	Press	Wives	Total
Methodist Men	* 1½	2	3½	1	8	16
Presbyterian Men	8	1	2	-	9	20
Methodist Ladies	3	-	2	-	-	5
Presbyterian Ladies	3	-	-	-	-	3

One physician gave half-time to evangelistic work.

STOKES' 1893 DISTRIBUTION OF MISSIONARIES IN KOREA
TABLE IV

While Presbyterians were richly blessed with nine evangelistic male workers, the Methodist Mission had only one person giving full time to this work and another man who gave about half of his time. Actually, the Presyterian Mission had *nine* evangelistic men at this time and no one assigned to education. Mr. J. S. Gale, though not ordained in 1893, was nevertheless an evangelistic missionary, planting churches in and around Wonsan. The first full-time educational worker in the Northern Presbyterian Mission was actually appointed in 1896.

Since it is as true in planting churches as in planting grain that good fences make good neighbors, the Methodist and Presbyterian Missions early realized that a comity agreement was necessary for the efficient use of available resources and the elimination of unnecessary competition. In 1892 the first comity agreement between the Northern Methodist and Northern Presbyterian Missions was signed. It provided that towns of over 5,000 population be served by both missions, but towns of under 5,000 were considered occupied if there

[28] *Ibid.* Quoting P. N. Report 1893, pp. 142-146, and M.E.K.M. Minutes, 1893, pp. 18-19.

was already an established denominational group visited regularly by missionaries.[29]

VI. STEWARDSHIP OF MEN AND MONEY

Until 1905 the Northern Methodist Mission had no fixed policy in self-support, but in 1905 it took a stronger action adopting self-support as a policy in order to make the Church self-sufficient.[30]   The policy of self-support was adopted by the mission quite late, after churches had become accustomed to financial assistance from the mission. However, as Stokes says,

> In most places there was a healthy response to this new challenge and a marked increase in contributions was reported . . . [but] there were only a few churches that really became self-supporting.[31]

Coming as late as it did, it was naturally more difficult to enforce, and the Methodists did not adhere to a rigid policy of self-support as Presbyterians did through their Nevius plan. The action taken in 1905 never was practiced universally by the Methodist Mission. Throughout its history, if a need for building a church or supporting a pastor was seen and the funds were available, that help has been given.

Korean nationals and missionaries often say or imply that the Presbyterian Church grew rapidly because the mission followed a rigorous policy of self-support (defined as encouragement of a church to support its own organization), while the Methodist Church was denied rapid growth because it did not follow this policy. The policy of self-support had its effect on church growth in Korea, but we must always remember that the Presbyterian Church shows great growth primarily because of the response predominant in northwest Korea, while the policy was maintained in other areas also. In addition, we have shown that in one area of the Presbyterian Church, the churches were assisted in their growth by the judicious use of financial aid.

[29] Harry A. Rhodes, *History of the Korea Mission Presbyterian Church U. S. A. 1884-1934*, p. 441.
[30] Stokes, *op. cit.*, p. 156. Quoting M.E.K.M. Minutes, 1905, p. 19.
[31] *Ibid.*, pp. 156, 177-179.

Northern Presbyterian missionaries in Korea were required by their own by-laws to refrain from using private or mission money for both the construction of churches and the employment of national church leaders in local church positions. Foreign aid was not used to support the organizational structure of the Church, nor was it used extensively in primary education. In many instances, the mission did provide a small fraction of the total cost in building churches. But generally in all phases of the financial relationship between the younger Korean Church and the ambassadors from the American Church, self-support was advocated by the mission with intent to plant a vigorous, self-reliant Christian body.

Because of the alleged cause and effect relationship between self-support and rapid growth in comparing Korean Methodist and Presbyterian Churches, we must here examine more closely the policy of self-support the Presbyterian missionaries adopted as a result of hearing the experiences of Nevius.

Presbyterian William B. Hunt, who worked beside Methodists in Whanghai Province, writes that, while the Methodist Church in Pyongan and Whanghai Provinces made early gains by building churches and paying helpers with American funds, that same Methodist Church was considerably weaker in 1909. In the Pyongyang "western district," Presbyterians had ten times the Christian strength as Methodists had in 1909. Hunt says that Western funds used for paying Methodist helpers attract a type of helper who is adroit in using the missionary's name in civil court cases and who is really a business man first and a preacher second. He says that instead of making "better Christian manhood and womanhood" if the work should be supported by the nationals, missionaries using foreign funds make an "inferior, pauper sort of person.[32]

Criticism of the use of foreign funds is written with great feeling because Hunt experienced the effect of the Methodist

[32] William B. Hunt, Letter to the Board of Foreign Missions of the Presbyterian Church in the U. S. A. (Chairyung, Korea: February 1, 1909).

policy on his work. If he pictures the conditions correctly
— and there is no reason to doubt him — the use of foreign
money particularly in the northwest was an important factor
in the slow Methodist church growth. When money from
abroad built churches and paid pastors' salaries, the Methodist Christians came to understand that this is the way
churches are planted. The Church could grow only as
fast as buildings and support could be given by the missionaries. It is obvious that in this northwest area, if Methodists had been given a chance, the national Church would
have broken out, supported its own workers, and would have
expanded at a rapid rate. Western money used in the northwest of Korea was like a trap, surrounding the Church and
keeping it from growing.

One of the most important reasons why the Nevius method
worked so well in the northwest is that, because of a strict
comity agreement, there was relatively little competition
from other missions using different policies. The Presbyterians had most of the territory to themselves. The liberal
use of foreign funds in adjoining territory was only a mild
form of competition. It would have been much more difficult
for the Presbyterians to hold the hard line of self-support
had there been churches supported by foreign funds, mixed
in Presbyterian territory.

However, self-support principles did work well in northwest Korea. In fact, they were most thoroughly practiced
there where the Church was growing so. Dr. Rhodes raises
the question as to "whether the Church flourishes because
of the system or the system is possible because of the flourish-
ing condition of the Church."[33] While we know that the
Nevius method accompanied church growth in the northwest,
we have seen that it is a vast oversimplification to say that
it caused church growth.

Look at the churches in the Seoul area in 1930. The
number of Northern Methodist communicants and catechumens in this region was 4,200.[34] For Northern Presbyterians

[33] Rhodes, *op. cit.*, p. 89.
[34] Stokes, *op. cit.*, p. 380. Quoting MEKAC Journal 1930, p. 270.

it was 3,522.[35] Both missions were working in the same section of Korea among an approximately equal population. If strict adherence to self-support principles caused the rapid growth of one Church and nonadherence the slow growth of the other, why then in these two sections of one area, Seoul, each with an equal number of people, are the rates of growth about the same? Self-support is not a policy that in itself alone produces church growth everywhere it is used.

In his doctoral dissertation, Dr. Sung Chun Chun says that the principle of self-support did not cause church growth, but in fact "hindered" it. He suggests that one reason it hindered church growth was that it was strictly enforced throughout all of Korea. Because strict self-support was not always the best policy in some parts of the nation, the growth pattern of the Church was different from that seen in the northwest and in these places self-support did hamper church growth.

> Without specific helps toward self-support, the Nevius plan assumed that the churches in Korea would naturally become self-supporting. However, particularly in south Korea, the poor tenants had little opportunity to develop the prerequisite for self-support. This meant that the program of missionary effort was hampered by the Nevius plan. The majority of the population in Korea is composed of poor farmers who desperately needed guidance prior to attaining any degree of self-support.[36]

Dr. Chun is not the only one who feels that the principle of self-support was not the best policy for immediate church growth in the farming area of the south. We have previously shown that the wise use of the Adams Fund actually helped the churches of North Kyungsang Province to grow. Such evidence supports Dr. Chun's appraisal of the situation.

The policy of self-support appeals to missionaries, sending

[35] *Ibid.* Quoting Presbyterian Church U. S. A. Chosen Mission Minutes and Reports of Annual Meeting, 1931, pp. 123-124.

[36] Sung Chun Chun, *Schism and Unity in the Protestant Churches of Korea,* p. 71.

Churches, and mission boards today. Self-support, while not some mystic reason for church growth, is sound in that payment of pastors' salaries, church building costs, education expenses of catechists and pastors, and further evangelism expenditure, when made from mission funds, may put severe limits on the growth of the Churches. The young Church suffers and is able to grow only as fast as the funds from abroad will permit.

The Northern Presbyterians, who gave less subsidy than Methodists, had no such limitations. They had an indefinitely reproducible pattern because it was indigenous and free of foreign funds. The building of a church or the hiring of a pastor did not have to wait on an appropriation from the mission. The principle liberated Korean genius and produced local leadership. Local churches were not dominated by missionaries. Of course, missionaries visited churches, gave advice to them, and admitted their new members, but it was the local leader's responsibility to conduct worship services and to handle the problems of his congregation from week to week. A self-governing Church in a responsive population reproduced itself again and again, because church leaders realized their leadership would be enhanced if the Church were larger. From the self-government principle naturally extends the principle of self-propagation. The faith which burst into flower all over northwest Korea would have been crushed by dependence upon Western leadership or Western funds.

We conclude that in slower-growing areas the Nevius Method probably hampered church growth by its rigid enforcement of a scheme that did not fit them. Western funds did help where they were used wisely in a slow-growing area, but where there was great responsiveness, self-support, though it did not cause growth, enabled growth to go on unhampered by budgetary restrictions imposed by the giving of American churches and the divisions of funds by American boards.

Chapter VIII. Growth of Other Protestant Churches in Korea

FIGURE 17 SHOWS US A PICTURE OF THE ORGANIZED PROTESTANT Christian Churches in Korea over a nine year period: 1930 to 1939. This is also a fair representation of the relative numerical strength of these denominations in Korea at the present time. The statistics came from the Federal Council of Churches in Korea. Statistics for the Roman Catholic Church are briefly discussed in the Appendix.

In a study of church growth in Korea, Figure 17 also shows that we are not amiss in concentrating on the Presbyterian and Methodist Protestant Churches, as here they received the greatest growth and in many ways have dominated the Christian scene in Korea. Four other denominations also received significant growth, and so a brief look at these Churches existing in Korea before 1941 will be necessary.

I. THE SALVATION ARMY

In 1930 the Salvation Army had thirty-five missionaries, and in 1931 it had one hundred thirty-seven centers throughout the Korean peninsula, where special evangelistic campaigns were carried on. The Salvation Army shows moderate growth in membership, but the organization is very well known for its Christian service in temperance, rescue, and relief work. In 1919 a Boys' Industrial Home was established, and by 1931 one hundred twenty boys were being trained in several industrial trades. This mission, established in 1908, has always been very friendly and cooperative with the other denominations in Korea.

II. CHURCH OF ENGLAND

The Church of England's mission to Korea began at the consecration of the first bishop of the Diocese of Korea in 1889. This man was Bishop Charles John Corfe. Bishop

189

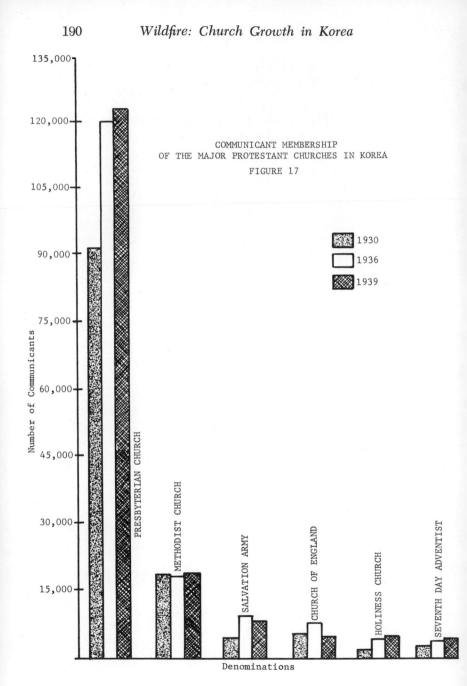

COMMUNICANT MEMBERSHIP
OF THE MAJOR PROTESTANT CHURCHES IN KOREA
FIGURE 17

Corfe labored seven years before the first Anglican convert was baptized. This first convert was Mark Kim, who later became the first Korean Anglican priest. Bishop Corfe resigned, and one of his priests, Arthur Turner, was raised to bishop, but died five years later. From 1910 until 1930, Mark Napier Trollope was the bishop who was

> . . . statesman, scholar, great organiser, great Bishop and almost second founder. He had been the first priest on Bishop Corfe's staff and had baptized the first convert.[1]

The Church grew only moderately and by 1939 had slightly over 5,000 communicants. To care for these members there were only fourteen missionaries and eighteen Korean priests. Part of the difficulty was due to lack of missionaries and money. "The Church of England had sent her volunteers into almost every corner of the world, but there never seemed to be enough for Korea."[2] By comparison, at this time there were 251 Presbyterian missionaries in Korea. In addition, there were 357 communicants to one missionary of the Anglican Church and 545 communicants to one missionary of the Presbyterian Church. We can see from this that the number of missionaries is not the only answer to church growth.

The Anglican Church also felt pressure at the hands of the Japanese, and, because of anti-British feeling, the European missionaries felt that they had become a hindrance to the Church and "a danger to the physical safety of ten thousand Korean Anglicans."[3] Accordingly, most of the Anglican Mission withdrew from Korea early in 1941.

III. THE HOLINESS CHURCH

The Holiness Church is the literal translation of the Korean name for the Church established by the Oriental Missionary Society. This Church is in doctrine closely related to the Methodist Church. The Oriental Missionary Society first sent their missionaries to Japan, and then to

[1] *The Anglican Church in Korea,* p. 6.
[2] *Ibid.,* p. 7.
[3] *Ibid.,* p. 8.

Korea in 1907. In 1931 they reported eighty-seven preachers and fifty-seven Bible women working throughout the thirteen provinces and Manchuria. A strong Bible Training Institute was established in Seoul, where one hundred two students were studying at that time. If the figures are correct, this was a period of rapid growth, for there was a doubling of membership from 1930 to 1931.[4] This rapid growth did not continue, as the Holiness Church had slightly over five thousand members in 1939. In that year the Oriental Missionary Society had just four missionaries, two less than in 1930. So this Church saw good growth in proportion to its missionary staff.

IV. SEVENTH DAY ADVENTIST CHURCH

The mission of the Seventh-Day Adventists, established in 1904, did not see great church growth until after the Second World War. However, it did establish medical work in South Pyongan Province and in Seoul, and it continues today to provide fine medical service in the capital of South Korea. A printing plant was also established in Seoul by the Seventh Day Adventist Church.

[4] Federal Council of Missions in Korea, *Korea Missions Yearbook,* p. 128.

Chapter IX. Relationship of Mission Policies to Church Growth

BECAUSE SO MUCH HAS BEEN WRITTEN AND SAID ABOUT THE methods of the Protestant missionaries in Korea, we must consider how these various policies are related to the growth of the Churches. We will do this in particular relating to the Presbyterian Church in Korea.

I. THE NEVIUS METHOD

When one thinks of the policy of the Northern Presbyterian Mission in Korea, "Nevius Method" is the first term that comes to mind. Indeed this method was built into the policy of the Southern Presbyterian and Southern Methodist Missions, as well as into that of the Northern Presbyterian Mission. The Nevius Method is so interwoven with Protestant missions in Korea that we have already mentioned it many times. So important is it that, at the risk of repetition, I will summarize the method here.

The Nevius Method is described in four principles by the first Horace Underwood, who knew Nevius personally and entertained him when he visited Korea in 1890.

> First, to let each man "abide in the calling wherein he was found," teaching that each was to be an individual work-er for Christ, and to live Christ in his own neighborhood, supporting himself by his trade.
>
> Secondly, to develop Church methods and machinery only so far as the native Church was able to take care of and manage the same.
>
> Third, as far as the Church itself was able to provide the men and the means, to set aside those who seemed the better qualified, to do evangelistic work among their neighbors.
>
> Fourth, to let the natives provide their own church build-

ings, which were to be native in architecture, and of such style as the local church could afford to put up.[1]

Dr. Charles A. Clark, who has studied and written extensively about the Nevius principles in Korea, has also summed up those methods briefly by saying that they are:

> Bible emphasis, personal evangelism through wide itineration, self-propagation, self-government, strict discipline, cooperation and union, non-use of secular motives such as help in lawsuits, etc., and helpfulness in the economic problems of the people.[2]

These are the principles followed by the Presbyterian Mission, but since that mission was not one person but a group of highly individualistic missionaries, it was felt that these principles had to be codified into strict rules. This was done in the rules and by-laws of the Korea Mission in 1891. (Also see "Nevius Method" in glossary.)

So the Nevius Method as followed by the Northern Presbyterian Mission, while quite similar to that espoused by Nevius himself, was really the Korea Mission's adaptation of these principles. For instance, the principle of inspiring self-support was advocated by Nevius, but not to the point of rigidity, for he himself, when he had eight hundred communicants in sixty churches (he called them outstations), used mission funds to pay two helpers' salaries. The Presbyterian Mission also used its funds for salary payment of helpers, but to a much lesser extent. In addition, the mission had strictly enforced rules which spelled out the limits for use of American money. Dr. John L. Nevius' method was not born in the mind of a theorist to be set down as rules, but was produced as a practical measure to do a better job of planting churches. As the Presbyterian Mission adopted Nevius' policy ideas, it also adapted them to its own particular kind of church planting.

Although the mission codified Nevius' methods, as the conditions changed, so the rules also changed. Dr. C. A.

---

[1] Horace G. Underwood, *The Call of Korea*, pp. 109-110.
[2] Charles Allen Clark, *The Nevius Plan for Mission Work in Korea*, p. 241.

Clark remarks on some of these changes, especially as they applied to the early mission school for boys in Seoul. The rules of 1891, Section C12 say, "No more should be done in the way of board, clothing, etc. than is absolutely necessary to secure the end desired by the school." But the rules of 1898, seven years later, say that "not over half of the running expense of the school (not the individual expense of the pupil) shall be paid from mission funds."[3] Dr. Clark indicates several other changes not only in school policy, but also in regard to the Winter Bible classes for leaders and then in regard to lay leaders in the churches:

> In Sec. C. VI, it says that "all teachers, if possible, shall be Christians," for, in those days, persons competent to teach were very hard to find. In 1901, on the basis of its experience and practice, it ruled, "All teachers must be Christian."
>
> In Sec. D. VII, [1891] the Mission planned to pay the full cost of entertaining [housing and feeding] those studying in the Classes, since this was Dr. Nevius' [procedure]. This was done only a very short time. In 1901, the Mission goes beyond Dr. Nevius' plan and writes into the law, what had long been its practice, that "The Korean Christians shall defray the expenses of the Classes."
>
> The emendation made in 1896 in Sec. B XII is most significant, where the members of the Mission are refused the right to pay native agents without Mission permission, *even though they use personal funds to do it.*[4]

Let us be sure we attribute these changes in Nevius' method to the rightful cause. The changes may have been improvements. Certainly on paper they looked like improvements intending to increase the spiritual strength of the Church. But these refinements could be enforced only in an area where the Church grew rapidly and where it had power in the numbers of committed Christians in its ranks. After the Church grew, a young person who could not afford to pay his way to a Bible Institute could call on Christian relatives to help pay his expenses. The large Church also had

[3] *Ibid.*, p. 95.
[4] *Ibid.*

enough Christians in it to furnish Christian teachers for the schools, and so a more definite wording of the by-laws could be made. These modifications of the Nevius Method would have been impossible or, if enforced, disastrous in an area of little response.

Nevius' ideas and the regulations which they produced were not intended to be a set of prohibitions. Because self-support is often claimed to be the key principle of the Nevius Method, missionaries often erroneously conclude that they are practicing the Nevius Method if they withhold Western funds from the national Church. Nothing could be further from the original truth. Nevius' method was a plan intended to be practical in all respects, including the disciplined use of foreign funds for planting churches. In fact, this is the title of Dr. Nevius' book: *The Planting and Development of Missionary Churches.* Planting churches is still the purpose of the United Presbyterian Church in the U. S. A. Since 1957 this purpose has been expounded in its manual as follows:

> The supreme and controlling aim of the Christian Mission to all the world is to make the Lord Jesus Christ known to all men as their Divine and only Savior, and to persuade them to become His disciples and responsible members of His Church in which Christians of all lands share in evangelizing the world and permeating all of life with the spirit and truth of Christ.[5]

II. BIBLE CLASSES

The use of the Bible as the basis of training new Christians and intensive Bible teaching are included in Nevius' plan. We have seen how, because the churches "spread like WILDFIRE," it was impossible for missionaries alone to minister to the hundreds of congregations scattered all across the mountainous countryside, particularly in the northwest.

[5] "The Aim," Chapter IIB, Art. 13, *Manual of the Commission of Ecumenical Mission and Relations of the United Presbyterian Church in the U. S. A.* (amended in February 1957 to read according to the statement written at the 1956 Lake Mohonk Consultation called by the Presbyterian U. S. A. Board of Foreign Missions).

Bible Training Classes were set up early in the mission's history. These classes, also especially in the northwest, were a powerful force in producing a strong Church. Since the people of Korea had inherited a Confucian respect for good literature and had lived by their classics for centuries, they eagerly responded to the opportunity to learn from this ancient, Oriental book, the Bible, when it was given to them. They respected the Book that spoke to them all the Words of this Life.

III. MISSIONARY ITINERATION

Another Nevian principle that fit well with the growing Church in Korea is that of itineration. Itineration was actually thrust upon the missionaries by the early calls of Koreans from all over the country for instruction in the new faith. There is no question that the travel of missionaries to small groups of new Christians and their residence in these communities for an amount of time sufficient to give spiritual guidance and instruction, were most important features in the Korean Church. Without fast, modern means of transportation, missionaries learned to live out among rural people and to take along only those things they considered necessary for good health. (From a Korean point of view these "things" were often amazing!) In 1895 Dr. J. H. Wells, who had been in Korea only six months, wrote that he had done six hundred miles of itinerating during that time.

Itineration did two things. First, it put the foreigner out among Korean people so that he not only learned the Korean language, but also came to understand the people in a way impossible for one who remains isolated in a large missionary home in a Korean city. Second, itineration established a strong Church. The men traveled to village churches with a purpose. They knew their inability to give constant oversight. They knew that in their short time at each church, they must train Korean leaders who would take over the church organization and continue teaching Bible, and do both well.

Rural people were more responsive than city dwellers to the Christian faith, and only *mobile* missionaries, who trained these leaders, helped establish a strong Church in the country areas. The importance of travel to rural churches can be seen when we observe those in positions of leadership of large city churches. Most leading pastors today received their first training in a little country church; most church leaders came from the country rather than from the city.

IV. MISSIONARY ENCOURAGEMENT OF NATIVE INITIATIVE

The Nevius Method also stressed self-government. The Northern Presbyterian Mission, early in its history, began negotiations for a church organization fully controlled by the Korean people. In 1907, after long negotiations with the home Churches involved, an autonomous Korean Church was set up.

The self-support principle included in the Nevius Method has attracted wide attention. It is often erroneously thought to be the sum total of the Nevius Method. This principle has become so famous not because it is basic to the Nevius Method, but because it is a radical departure from previous missionary methods. While considering the Methodist Churches in Korea, we saw that self-support is the best and only policy to follow in a responsive area where the growing Church can afford to pay its own way. Under such conditions, the use of Western funds would be disastrous and would severely limit church growth.

When considering the Presbyterian work in North Kyungsang Province, an area of moderate response where a small group would be hard put to support a church because of poverty conditions, we saw that the wise use of foreign money did aid church growth. However, in a practically nonresponsive area such as Kyunggi Province (which includes Seoul), it seemed to make no difference whether foreign funds were used or not. Neither foreign money nor a rigorous self-support policy produced church growth in this area.

Self-propagation, another policy of the Nevius Method, was taught by the missionaries from the very beginning. Many of these missionaries required that a person wishing baptism must lead someone else to Christ before he could be admitted to membership through baptism. The vestiges of this requirement can be seen in 1962, when Korean women attending a circle meeting of their local church are asked to report how many people they led to Christ during the month. The Korean Christians of both the past and present feel a strong responsibility to witness for their Savior.

V. EDUCATIONAL POLICY

The Nevius Method has been criticized by Dr. Chun as favoring "isolationism" of the Korean Church. He says, "Information concerning social and theological developments abroad was curtailed because few students were sent overseas for further education."[6] This criticism directs our attention to the educational policy of the Northern Presbyterian Mission. The mission's members have been accused before of being concerned more with planting churches than with educating church leaders on the graduate level. Missionaries were not unaware of the problem, but they found they had to make a choice. Those congregations which were multiplying so fast sent few leaders to institutions of higher learning in Korea; therefore, fewer men were qualified to go abroad for further study than some would have desired. If manpower and resources only had been unlimited, both church extension and higher education could have been realized, but the fact was that personnel and funds from the American Church were limited, and so the mission was forced to make a choice.

One either plants churches and concentrates on training nationals to lead them, or one concentrates on higher education at the risk of getting little church growth. Educational work does not have to be a deterrent to church growth, but it often is. Because of its concentration on education, the Northern Methodist Mission was unable to seize the opportunity for establishing multitudes of churches in the responsive population of the northwest.

To explain this dichotomy of education and church plant-

[6] Sung Chun Chun, *Schism and Unity in the Protestant Churches of Korea,* p. 71.

ing, Dr. Chun himself quotes the Rev. Mr. Clarence F. Reed, first superintendent of the Methodist-Episcopal South Mission in Korea, who wrote:

> I would make evangelistic work rather than ministerial work the leading feature of the Mission. In China the institutions, schools, hospitals, etc., get our best men and the bulk of our money. Good schools and hospitals are excellent institutions; but I have observed that as a rule a very small percent of their work is conserved in the Church and that the missions which make these features prominent count their memberships by the hundreds while the missions chiefly engaged in evangelistic work count their numbers by the thousands.[7]

Chun continues: While the American Presbyterian and Methodist-Episcopal South Missions were church planters following *this* point of view, "Some Canadian Presbyterians and the [Northern] Methodist Episcopal Mission were of the opposite school of thought, especially as time went on. They considered education, both religious and secular, of primary importance. Conversion should follow naturally."[8] Perhaps conversion *should* follow naturally, but unfortunately it seldom *does*.

The problem of higher education versus evangelism cannot be solved by choosing one or the other, but by determining a proper proportion of both in view of the local potential for church growth. Since both education and evangelism are good in themselves, a choice between them is difficult and is, indeed, unnecessary. If a Church obeys the Great Commission given by our Lord and centers its primary concern on making disciples, it will plant many churches and follow with a good educational program. If a Church is preoccupied with a good educational program, expecting evangelism and church growth to follow naturally, it will plant fewer churches — and in many populations, very few indeed. To those who would criticize the Korea Presbyterian missionaries for emphasizing evangelism rather than education, I would answer that the missionaries who pre-

[7] *Ibid.*, p. 65. Quoting Methodist Episcopal South Board Annual Report 1897, p. 28.
[8] *Ibid.*, p. 65.

ferred to devote themselves to the extension of the Church were following the Biblical wisdom of the Great Commission.

Instead of education producing churches, the independent churches particularly of the northwest established by Presbyterian Christians, founded their own educational institutions at the primary level. If we include primary schooling in a consideration of educational policy, we find that Presbyterian churches multiplied, established their own schools, and actually did more educational work than Methodists. In 1927 the Federal Council of Missions records 233 church-related schools in the Northern Presbyterian area and exactly 100 schools in the territory of the Northern Methodists.

The educational policy of the Northern Presbyterian Mission was simply "to win the lost and educate the saved," a policy at variance with that of the home mission board. The Board of Foreign Missions in New York City was in favor of a broader educational policy which did not concentrate on education for Christians but was rather aimed at the whole Korean population. They made it plain that they thought the Korea Mission was narrow-minded in its policy of directing its education toward Christians and their children only. Of course, the Korea Mission did not exclude non-Christian children, but it did not aim its program at the non-Christians either.

The attitude of the board is understandable when we remember that the people in many important countries around the world were not as responsive to Christ as those of northwest Korea. Of necessity, education was used in those countries as a method of evangelism. In fact, the introduction of missionaries into some countries was accomplished only through their declared intent to be educators of the public. The image generated in those lands concerning mission education was that held by the board. But in Korea, where missionaries easily entered the nation and where Korean people flocked to the Christian churches, the situation was different. It was most different in the northwest, where the missionaries steadily pressed to win the lost and educate the saved to the extent of establishing their own college in Pyongyang for the children of Christians. This college was forced by the recent division of the nation to move to Seoul in South Korea, and it continues to operate today as a Christian college.

The world-wide mission educational pattern, arising in unresponsive populations and embraced by the Korea Methodist Mission and by the Presbyterian Board, looked good, and with the passing of the years even Presbyterians in the less responsive areas of Korea pressed for and finally obtained a college which welcomed Christians and non-Christians alike who desired a liberal education. This college, also located in Seoul, is now a respected university with a distinctive Christian witness.

In the process of obtaining these schools with their markedly different goals, the missionaries of Pyongyang Station lined up against the missionaries of Seoul Station in a heated debate lasting several years — a disagreement that involved the entire Northern Presbyterian Mission. This debate finally was settled and fought to a draw on the floor of the American General Assembly. The argument over two different types of educational institutions (one in Pyongyang intending to educate mainly Christians and the one proposed in Seoul to educate both Christians and non-Christians) did not arise from a difference in personality of the missionaries involved nor from a theological difference in goals. Rhodes states that "any difference as to methods and policies between our missionaries in the two stations was due as much to the difference of environment of the two cities as to any difference of the missionaries themselves."[9]

This difference in the environment of the two cities was seen primarily in their church growth. The city of Pyongyang in the northwest was the center of a growing, thriving, strong Church. In contrast, the city of Seoul had only a handful of Christians. The lack of good growth in Seoul led these missionaries to turn to other forms of "good mission work." An educational institution devoted only to the education of a few Christians in Seoul would have been unnecessary and poor stewardship, while in the northwest an institution dedicated to the training of Christian leaders was not

[9] Harry A. Rhodes, *History of the Korean Mission Presbyterian Church U. S. A. 1884-1934*, p. 479.

only possible but the best educational plan for that area, because there was such a large community of Christians from which to obtain students. Students were never turned away on the basis of religion, but it would be hard to imagine a mission-supported school, in the midst of the great northwest churches, not dedicated to teaching Christian students. The bearing of church growth on educational policy has seldom been so clearly illustrated.

No educational institution anywhere is as effective in evangelism as an evangelizing Church. It can be safely argued that the colleges and schools established in Korea were not needed as evangelistic tools, because the Church was already spreading by means of a people movement, more effective than formal education has been anywhere in the world for expanding church membership. Christian education of the public has its own merits, of course, but, to aid church growth in the best way, students within the membership of a fast-growing Church should be placed in a college where the faculty are Christians interested and engaged in church extension, and where the students also are mostly Christian. This manner of education seems to produce church leaders vitally interested in the growth of their Church. This is the sort of education that the majority of Presbyterian missionaries wanted to set up.

VI. MEDICAL POLICY

Korea was first opened to Protestant missions through the medical skill of Dr. Horace Allen, who treated a prince, saved his life, and won a royal welcome for Christian missions. Other doctors were sent by both the Presbyterian and Methodist Missions. The first medical missionaries who sailed to far-off Korea were interested in using their medical training for the evangelistic advance of the Kingdom. They traveled with their fellow American preachers, and their main purpose was to win a welcome for the Christian enterprise. As they treated their Korean patients, they hoped to win them to Christ.

Quite early, when it became apparent that hostility was being replaced by cordial acceptance, the Northern Presbyterian Mission wanted to give up medical work in large hospitals. As early as 1891 Dr. Gifford says:

> The day for preliminary work so ably conducted by Dr. Allen and Dr. Heron is now past and a foothold in the land is secured. The Koreans know we are here for evangelizing and consent to this.[10]

The mission saw medicine not so much as a Christian service of love, but as a way of gaining a foothold in this land where a Church could be produced. Soon they no longer saw the necessity of using medicine as a means for evangelism. The Church was already growing much faster by other means, namely by the witness of new Christians in a people movement. In 1902, when the board, through a private gift, wished to give Korea a large grant making possible a hospital in the capital city, the mission (especially those members in the northwest) opposed accepting the grant on the grounds that the hospital in Seoul would cloud the main purpose and make "medical work" appear as important as church multiplication. Nevertheless, the hospital was established.

This action clearly indicates that receptiveness of various populations and speed and completeness of church growth in different sections of a country all have a bearing on medical policies. For the northwest, the thinking of the northwest Korea missionaries was correct. There, in the midst of pentecostal growth, it would have been foolish to divert any part of the available resources to a program for preparing people to hear the Gospel. Not only were people already hearing it, they were obeying it. If the board had money for a medical missionary, it would be better spent in sending a man to father and train fifty churches, but the thinking of missionaries in Seoul and in the less responsive parts of Korea was also correct for their part of the land. With the very limited response they were getting, a hospital may have been a real advantage for them. If it became a semi-secular hospital staffed by persons who were Chris-

[10] D. L. Gifford, Letter to the Board of Foreign Missions of the Presbyterian Church U. S. A., (Seoul, Korea: June 17, 1891).

tian only on Sunday, its value to the Christian enterprise might be that of compassion. But if, together with being a splendid medical plant, its staff were warmly Christian and openly engaged in church planting, this value would be tremendously increased.

In some places medicine aids the advance of the Church today. I know of men and women who have been won to Christ through treatment received in hospitals connected with the Korean Church. The large mission hospital at Taegu has been instrumental in planting over one hundred churches during its history of continued evangelistic effort. The superintendent, Dr. Howard Moffett, describes the evangelistic work of that hospital:

> "At the center of all our hospital work and program . . . is our evangelistic effort." The staff is voluntarily organized into a "preaching society," in which all participate. A typical medical-evangelistic mobile clinic trip included four doctors, two nurses, one pharmacist, one hospital chaplain and a driver-mechanic. The group took a week's exhausting trek through three provinces, treating patients in the villages, holding roadside demonstrations on health problems, giving medical lectures, making health surveys, and holding evangelistic services every night. They worked from daybreak prayer meeting time until midnight. More than 1,200 patients were given free treatments, and hundreds asked to know more about the Lord Jesus Christ of whom the doctors and nurses spoke so freely.[11]

Yet, like education, medicine too often becomes big business, and the large institutions required by modern Western medicine tend to become more and more healing machines, less and less personal witness, and are being called into question by at least some home mission boards today. It is not wrong for the Church to be involved in medicine or education, if it can afford the institutions that result. But the question is: can we afford schools and hospitals at the expense of missing opportunities to help a Church expand? There are even times when these large institutions, which require so much personnel, equipment, and funds for their

[11] Samuel Hugh Moffett, *The Christians of Korea,* pp. 167-168.

maintenance, actually hinder the unfinished task of bringing the whole world to a knowledge of Christ and into His Church.

In summary, perhaps the test is this: if the school or hospital is helping the Church to grow, it is useful. If not, then its support by funds from overseas, earmarked for the extension of the Church of Jesus Christ, should be seriously questioned.

Chapter X. Growth of Protestant Churches in Korea from 1940 to 1960

THE TWO DECADES BETWEEN 1940 AND 1960 REPRESENT AN UN-usually turbulent period in the history of the Church in Korea. A world war, a war in Korea herself, and subsequent divisions in the Church have made it almost impossible to obtain accurate statistics of church membership during this period. Records were destroyed by the Japanese during the Second World War, and other records were destroyed in the Korean War. In the Presbyterian Church division, both sides tend to overclaim their membership. Only a picture in outline can be given of the growth of the Protestant Church during these troubled times.

I. WORLD WAR II
1940-1945

This was a time of increasing Japanese pressure on the Church, whose Presbyterian branch had formally submitted to bowing at the shrines in 1938. The outbreak of World War II in 1941, with its colossal American defeats, brought even stronger oppression upon the Churches. Many church leaders were imprisoned.[1] The Presbyterian Board of Foreign Missions reports that at this time 1,200 out of the 5,000 Protestant Churches closed.[2] The Presbyterian Church dropped in communicant membership from 134,000 in 1939 to 110,000 in 1942 (Figure 3), when all denominations were united by the Japanese government into the Korean branch of the United Church in Japan (Kyodan). I do not have the figures for the Methodist and Holiness Churches during this same period, but it would seem reasonable to assume that

[1] Yang Sun Kim, *History of the Korean Church in the Ten Years Since Liberation*, 1945-1955, translated by Allen D. Clark, p. 1.
[2] Annual Report of the Board of Foreign Missions of the Presbyterian Church in the U. S. A. (New York: 1946), p. 20.

the climate for church growth was just as unfavorable to them as to the Presbyterians. The Rev. Mr. Yang Sun Kim says that churches were limited in the number of hours a week for worship; there was forced labor, and many of the Christians went underground, so that Protestant Christians were reduced to half of their previous number.[3] I presume that Kim means *known* Christians.

The 1942 Minutes of the General Assembly of the Korean Presbyterian Church record the fact that the Church was forced to turn in up to one thousand church bells to be used in the war effort. The Minutes also tell how a collection was taken, amounting to about $70,000.00 (U. S. dollars) for the purchase of an airplane for the Japanese air force. There were so many demands by the Japanese government upon the General Assembly that a general council had to be formed to meet them. This period was marked by decline instead of by church growth.

II. APPROACHING COMMUNIST INVASION
1946-1950

The end of World War II brought only temporary relief to the Church in Korea. The decision to allow the Russians control above the thirty-eighth parallel proved disastrous for the Church as it later did for the nation as a whole. It will be remembered that a very large share of the communicant membership of the Church in Korea was above the thirty-eighth parallel. Even as early as a few months after the end of the war, the Communists had made travel and communication across the thirty-eighth parallel so difficult that it was impossible for a General Assembly of the Presbyterian Church or a General Conference of the Methodist Church to be held.

Presbyterians met in the north separately from the United Korean Church that met in the south, which attempted to continue in this united body of Methodists and Presbyterians, forced on Korean Christians by the Japanese government. But the united body divided along its former denominational

[3] Kim, *op. cit.*, p. 1.

lines. By June 12, 1946, a southern division of the Presbyterian General Assembly met, as it did annually thereafter.

The Presbyterian Church in the north, whose leaders
sought to do their best for their country's rehabilitation, formed
political parties and used its moral influence on the puppet
government of Il Sung Kim. On the issue of a Sunday election,
the Church met with Communist opposition, which resulted
in many arrests.

A Christian League was formed of those supporting the
Communist government, in order to weaken the Church by
indirect means. By 1949 this League gained control of the
churches and presbyteries in the north. The League also
controlled the seminaries of the Presbyterian and Methodist
Churches.[4] During this time many Christian leaders saw the
handwriting on the wall and fled for their lives to the south.
In both north and south, 1946 to 1950 were years of confusion, with little church growth in the Presbyterian and
Methodist Churches and presumably in the others.

III. THE KOREAN WAR
1950-1952

During the war fought in Korea between United Nations
and Communist forces, the Church was beaten and scattered.
Church buildings were destroyed. Over four hundred Christian pastors met martyrdom at the hands of the Communists.
The Christians were the main object of Communist persecution. Cities were laid waste as the armies advanced and
retreated over most of the peninsula. The suffering of the
people and the soldiers was indescribable. Only the extreme
south and the extreme north remained untouched by war.
By 1952 the war had settled into fierce battles along the
division line which still exists today in 1964. Despite the
bloodshed of 1952, people on both sides of this line observed
its settled and solid condition and were able to begin re-
building accordingly in that year. Before the line was fixed
in late 1951, anything like church growth was unlikely, but

[4] *Ibid.,* p. 15.

the fact remains that the great Church in Korea did will to survive.

IV. THE CHURCH REBUILDS AND DOUBLES
1953-1960

The city of Seoul once had only a few churches, but now refugees poured down from the north, planted churches in this city, and brought the number of churches in Seoul to the largest number of any city in the Orient. Refugees from North Korea, in their flight from terror, had walked all through the south and now began to settle in the towns and cities there. Most important, they began to plant more churches. During this reconstruction period the Church grew because of this influx of refugees, but it also grew because of an awakening in the whole Church. Once again the churches spread like WILDFIRE.

In southwestern Korea, the area of the Southern Presbyterian Mission, church membership remained essentially static until 1948 and then began a period of tremendous growth which continued until 1958. The Church grew from a communicant membership in 1948 of 14,818 to one of 40,-781 in 1958, almost trebling in ten years.

Recently I asked a missionary — one who experienced the growth in North Chulla Province in southwest Korea following World War II — just how the Church grew. His answer painted a picture similar to that seen in the northwest during the days of Dr. Samuel A. Moffett. He said that in 1954 the church members and officers walked out to call on the members of their villages, particularly on Saturdays, and urged them to attend the Jesus-believers' church. These church leaders brought their relatives, friends, and fellow clansmen into their congregations. Also during this postwar period, the missionaries traveled to these churches in rural villages, examined candidates for baptism, and baptized as many as ninety adults in one church on one Sunday. Once again Korean Christians led their own to Christ, and missionaries were kept busy doing the best they could to help build a strong Church. But this time, there was a strong body of experienced pastors, seminary graduates who could train the young Church, growing by a people movement. However, the missionaries, by virtue of their mobility in cars, were out in front doing much of the training of these new Christians.

The number of churches in the Andong Station area of North Kyungsang Province increased from about eighty to over four hundred in a few years following the end of the Korean War in 1953. Various reasons have been given for this huge growth during that time. A popular one is that, following the war, American Churches sent massive relief supplies to war-stricken South Korea, and many persons joined the Church in thankfulness for this material help. Let us evaluate this reason. The material help American Christians gave to the people in their time of need did serve as an example of Christ's love, and many recipients of this aid responded to that love and became Christians. It is evident, though, that the relief goods alone did not bring about a response to the Gospel. Material help was given to multitudes who were and remained non-Christians. At the most, this help was only a minor aid in winning the responsive. When relief goods were no longer distributed in great quantities, there were no great reversions or falling away from the Church. This fact testifies that relief aid was not the foundation of the growing Church, but only provided a favorable atmosphere for responsive people. In many lands massive aid has been given and no one has become Christian.

Other reasons for a favorable climate for church growth include the fact that the United States was the nation that kept South Korea from being swallowed up by the hated Communists, whose policies had already left scars on the people. America was a savior and also was known as a Christian nation. Christianity also was popular with the people because the first president of the Republic of Korea (elected in South Korea in 1948) and many high officials of that government were Christian. Many of the Christian leaders who came south were also political leaders and heroes for their stand against Communism.

A final reason, which does not exhaust the "whys" of rapid church growth following the war, is that any country torn by war has had its old traditions smashed, generally leaving it unusually receptive to something new. Andong was known to be a center of conservative Confucianism, but the town and countryside around it were ravaged by war, and much of the city was destroyed. This uprooting produced the uncertainty and dissatisfaction which war always brings, and as so often happened, people turned to the Church for guidance. Missionaries who came to Korea directly after the Korean War can recall vividly that, at *any* place they preached, there were always those who desired to accept Christ as their Savior. The numerous churches which have sprung up around Andong since the war witness to an extraordinarily favorable climate for church growth throughout the country.

The Korean War made Korea well known around the world so that many American denominations sent their own missionaries to Korea following the war for the purpose of planting new Churches. One such denomination was the Southern Baptist Church. While Korea had for many years an independent missionary, who loosely connected himself with the Baptist Church, the Southern Baptist Convention did not enter Korea until after the war. I have seen no statistics for Baptist membership in Korea previous to this. Given in Table VII in the Appendix are the only statistics I have available. The sharp decrease from 1958 to 1959 is explained by a division in the Baptist Church.

While there may have been sections of slow growth, I do not know of any. The Rev. Mr. Yang Sun Kim says in 1955 that the Korean Church, long known for its emphasis on evangelism, sought for spiritual revival after living through the Communist invasion. Although complete statistics are not available, we know that tremendous growth marked the period. (See Table VII in the Appendix.) Mr. Kim says: "The spiritually revived Korean Church today has twice as many churches and members as before June 25th."[5] He refers, of course, to the day of Communist invasion on June 25, 1950.

Unfortunately, the wide-spread uncontested growth of the Churches during this period has been obscured by serious

[5] *Ibid.,* p. 22.

divisions in the Presbyterian Church. These divisions, coming in a Protestant world centered on church mergers and ecumenical relations, have captured the limelight. When people think about Korea today, they think about church splits and the sin of division, rather than rejoicing in the spiritual vitality of a Protestant body which has doubled in eight years.

The foundation of the divisions lay in the shrine issue. Those who bowed before the shrine were taken to task by those who had not bowed, and full repentance was demanded. The leadership of those martyred by the Communists was missed, and division resulted. A new General Assembly was formed in 1951 and again in 1954. In 1959 another major division began around the seminary and grew into the "ecumenical" and "conservative" branches of the Church. Part of the 1951 and 1959 divisions united, but part did not, so the Presbyterian Church is now split in four ways. Dr. Samuel Hugh Moffett gives us an approximation of the total Presbyterian community in 1961 as follows:[6]

Presbyterian Church in Korea	375,000
Reunited Anti-Ecumenical Assembly (1951 and 1959 schisms)	220,000
Presbyterian Church in the R.O.K. (1954 schism)	114,000
Continuing Koryu Presbyterian Church (1951 schism)	66,000

MOFFETT'S 1961 MEMBERSHIP
OF DIVIDED KOREAN PRESBYTERIAN CHURCHES
TABLE V

[6] Samuel Hugh Moffett, *The Christians of Korea,* p. 116.

The total of these estimations made in 1961 is Presbyterian community of 775,000.

Attempts are still being made to unite the Korean Church, but hopes for a speedy reunion seem dim. While there are now some doctrinal issues, the divisions are largely centered around personalities struggling for power. The divisions have extended even into small villages where two elders, who for other reasons might not be getting along, have taken sides and divided their congregations down the middle, aligning themselves with opposing General Assemblies.

Dr. S. H. Moffett points out that division following persecution is a pattern commonly seen throughout the history of the Church. Only the perspective of time will enable us to understand how these church splits have affected church growth in the Presbyterian Church in Korea.

V. THE CHURCH TODAY
1961-1964

With statistics as confused as they are, it is difficult to determine whether the Presbyterian Church is growing in 1964. From my own observations in Korea, however, I believe that it is growing, but not fast. In isolated cases, schism has actually favored growth because churches have separated into two congregations, which have begun evangelizing in different sections of their community, each spurred on by the other. But for the most part, the splits are undoubtedly a deterrent to new people becoming interested in the Church. I have heard several ministers tell of unbelievers who have said they would not become Christians because "those Christians are always fighting." I once spoke to a man out in the country who said, "Well, someday I may want to become religious, but I don't want to have anything to do with a church that fights."

While the Methodist Church has had internal difficulties, she has not split and has shown consistent good growth. Her figures indicate a good spurt of growth following the Korean War but also a tendency to plateau in the last few years.

The Holiness Church, served by the Oriental Missionary Society, has shown good growth in the postwar period. Part of this growth may be due to an extensive program of relief goods and aid carried on by the Oriental Missionary Society following the Korean War and continuing to the present time. In 1961-1963, however, this Church also has been rocked by a split. Because of this strife, the statistics are obviously unreliable, for some of the same members are counted by both Churches.

Part of the recent plateauing of the Protestant Churches may be due to excessive channeling of missionaries into institutional work. Missionaries in all three of these missions have become highly involved in institutional work in recent years. Very few of them take long trips out among the churches in the country, as was previously done. Due to the better roads and improved transportation of today, however, many men working in institutions do visit country churches regularly on weekends. The image of the missionary is that of an institutional Christian. It also seems likely that the Church has not yet learned how to use missionaries and its own Korean evangelists and pastors to multiply churches.

I believe that the climate for church growth continues favorable and is likely to be so in future years. At present Korean Christians seem much more concerned than United States Christians as a whole with the extension of Christ's Kingdom. If the Korean Church can recapture its former intensive degree of concern to carry the Gospel to every hamlet in the hills and every section in the towns, reaching out to new homogeneous units in the population, starting new Sunday Schools, branch churches, and preaching points, and discipling whole families or large parts of them, great and sound growth is still abundantly possible.

Chapter XI. Conclusions

A STUDY OF PAST CHURCH GROWTH IN KOREA WOULD BE IN-complete if it did not focus our attention on lessons learned for the future. Here I have drawn some tentative conclusions from the study, tentative because this study has just begun. As long as churches can grow, there will be a need for the study of their growth, in order that the Church may plan for the future.

I. NEED FOR A TRUE PICTURE OF CHURCH GROWTH

The most common mistake made in studying church growth is that of noting the growth of a certain church, then as-signing the cause of that growth to missionary method or to some environmental factor that may coincide with the growth for that particular time. Under closer observation these co-incidental reasons may be found to be not the cause of growth. Simple, sweeping statements are apt to be not only untrue but also a failure to give credit to God for growth. Broad, general statements as to why the Church grows in a country, or even concerning why a particular denomination grows, are useful only if the Church in question grew at a similar rate everywhere. But fast-growing sections next to slow-growing sections of the same Church are an indication that further research needs to be done if a true picture of church growth is to be found.

We have seen in Korea that the assignment of a particular missionary method as the cause of church growth led to its missionwide enforcement. This procedure was seen to be an error, because the whole countryside where the mission worked was not homogeneous, and therefore this policy, the Nevius Method, had different effects on different areas of the Church. In some areas, this method assisted growth; in others, growth was hindered.

216

Likewise the assignment of some environmental factor as a cause of growth or nongrowth is very misleading. The Conspiracy Case, often cited as a growth retarder in the year 1912 in Korea, actually had a double effect on the Church. It slowed growth in some places; but where the Conspiracy Case originated and the oppression was fiercest, the Church grew at the same rapid rate following 1912 as before. In fact, rapid growth in this vital church around Sunchun may have been assisted by persecution.

My own study of the Presbyterian Church's growth by provinces will need correction later when more research uncovers districts of the provinces with pockets of fast growth in special years. Even further, a true picture of church growth can be seen well only when a study in depth of individual congregations is completed. What we are looking for in the picture is an accurate description of how the Church grows in true, homogeneous units within the society.

II. NEED FOR RESEARCH IN CHURCH GROWTH

It is imperative that we discover *how* the church grows in each one of these homogeneous units of society, because even within one nation the differences of social structure, economic level, and sociological features are much more responsible for church growth differences than any other factor might be. When we experience church growth, we easily give way to the tendency to claim immediately a missionary-related cause for this growth, without an adequate understanding of the characteristics of the particular unit of society in that local area.

Religious Attitudes of the People. We must understand the religious climate of the society where the Church is growing. Not only must we study the doctrines and creeds of this people's religion, but we must also understand how it affects the person himself in this society. A study of Buddhist sacred writings alone is not sufficient, but we must know in addition the dynamic forces of a particular type of Buddhism on the people in a society, to understand their response or lack of it to the Gospel.

I suspect that animism and Shamanism prevalent in Korea

have not been seen by missionaries as a very important part of the individual Korean's life. We must know of what a person's religious life consists and what his understanding of the words we use is, when we advocate a change from animistic beliefs to Christian beliefs. Missionary writings are all too sparse at this point.

The message of Christ is the same Gospel wherever and to whomever it is proclaimed, but we should present it in a different way and use different words and methods when speaking of it to a predominantly animistic people. The animism of northwest Korean people is one of the keys to the great growth there, but only rarely has it been mentioned, and then in passing, by writers who have observed and participated in this past growth. Animism gave the people an awareness of a higher being, with the *shamans'* attempts to control the spirits, but it was not and is not satisfying. The people in the northwest were not satisfied with their animistic worship; they were glad to find a high God of love to replace the gods of fear they had known.

Recently a Korean *shaman* tried unsuccessfully three times to control the evil spirits causing miscarriages in a woman. When the woman came back during her fourth pregnancy to have the spirits controlled, the *shaman* was at a loss. This time the female *shaman* saw that her trances and dances would be useless, so she told the pregnant woman, "The only thing for you to do now is to believe in Jesus, like they do in that little Methodist Church over there." The woman became a Christian through the witness of this professional animist. No wonder the people are dissatisfied with their spirit religion.

Animism is not weak. I have witnessed the burning of animist objects for worship by a new Christian, and, while the burning was meaningless to me at the time, I could see that this was a solemn occasion for the participants, and I could sense the power struggle that was going on. I have seen a figure of a *shaman*, carved for tourists, cause a violent reaction of fear as well as disgust in a Christian.

I have seen enough in this study and have had enough experience to realize that animism has a most important relationship to church growth in Korea. But I confess a lack of understanding. What is needed is a study of the dynamics of church growth, showing how Christianity wins or loses the power struggle with the animistic forces in Korea. Increased understanding is demanded if our presentation of the Gospel is to be successful. The continuing animism of the country people of Korea must be taken more seriously in the future.

Structure of the Society. We must also understand more fully the structure of the society in which the Gospel is preached. For instance, a study of who owns the land and who has the economic power in the village is important to church growth. It is much more than a coincidence that churches in Korea grew better among the landowners. A landowner is free to make his own choice. A tenant farmer could lose his means of livelihood if the landlord objected to Christianity, as most of the *yangban* landlords did.

Western theology is geared to an individualistic society. Those trained in this theology easily misunderstand the phenomenon of a church growing along the family pattern of the East. Missionaries must fully acquaint themselves with the family pattern of the society in which they work. Missionaries, myself included, have been quite surprised to wake up to the intricate family relationships of those who "happened" to be employed by a mission station. I have been surprised by the endless family ties of the leaders in the presbytery where I serve. This surprise comes from an inadequate understanding of the society and its personal interrelationships. The family structure has been used by God in Korea to win men and women to Christ. If we are to be His servants, to assist in further winning, we must study the family structure pattern, and develop a theology congenial to it.

Test for Responsiveness to the Gospel. In order to place our effort directly on achieving rapid church growth, we must learn to recognize where the people are responding to Christianity. Too often missionaries wrote, "Church growth is just around the corner; the people are ready to believe," when they were only indulging in wishful thinking, as proved by later nongrowth.

The only real test of the responsiveness of a people is whether the Church is growing or not. Citing isolated examples of men turning to Christ and trying subjectively to feel the mood of the people will not give any assurance that a people is responsive. However, when churches in a certain geographical area or when churches composed of a certain segment of society are growing, then and only then, can we conclude that the people are responding to the Gospel. It would be extremely difficult for an observer to assess wrongly the responsiveness of a people in an area for which he has a graph showing communicant membership for at least five years.

Until someone discovers an accurate formula that will show when a person is dissatisfied with his own beliefs and ready to turn to Christianity, the only true indication of a responsive people is whether there is growth in the Church among that people.

III. NEED FOR MISSIONARY ACTION

We try to discover where responsive people live and what kind of people they are for only one purpose: to turn them to Christ. Research in itself is useless. If this book does not help the Church to grow, writing it has been a waste of time. But finally, when through honest study we find that one area is growing while another in the same country is not, what do we do about it? The answers are simple.

(A) We should use those approaches which most effectively communicate the Gospel, remembering that just as there is no teaching without learning, so there is no effective evangelism without conversion.

(B) We should concentrate our limited forces on areas where there is response. This will mean thinning our personnel for church extension in the nonresponsive areas, since our missionary forces are limited, but the result will be more church growth in both areas. It is a sinful waste to keep two areas equally staffed just because there is the same number of citizens in each, when there is a great difference in potential for growth of the Church. If we say we must do our best to aid growth in the nonresponsive area, thereby holding back resources from a church-growing area, we deceive ourselves.

Many do not yet realize that a powerful, growing Church made up of people from a responding population in a nation will win more Christians, even from a relatively nonresponsive area of that nation, than will a handful of professional personnel, both foreign and national, no matter how good servants or evangelists they may be. The Presbyterian Church of northwest Korea gave strength to its denomination all over Korea. Remember how, from 1895 to 1910, the churches "spread like WILDFIRE." Following the Communist invasion in 1950, hundreds of churches were planted in previously nonresponsive areas by these displaced Christian refugees from the northwest.

Nothing wins men to Christ like good church growth. Yet this principle has been denied in the practice of our Churches and missions. Not only have we failed to realize that church growth can be achieved by concentration on responsive areas, but we also have deceived ourselves into conducting auxiliary activities in nonresponsive areas. These activities, while good in themselves, do not produce church growth. No one questions the validity of educational and medical work for serving human needs, but if church growth is our object and there are responsive populations where we can act, we are mistaken in using these Christian services in nonresponsive areas hoping to "soften up" the people so that they eventually will become Christians. We are mistaken in using these expensive institutions as indirect evangelistic tools in nonresponsive areas where nearby are populations which would respond to direct evangelism if we would send many workers there.

These conclusions imply that mission boards and personnel-assigning committees, concerned with discipling the nations and winning as many as possible to Jesus Christ, should concentrate their efforts on those areas where growth is possible. Decisions constantly must be made to balance the missionary effort around the world. The criterion for these decisions must be the possibilities of church growth. Missionaries must be sent to areas of response, even to the point of reducing our forces in areas where church growth is presently impossible, and Christian service alone can be carried on. We must do these things because of the Great Commission given to us by our Lord and because of our belief that it is in the nature of God to desire as many as possible to come to Himself.

Local missions should be alert enough to recognize areas where growth is possible and flexible enough so that personnel and funds might be sent to reap the ripe harvest in these areas. In this new day of mission, the younger Churches themselves must concentrate on their areas of high potential, using national and foreign personnel in these places. The assignment of missionaries in many areas has been turned over to national Church organizations, but quite often the criterion for assignment is more vague than it has been in the past. Now, even more than ever, younger Churches must use foreign personnel and funds as well as their own national personnel, for the purpose of assisting the Church to grow, if the Church around the world is to carry out God's plan of reconciling men to Himself and building His Church.

Appendix

Year									
1915	14023	13587	7600	3936	5949	2911	4274		8003**
1916	14181	16137	7893	3781	5810	3001	4268		8131**
1917	15549	18459*	8833	3966	5981	3465	4154		7823**
1918	17112	16724	9243	3724	6311	3972	4125	3115	4180
1919	17759	15612	9545	3541	6250	4632	3936	3653	4119
1920	18171	15312	8481	3351	7113	5058	3836	3261	4442
1921	15718*	15862	9148	3823	7588	5825	4169	3796	4643
1922	18433	16532	8767	3818	7557	4560	4500	3418	4561
1923	19000	16693	9198	4026	8009	4105	4590	4672	5956
1924	19982	16766	9192	3849	8256	4404	4744	4529	6539
1925	21922	18336	9932	4906	8625	5333	4122	4099	7225
1926	22517	19326	9156	4155	8225	4991	5632	4123	7360
1927	23580	22683*	8353	3979	8311	6445*	5641	4979	7120
1928	21570	18083	8039	4128	8942	5484	5467	5040	6584
1929	21908	18184	9120	4180	9411	5194	5453	5445	6441
1930	22493	18199	9055	4124	9288	5504	5445	5526	6916
1931	23094	18454	9063	4614	9506	5861	6081	5716	6776
1932	25729	20593	10420	5055	10592	6428	6567	6325	7527
1933	24302	20932	10162	5216	11365	6543	7184	6445	7305
1934	25530	22097	10037	5672	12267	7274	7532	7124	8157
1935	29296*	22109	12308	5146	12282	6394	7700	7671	8449
1936	28873	23015	12871	5295	10359	6721	7949	7980	8857
1937	30668	24206	13264	5571	12405	7201	8443	8800	8735
1938	31853	25487	15537	6656	13658	6107	9039	8657	8971
1939	33422	25746	15822	6861	12949	7412	8921	7638	8399
1940	34079	25822	18198		10596*	7838	3925*	3925*	7877
1941	32624	21907	18903	7057	13067	7579	7183	8128	8063
1942	29129	20327	17204	5714	9914	7868	6370	8353	6293

* Probably incorrect
** Separate statistics unavailable

TABLE VI

COMMUNICANT MEMBERSHIP OF THE PRESBYTERIAN CHURCH IN KOREA BY PROVINCE 1886-1942

Year	A North Pyongan Province	B South Pyongan Province	C Whanghai Province	D Kyunggi and North Choongchung Provinces	E North Kyungsang Province	F Hamkyung Provinces	G South Kyungsang Province	H North Chulla Province	J South Chulla Province and Cheju Island
1886									
1887									
1888									
1889				9					
1890				25					
1891				65					
1892				104					
1893				100					
1894	3**			119					
1895	52**			127					
1896	73***			136					
1897	243***			389					
1898	377***			949			6		
1899	1058***	671		1199	2		7		
1900	202	2213		1430	4	5	18		
1901	420	2994		1547	7	23	43		
1902	677	3100		1582	12	92	30		
1903	1027	3765		1512	33	115	110*		
1904	1265	4703		1678	59	311	292	124	8
1905	1958	5468		1938	112	308	363	240	27
1906	3121	6685		2174	235	492	464	316	64
1907	4039	6089	2255	1612	564	814	747	415	189
1908	5408	7642	2974	1963	807	932	2149	1255	708
1909	6703	9142	2921	2422	1615	1141	1885	2278	1000
1910	7901	10842	4740	2975	2886	1691	2840	3156	1352
1911	9853	12599	5021	3222	3354	2271	3519	3464	2045
1912	11072	12601	5718	3961	4138	2325	3679	3974	3181
									9514**

EXPLANATION OF TABLE VI

The figures in Table VI are highly reliable. They have been derived from records of the Korea Mission of the Presbyterian Church in the U. S. A. for the years 1886 to 1907, and from General Assembly statistics of the Presbyterian Church in Korea for the years 1907 to 1942. At only two places has reclarification because of internal evidence been necessary.

(1) The figure for communicant membership in South Pyongan Province in 1927 should be reduced by three thousand from the figure reported in the General Assembly minutes, in order to bring it to a more reasonable figure. Any sudden jump in figures for one year, which shows a similar plunge the next year, is suspect. This figure for 1927 is an obvious statistical error. We find in *one* out of four presbyteries of South Pyongan Province, a number for one category which is out of proportion with the preceding and following years. The 1926 column of "members under discipline," which is added in the total number of communicant members, reads 150, while the same column in 1927 shows a jump to 3,163. In 1928, 994 is given but it is a figure that includes those who are reported as missing as well as those disciplined. In other words, "members under discipline" are not reported separately.

Note that in 1928 the error was corrected not by showing a large increase in those removed from discipline, as would be normal procedure if actually 3,000 were under discipline that year, but by a mere reduction of the communicant membership statistics. Since this is one category in one of the four presbyteries included in South Pyongan Province, we conclude that there was a statistical error which was corrected the following year.

(2) The jump in South Pyongan Province in 1917 is a result of the addition of a new category of members that includes those recently suspended. These suspended members had been left off the rolls to avoid the per capita tax, but are now included in an "imperfect" membership column, which C. A. Clark feels gives a truer picture of the Church and which I follow.* The jump in all presbyteries is explained by this.

The two thousand members that seem to come out of nowhere in South Pyongan Province make the graph rise sharply from 1916 to 1917 and from 16,000 to 18,000. They are a jump in "imperfect members" which accompany this statistical redefinition. The 18,000 dropped back to 16,000 the next year. No explanation was given; neither were more members suspended than the previous year. So we must conclude that the sharp drop was also a change in definition of which people are included in the membership rolls.

* Charles Allen Clark, *The Korean Church and the Nevius Methods,* pp. 305ff.

THE ROMAN CATHOLIC CHURCH IN KOREA

There is a need for a careful study on the marvelous growth of the Roman Catholic Church in Korea. The glimpse I have had of just a few Roman Catholic sources promises that this study should be both instructive and fascinating.

The Roman Catholic Church has a history of martyred priests and Korean believers. This Church was established and almost completely wiped out by bloody persecution long before Protestant missionaries entered Korea. In the wake of political changes that allowed Protestants to enter Korea in 1884, the French Roman Catholic missionaries around Seoul and Taegu saw their Church grow to about 30,000 Catholics by 1900, when the Protestants still had only a handful. After 1900 the growth was not so spectacular, because by 1939 the French Mission had only a 90,000 Catholic community.

The American Catholic Mission came into Korea in 1923, established a mission in Pyongyang and saw remarkable growth in this northwest area by claiming over 24,000 Catholics in 1939. This was a trebling of believers from 1930.

The Roman Catholic Church in Korea provides a rich field for research in church growth for someone with a reading knowledge of French and a will to search for the facts.

Year	Presbyterian Church	R. O. K. Presbyterian	Koryu Presbyterian	Methodist Church	Holiness Church	Baptist Church
1952	231473			23166	7025	
1953	250000	16944		29105	11339	
1954	103594*			34781	13519	
1955		21937		38391	14904	
1956		68610*	15350	40792		
1957	550853*	30892	17366*	42582	16634	4458
1958	110788	31637	15998	44040	17642	2901**
1959	110788	31637	17401	44726	17855	2806
1960			17503	45883	18444	4843
1961					18907	5125
1962	86434				18649	

COMMUNICANT MEMBERSHIP OF MAJOR PROTESTANT CHURCHES
IN SOUTH KOREA 1952 - 1962   TABLE VII

* Statistics that are questionable. The sources for these statistics offer
no explanation for the great variances. They are probably inaccurate
because of the divisions in the Presbyterian Church during this decade.

** Probably a division in the Baptist Church.

Bibliography

A. LETTERS

Letters of the Presbyterian Church in the U. S. A. Korea missionaries written to Board of Foreign Missions staff. Microfilm. New York: United Presbyterian Library, 1884-1911.

B. REPORTS

Annual personal, station and mission reports written to the Board of Foreign Missions of the Presbyterian Church in the U. S. A. from its missionaries in Korea. Microfilm. New York: United Presbyterian Library, 1884-1911.

Annual personal and station reports written to the Board of foreign Missions of the Presbyterian Church in the U. S. A. and the United Presbyterian Church in the U. S. A. New York: Files of the Commission on Ecumenical Mission and Relations of the United Presbyterian Church in the U. S. A., 1912-1962.

Fifth Annual Meeting of the Federal Council of Protestant Evangelical Missions in Korea. Seoul, Korea: Y. M. C. A. Press, 1916.

General Council of Protestant Evangelical Missions in Korea, First Annual Meeting. Seoul, Korea: September 11, 1905.

General Council of Protestant Evangelical Missions in Korea, Second Annual Meeting. Seoul, Korea: September 10, 11, 1906.

General Council of Protestant Evangelical Missions in Korea, Seventh Annual Meeting. Seoul, Korea: September 27-29, 1911.

Korea Mission of the Presbyterian Church U. S. A. Annual Meeting Reports of 1909, 1913, 1914, 1916, 1918, 1949-1953, 1954-1956.

Korea Section of Annual Reports of the Board of Foreign Missions of the Presbyterian Church U. S. A. and the Commission on Ecumenical Mission and Relations of the United Presbyterian Church in the U. S. A. New York: United Presbyterian Library, 1885-1962.

Statistics from the Printed Minutes of the General Assembly of the Presbyterian Church in Korea. Seoul, Korea: Photographed from General Assembly files, 1913-1942.

Statistics from the Printed Minutes of the Presbytery of the Presbyterian Church in Korea. Seoul, Korea: Photographed from General Assembly files, 1908-1912.

C. THESES AND MANUSCRIPTS

Chun, Sung Chun. *Schism and Unity in the Protestant Churches of Korea.* New Haven, Conn.: Yale University doctoral thesis, May 1955.

Clark, Allen D. *A Study of Religion and the State in the Japanese Empire with Particular Reference to the Shrine Problem in Korea.* Princeton, New Jersey: Princeton Theological Seminary thesis, 1939.

Kang, Won Yong. *A Study on the Family System of Korea: The Christian Approach to Its Changing Situation.* New York: Union Theological Seminary S.T.M. thesis, 1956.

Kay, Il Seung. *Christianity in Korea.* Richmond, Virginia: Union Theological Seminary thesis, March 1950.

Kwon, Elizabeth Younghee. *A Study of the Growth of the Presbyterian Church in Korea.* Los Angeles, Calif.: University of Southern California master's thesis, August, 1962.

Lautensach, Herman. *Korea Land, Volk, Schicksal.* Translated by Glenn Wass. Verlag-Stuttgart, Germany: K. F. Koehler, 1950.

Pollard, Harriet E. *The History of the Missionary Enterprise of the Presbyterian Church U. S. A. in Korea with Special Emphasis on the Personnel.* Chicago, Ill.: Northwestern University master's thesis, 1927.

Rhodes, Harry A. *History of the Korea Mission Presbyterian Church U. S. A.* Vol. II, 1935-1950. Vol. III, 1950-1954. New York: United Presbyterian Library. Mimeographed, 1954.

Stokes, Charles Davis. *History of Methodist Missions in Korea,* 1885-1930. New Haven, Conn.: Yale University doctoral thesis, 1947.

Ye, Yun Ho. *A New Cult in Postwar Korea.* Princeton, New Jersey: Princeton Theological Seminary. Mimeographed, February 16, 1959.

D. PAMPHLETS

Brown, Arthur Judson, and Samuel M. Zwemer. *The Nearer and Farther East.* New York: Macmillan, 1908.

Clark, Charles Allen. *Digest of the Presbyterian Church of Chosen.* Seoul, Korea: Presbyterian Publication Fund, Christian Literature Society, 1934.

Goforth, Jonathan. *When the Spirit's Fire Swept Korea.* Grand Rapids, Michigan: Zondervan, 1942.

Jones, George Heber and Arthur Noble. *The Korean Revival.* New York: Board of Foreign Missions of the Methodist Episcopal Church, 1910.

Korea Mission of the Presbyterian Church U. S. A. *Presentation of Difficulties Which Have Arisen.* . . . A petition, statement and correspondence by the missionaries and Board of Foreign Missions of the Presbyterian Church U. S. A. Printed for private use, 1918.

Moffett, Samuel A. "Men and the Modern Missionary Enterprise."
    Lectures given February 19-21, 1907 in Omaha, Nebraska.
    IX & XXIII.
Mott, John R. "The Rural Mission of the Church in Eastern Asia."
    Nos. XIII, XIV and XV of Part Four, *Cooperation for the
    Christian Advance in Rural Korea.* 1931.
Pyun, Y. T. *My Attitude Towards Ancestor Worship.* Seoul, Korea:
    Christian Literature Society, 1926.
Report on Korea. The Commission on the Orient of the World's Sun-
    day-School Association. Presented at the World's Seventh
    Sunday-School Convention, Zurich, Switzerland: July 8-15,
    1913.
"Students and the Modern Missionary Crusade." Address delivered
    before the fifth International Convention of the Student Vol-
    unteer Movement for Foreign Missions at Nashville, Tenne-
    see: February 28-March 4, 1906. New York: S.V.M. for
    Foreign Missions, 1906.
The Anglican Church in Korea. Privately printed in 1958.
The Korea Digest. Korea Mission of the Presbyterian Church U. S. A.,
    1937.
Transactions of the Asiatic Society of Japan. Tokyo, Japan: The Haku-
    bunsha, 1890. Vol. 18.

E. ARTICLES AND MAGAZINES

Gale, James Scarth. "A History of the Korean People." Published seri-
    ally in the *Korea Mission Field.* Seoul, Korea: Christian Liter-
    ature Society of Korea, July, 1924-September, 1927.
Hooper, James Leon. *Mission Study.* Extracts from the material of the
    Board of Foreign Missions of the Presbyterian Church in the
    U. S. A. New York: 1949.
International Review of Missions. Vol. 27. 1938.
Korea Mission Field. Seoul, Korea: Evangelical Missions of Korea,
    1905-1941.
Korean Repository. 1896-1898.
The Korea Field. Seoul, Korea: November, 1901-April, 1904. June,
    1904-August, 1905.
Yang, Key P. and Gregory Henderson. "An Outline History of Korean
    Confucianism, Part I, The Early Period and Ye Factionalism,"
    The Journal of Asian Studies. Vol. XVIII, No. 1, November
    1958.

F. BOOKS

Allen, Horace N. *Things Korean.* New York: Revell, 1908.
Bishop, Isabella Bird. *Korea and Her Neighbors.* New York: Revell,
    1897.
Blair, Herbert E. *Stewardship in Korea.* Seoul, Korea: Christian Liter-
    ature Society of Korea, 1938.

Blair, William Newton. *Gold in Korea*. New York: Central Distributing Department of the Presbyterian Church in the U. S. A., 1946.

Blakeslee, George (ed.). *China and the Far East*. New York: Crowell, 1910.

Brown, Arthur Judson. *Report on a Second Visit to China, Japan and Korea*. New York: Board of Foreign Missions of the Presbyterian Church in the U. S. A., 1909.

————. (ed.). *The Korean Conspiracy Case*. New York: Board of Foreign Missions of the Presbyterian Church U. S. A. 1912.

————. *The Mastery of the Far East*. New York: Scribner's, 1919.

Brown, George Thompson. *Mission to Korea*. Nashville, Tennessee: Board of World Missions, Presbyterian Church U. S., 1962.

Butterfield, Kenyon L. *The Rural Mission of the Church in Eastern Asia*. New York: International Missionary Council, 1931.

Campbell, Arch. *The Christ of the Korean Heart*. Columbus, Ohio: Falco Publishers, 1954.

Clark, Allen D. *History of the Korean Church*. Seoul, Korea: Christian Literature Society of Korea, 1961.

Clark, Charles A. *First Fruits in Korea*. New York: Revell, 1921.

————. *Religions of Old Korea*. New York: Revell, 1932.

————. *The Korean Church and the Nevius Methods*. New York: Revell, 1930

Cooper, S. Kate. *Evangelism in Korea*. Nashville, Tennessee: Board of Missions, Methodist Episcopal Church South, 1930.

Cynn, Hugh Heung-Wo. *The Rebirth of Korea*. New York: Abingdon, 1920.

Dixon, Roland B. *The Racial History of Man*. New York: Scribner's, 1923.

Downs, Darley (ed.). *The Japan Christian Yearbook*. Tokyo, Japan: The Christian Literature Society (Kyo Bun Kwan), 1941.

Drake, Henry Burgess. *Korea of the Japanese*. London: John Lane the Bodley Head, Limited, 1930.

Eddy, Sherwood. *I Have Seen God Do It*. New York: Harper, 1940.

Fairservis, Walter A. Jr. *The Origins of Oriental Civilization*. New York: New American Library (Mentor: Ancient Civilizations), 1959.

Federal Council of Missions in Korea. *The Korea Missions Yearbook*. Seoul, Korea: Christian Literature Society of Korea, 1928, 1932.

Fenwick, Malcolm C. *The Church of Christ in Corea*. New York: Hodder & Stoughton — Doran, 1911.

Fulton, C. Darby. *Star in the East*. Richmond, Virginia: Presbyterian Committee of Publication, 1938.

Gale, James S. *Korea in Transition*. Copyrighted by the Young People's Missionary Movement of the United States and Canada. New York: Educational Department Board of Foreign Missions of the Presbyterian Church in the U. S. A., 1909.

Gehman, Richard. *Let My Heart Be Broken.* New York: McGraw-Hill, 1960.

Gilmore, George W. *Korea From Its Capital.* Philadelphia, Pennsylvania: Presbyterian Board of Publication and Sunday-School Work, 1892.

Grajdanzev, Andrew J. *Modern Korea.* New York: International Secretariat, Institute of Pacific Relations, distributed by John Day Company, 1944.

Grant, William D. and Charles Cuthbert Hall (ed.). *Christendom Anno Domini MDCCCCI.* New York: Chauncey Holt, 1902. Vol. I & II.

Griffis, William Elliot. *A Modern Pioneer in Korea.* New York: Revell, 1912.

————. *America in the East.* New York: S. Barnes, 1900.

————. *Corea, the Hermit Nation.* New York: Scribner's, 1888.

————. *Corea Without and Within.* Philadelphia, Penn.: Presbyterian Board of Publication, 1885.

Gulick, Sidney L. *The Winning of the Far East.* New York: Doran, 1923.

Hamilton, Angus. *Korea.* New York: Scribner's, 1904.

Harrington, Fred Harvey. *God, Mammon and the Japanese.* Madison, Wisconsin: University of Wisconsin Press, 1944.

Historical Sketch of the Korean Methodist Church. In the Korean language. Seventy-fifth anniversary. Seoul, Korea: Annual Conference of the Korean Methodist Church, 1960.

Holton, D. C. *The National Faith of Japan: A Study in Modern Shinto.* New York: E. P. Dutton, 1938.

Ireland, Alleyne. *The New Korea.* New York: E. P. Dutton, 1926.

Jones, George Heber. *Korea, the Land, People and Customs.* Cincinnati, Ohio: Jennings and Graham, 1907.

Jubilee Papers. The Fiftieth Anniversary Celebration of the Korea Mission of the Presbyterian Church in the U. S. A. Seoul, Korea: June 30-July 3, 1934.

Kim, Yang Sun. *History of the Korean Church in the Ten Years Since Liberation.* Translated by Allen Clark. Seoul, Korea: Mimeographed 1962.

Korea. Philadelphia, Penn.: Women's Foreign Missionary Society of the Presbyterian Church U. S. A., 1897.

Korea Handbook of Missions. Federal Council of Korea and the Interchurch World Movement of North America, 1920.

Korea Mission of the Presbyterian Church U. S. A. *Quarto Centennial Papers Read Before Annual Meeting.* Pyengyang, Korea: August 27, 1909.

Korea Statistical Yearbook. Seoul, Korea: Economic Planning Board of the Republic of Korea, 1962.

Lasker, Bruno. *Asia on the Move*. New York: Henry Holt, 1945. Issued under the·auspices of the American Council, Institute of Pacific Relations.

Latourette, Kenneth Scott. *A History of Christian Missions in China*. New York: Macmillan, 1929.

Lee, Hoon K. *Land Utilization and Rural Economy in Korea*. Chicago: University of Chicago Press.

Linton, Ralph. *The Tree of Culture*. New York: Knopf, 1955.

Lowell, Percival. *Chosen, the Land of the Morning Calm*. Boston: Ticknor, 1886.

McCune, George M. *Korea Today*. Cambridge, Mass.: Harvard University Press, 1950. Issued under the Auspices of the International Secretariat Institute of Pacific Relations.

McCune, Shannon. *Korea's Heritage*. Tokyo, Japan: Tuttle, 1956.

McGavran, Donald Anderson. *How Churches Grow*. London: World Dominion Press, 1959.

————. *The Bridges of God*. New York: Friendship Press, 1955.

McKenzie, F. A. *Korea's Fight for Freedom*. New York and Chicago: Revell, 1920.

————. *The Tragedy of Korea*. New York: E. P. Dutton, after 1907.

————. *The Unveiled East*. New York: E. P. Dutton, 1907.

McVinacke, Harold. *The History of the Far East in Modern Times*. New York: Crofts, 1941.

Miller, Frederick S. *Our Korean Friends*. New York: Revell, 1935.

————. *The Gospel in Korea*. New York: Revell, 1939.

Moffett, Samuel Hugh. *The Christians of Korea*. New York: Friendship Press, 1962.

Moose, J. Robert. *Village Life in Korea*. Nashville, Tennessee: Publishing House of the Methodist Episcopal Church South, Smith and Lamar, Agents, 1911.

Nelson, M. Frederick. *Korea and the Old Orders in Eastern Asia*. Baton Rouge, Louisiana: Louisiana State University Press, 1945.

Nevius, John L. *Planting and Development of Missionary Churches*. From articles printed in 1885. Philadelphia, Penn.: Presbyterian and Reformed, 1958.

Nisbet, Anabel ·Major. *Day In and Day Out in Korea*. Richmond, Virginia: Presbyterian Committee of Publication, 1919.

Noble, Mattie Wilcox. *Victorious Lives of Early Christians in Korea*. Seoul, Korea: Christian Literature Society of Korea, 1927.

North, Eric M. *The Kingdom and the Nations*. West Medford, Mass.: The Central Committee on the United Study of Foreign Missions, 1921.

Osgood, Cornelius. *The Koreans and Their Culture*. Tokyo, Japan: Tuttle, 1951.

Paik, L. George. *The History of Protestant Missions in Korea,* 1832-1910. Pyengyang, Korea: Union Christian College Press, 1929.

Perry, Jean. *Twenty Years a Korea Missionary.* London: S. W. Partridge, 1911.

Rhodes, Harry A. *History of the Korea Mission, Presbyterian Church U. S. A.* 1884-1934. Vol I. Seoul, Korea: Chosen Mission of the Presbyterian Church U. S. A., 1934.

Roy, Andrew T. *On Asia's Rim.* New York: Friendship Press, 1962.

Ryang, J. S. *Southern Methodism in Korea.* Thirtieth Anniversary. Seoul, Korea: Board of Missions of Methodist Episcopal Church South, 1927.

Sauer, Charles A. *Within the Gate.* Seoul, Korea: Korea Methodist News Service. 1934.

Snyder, Laurence H. "Human Blood Groups; Their Inheritance and Racial Significance," *Source Book in Anthropology* by A. L. Kroeber and T. T. Waterman. New York: Harcourt, Brace, 1931.

Soltau, T. Stanley. *Missions at the Crossroads.* Grand Rapids, Michigan: Baker, 1955.

Speer, Robert E. *Missions and Modern History.* New York: Revell, 1904. Vols. I & II.

Swinehart, Lois Hawks. *Korea Calls.* New York: Revell, 1929.

The Christian Movement in Japan, Korea and Formosa. Tokyo, Japan: Federation of Christian Missions, 1923 & 1924.

The Economic Basis of the Church. London: International Missionary Council, Oxford University Press, 1939. Tambaram Series, Vol. V.

The Korean Situation. New York: Commission on Relations with the Orient of the Federal Council of the Churches of Christ in America, subject matter 1919.

Underwood, Horace G. *The Call of Korea.* New York: Revell, 1908.

Underwood, Horace H. *Partial Bibliography of Occidental Works on Korea.* Seoul, Korea: Literary Department, Chosen Christian College, 1931.

—————. *Tragedy and Faith in Korea.* New York: Friendship Press, 1951.

Underwood, Lillias H. *Fifteen Years Among the Topknots.* New York: Young People's Missionary Movement of the United States and Canada, American Tract Society, 1904.

—————. *Underwood of Korea.* New York: Revell, 1918.

Van Buskirk, James Dale. *Korea, Land of the Dawn.* New York: Missionary Education Movement of the United States and Canada, 1931.

Wagner, Ellasue. *Korea: The Old and the New.* New York: Revell, 1931.

Wasson, Alfred W. *Church Growth in Korea.* New York: International
    Missionary Council, 1934.
Weale, B. J. Putnam. *The Coming Struggle in Eastern Asia.* London:
    Macmillan, 1909.
White, Trumbell and James P. Boyd. "Corea," *Story of China and
    Her Neighbors.* 1900.

Glossary

Adherents
: The total number of baptized, children, inquirers, catechumens, and communicant members. Same as "community."

Andong
: Town in North Kyungsang Province, also Northern Presbyterian Mission Station.

Catechumen
: Person who promises to lead a Christian life, regularly attending worship services and studying prescribed Biblical material in order to be examined for church membership six months after being admitted to the catechumenate. Same as "probationer."

Chairyung
: Town in Whanghai Province of northwest Korea, also Northern Presbyterian Mission Station.

Cheju
: Large island off southern coast of Korea, now a separate province.

Choongchung
: Province in west central Korea, divided into North and South Choongchung in 1896.

Chundokyo
: Korean religion which has borrowed much from Christianity but is based mainly on patriotic motivation.

Colporteur
: Traveling Bible salesman.

Communicant member
: Person who after being a catechumen for six months or more is accepted after examination of his faith and practice into full membership of the church, either through baptism or, if previously baptized in infancy, confirmed.

Conspiracy Case
: In 1912, 105 Koreans, including many Christians, were convicted of conspiracy against the Japanese government. All but six judgments were reversed by a higher court.

Euiju
: Town on the China-Korea border in North Pyongan Province.

Haiju
: Town in Whanghai Province, also a Northern Methodist Mission Station.

237

Inchon	Port city twenty miles west of Seoul in Kyunggi Province, also a Northern Methodist Mission Station.
Independence Movement	Peaceful attempt in 1919 by the Korean people to free themselves from Japan's yoke by demonstrations. Many Koreans were shot and killed in the demonstrations and the leaders were imprisoned.
Inquirer	Person who gives up former religious practices and attends church regularly.
Kaesung (Songdo)	Ancient capital of Korea in Kyunggi Province, also a Southern Methodist Mission Station.
Kangkei	Town in the far north of North Pyongan Province, also a Northern Presbyterian Mission Station.
Kangwon	Province in east central Korea.
Koryo Period	935-1392 A. D. in Korea.
Kyunggi	Province in west central Korea containing Seoul.
Kyungsang	Province in southeast Korea divided into North and South Kyungsang in 1896.
Mudang	A *shaman,* one who attempts control of animistic spirits, especially in the sick, by dancing and chanting.
Nevius Method	Policy of mission work advocated by John L. Nevius, missionary to China, for the planting and developing of younger Churches, adapted by the Northern Presbyterian Mission in Korea. The policy's goal was a strong, indigenous Church with particular emphasis on Bible training for all Christians as in the annual Bible classes held in each area, wide itineration by the missionaries to care for the needs of the new churches, and the three "selfs":

1. Self-support required the Korean Christians to build their own churches and pay their own pastors.

2. Self-government early placed the Korean Christians in charge of their own affairs.

3. Self-propagation stressed the responsibility of each Christian to win those around him to Christ.

Probationer	Same as "catechumen."

Pusan	Large port city on southeast coast of Korea, also Australian Presbyterian Mission Station.
Pyongan	Province of northwest Korea divided into North and South Pyongan in 1896.
Pyongyang	Capital city of South Pyongan Province, also Northern Methodist and Presbyterian Mission Stations.
Russo-Japanese War	1904 war in which Japan defeated Russia partly on Korean soil, giving Japan a clear path to take Korea into the Japanese Empire.
Sajik Shrine	Confucian shrine located in a city park of Seoul.
Seoul	Capital city of Korea located in the west central section.
Shaman	See *"mudang."*
Shinto	State religion of Japan.
Shrine issue	Beginning in 1930, the Japanese occupation government forced all Korean students and teachers to bow in obeisance before the state Shinto shrines. This, according to the government, was not a religious act. Some Korean Christians and missionaries believed bowing to the shrine was a religious act. Churches were later required to bow at the shrines.
Sino-Japanese War	1894 war between China and Japan, fought partly on Korean soil.
Sorai	Village in Whanghai Province where the majority of the population rapidly became Christian.
Sunchun	Town in North Pyongan Province, also a Northern Presbyterian Mission Station.
Taegu	Capital city of North Kyungsang Province, also a Northern Presbyterian Mission Station.
Tangoon	Mythical originator of the Korean race and nation of four thousand years ago.
Tonghak	Literally "Eastern Learning." A reaction against the Western learning of the Catholics in 1850's which recurred as a revolt in 1894 against the corrupt government.
Tongnip	Korean Independence Army.

Whanghai	Province in northwest Korea.
Wonsan	Port city in Hamkyung province, also a Southern Methodist Mission Station.
Yangban	Landed gentry who were considered the upper class. The *yangban's* position was hereditary, and manual labor was beneath his dignity.
Yi Dynasty	1392-1910 in Korea.
Yungbyun (Yengbyen)	Ancient Buddhist center and town in North Pyongan Province, also a Northern Methodist Mission Station.

Index